KT-406-701

Issues in Foster Care

WITHDRAWN FROM THE LIBRARY UNIVERSITY OF WINCHESTER

KA 0245990 6

of related interest

Effective Ways of Working with Children and their Families
Edited by Malcolm Hill
Research Highlights in Social Work 15
ISBN 1 85302 619 0

Child Welfare Service Developments in Law, Policy, Practice and Research
Edited by Malcolm Hill and Jane Aldgate
ISBN 1 85302 316 7

Lesbian and Gay Fostering and Adoption
Extraordinary Yet Ordinary
Edited by Stephen Hicks and Janet MacDermott
ISBN 1 85302 600 X

State Child Care Practice: Looking After Children?
Carol Hayden, Jim Goddard, Sarah Gaira and Niki Van Der Speck
ISBN 1 85302 670 0

The Adoption Experience
Families who Give Children a Second Chance
Ann Morris
ISBN 1 85302 783 9

Issues in Foster Care

Policy Practice and Research

Edited by Greg Kelly and Robbie Gilligan

Jessica Kingsley Publishers
London and Philadelphia

All rights reserved. No paragraph of this publication may be reproduced, copied or transmitted save with written permission of the Copyright Act 1956 (as amended), or under the terms of any licence permitting limited copying issued by the Copyright Licensing Agency, 33–34 Alfred Place, London WC1E 7DP. Any person who does any unauthorised act in relation to this publication may be liable to prosecution and civil claims for damages.

The right of Greg Kelly and Robbie Gilligan to be identified as authors of this work has been asserted by them in accordance with the Copyright, Designs and Patents Act 1988.

First published in the United Kingdom in 2000 by
Jessica Kingsley Publishers Ltd,
116 Pentonville Road, London
N1 9JB, England
and
325 Chestnut Street,
Philadelphia PA 19106, USA.

www.jkp.com

© Copyright 2000 Jessica Kingsley Publishers

Library of Congress Cataloging in Publication Data
A CIP catalog record for this book is available from the Library of Congress

British Library Cataloguing in Publication Data
A CIP catalogue record for this book is available from the British Library

ISBN 1 85302 465 1

KING ALFRED'S COLLEGE
WINCHESTER

362.733
/KEL   KA024599906

Printed and Bound in Great Britain by
Athenaeum Press, Gateshead, Tyne and Wear

Contents

Introduction

Greg Kelly and Robbie Gilligan

All states that have the nuclear family – mother and/or father and dependent children – as their basic building block have to develop policies and services to cope with the contingency of the family failing to or being unable to care for the children. All societies that have laws against the abuse and neglect of children have to have services that will try to ensure that children are protected and nurtured and these services will need to include 'safe houses' where children can be cared for. One would expect, therefore, the development of policies and services for 'children in need' to be central to the political processes of our democratic states. In most societies, however, they have been at the margins of political life, thrust into centre stage by crises that have caught public attention usually because of the lurid and spectacular abuse of children or, more rarely, the suffering of families. Child-care policies, in the main, occupy the margins reserved for the poor and the economically weak of our societies.

In the United Kingdom and Ireland this culture of neglect punctuated by bouts of frenzied concern based around spectacular and therefore untypical cases has led to a staccato and chequered development of child-care policy. The emphases have ranged from the punishment of neglecting parents, to at least some efforts to help them through preventive policies, to a preoccupation with the detection of and protection of children from identified forms of abuse. Alongside have run policies that have punished children along with their parents, sought to rescue children from their parents with the emphasis sometimes on returning them to their families and at other times on ensuring they were well trained in an institutional setting and more recently on providing them with a 'fresh start' and a new family. Religion, politics, the law, the development of theory bases in psychology and social work have all influenced the approach to children in need. In this crowded and confused picture an absolutely key development has been the gradual acceptance that children have rights and needs of their own, separate from their parents and their families. Foster care, too, has been subject to a range of influences in its development but it can be seen as one of the early expressions of this recognition of the rights of the child. From the earliest years of its development foster care was an expression of the child's need for and right to the personalised family care that the workhouse and other crowded institutions could not provide.

Across the world countries are developing foster care as their preferred placement for 'out of home' care (Colton and Williams 1997). This, in part, reflects a growing appreciation of the needs of children. From the earliest years of its development, foster care has the capacity to deliver on children's key needs while also allowing, where appropriate, children to remain in touch with and identified with their birth families. The qualities of foster care that give it the potential to meet a wide range of children's needs are:

- it offers care in a family setting
- it offers care in the community
- it offers the opportunity to make attachment relationships to committed foster parents
- it can permit children to continue to be attached and identify with family of origin
- it can include the child's family in the care of the child
- it can provide care and support into adulthood
- it can channel extra support from the agency for the child and carers.

Foster care offers all these positive features for the agencies charged with caring for children. It has provided an established example of a service that has drawn flexibly on community resources to reduce reliance on institutional care, truly a 'community care' service. Foster care provides agencies with a highly flexible service. Agencies retain control over who they recruit and how they assess and support them. The term foster care now embraces many different forms of care provided by many different types of carer; these are summarised in Figure 1.1.

It is not surprising then that foster care has become the dominant placement of our child care systems. In England and Wales the proportion of children in care who are in foster care has grown from one-third to two-thirds in the last 20 years. In Northern Ireland, of the children in care and living away from their parents almost 80 per cent are in foster care and the actual number of

Who are foster carers:

- The child's relatives
- Largely untrained volunteers paid expenses
- Trained and supported volunteers
- Salaried foster carers

Types of foster care:

- Respite for parents
- Short-term care in emergencies
- Short-term care for assessment or preparation for long term
- Medium or long-term care
- Specialist placements for adolescents

Figure 1.1 The range of foster care

Ireland the percentage of children in care who are in foster care grew from 50 per cent to 75 per cent between 1977 and 1997. In all jurisdictions this growth has been mainly at the expense of residential care.

Foster care has truly become the 'work horse' of the child welfare systems in the UK, Ireland and many other countries. It may lack some of the qualities that are claimed for the 'thoroughbred' adoption, but adoption remains an exclusive privilege for a small minority in most care systems. In England and Wales, for example, the proportion of children placed for adoption in any one year has rarely risen beyond 5 per cent (Triseliotis 1999) and it has had an even less significant impact in other jurisdictions (Kelly and Coulter 1997). This book sets out to restate the importance of foster care, to understand its contribution historically and to re-examine what it uniquely can offer to the diverse problems of children in care and their families. In Chapter 1 Greg Kelly looks at the role of values, theory and research in the development of foster care and the challenges to it and in Chapter 3 he considers the range of outcome studies of foster care. In Chapter 2 Robbie Gilligan discusses children's experiences and views of foster care. In Chapter

4 John Pinkerton shows the enhanced role foster care can play in the too-often neglected area of support for young people leaving care.

Despite its spectacular growth, or perhaps, in part, because of it, foster care has many problems. The temptation with a willing workhorse is to overwork it. To mix the metaphors it could be argued that we are burning the candle at both ends. We are placing more and more children with greater and greater degrees of difficulty (one end of the candle) and we are drawing from a diminishing pool of what have been our traditional foster parents (the other end). It is in the nature of modern state child care that only children who have, or whose families have, the most serious problems enter and stay in public care. The more of these children we place in foster care the greater the strain, frequently signified by children's continued and severe behavioural problems. If neglected, these pressures can be a contributory factor in the worst of all possible scenarios, the foster care itself becoming abusive of the children it is responsible for caring for. Good foster care must, first and foremost, be safe care. In Chapter 8 Stephen Nixon discusses safe care, abuse and allegations of abuse.

The social workers who support foster carers, and the foster carers themselves, need to develop a range of skills to address the generality of problems that placements generate, and children and young people's behaviour problems in particular. In Chapter 6 Stan Houston introduces Solution-Focused Brief Therapy to foster care and in Chapter 7 Ken Kerr sets out some behaviour management techniques that workers might use and encourage foster carers to use with children. But we do not always have to be problem focused – foster care offers wonderful opportunities for creative work with children who may have suffered a lot but who also have their own gifts and talents. Robbie Gilligan, in Chapter 5, uses the concept of resilience to explore how we can build on children's strengths.

The supply 'end of the candle' is a vexed question. Foster care relies at least in part on a sense of altruism. Of course foster parents hope to get a sense of satisfaction from parenting children but they are motivated primarily by wanting to help abused and needy children. This sense of altruism is not easily measurable but many of the indications are that maybe it is on the decline in advanced Western societies. To thrive it needs people with space in their lives; we cannot do good if we have no time to do it. Foster care has traditionally drawn on the resources of families where women were full-time housewives and mothers and had the capacity to care for another child. As our lifestyles more and more demand two pay-packets the 'housewife and our lifestyles more and more demand two pay-packets the 'housewife and mother' family structure has declined and alongside this there has been a growth in one-parent families. One solution has been to meet the recruitment problem head on and pay foster parents a salary. It becomes increasingly difficult to sustain an argument that those who provide such a valued and difficult service to the community should not be paid. However, the resource implications of a fully paid service are enormous and it is difficult to shake off the feeling that something would be lost for children if we totally abandon, on the one hand, the potential for altruism that traditional foster care offers and on the other its reliance on 'ordinary' family life.

An alternative means of trying to increase the supply of foster carers is to look to those whom we may have reasonable cause to expect might have an increased sense of altruism, or at least sense of responsibility, for particular children: their relatives. In the United States 'kinship care' has increased dramatically as admissions to public care have grown and the availability of 'traditional' foster family homes has at best stagnated. In Chapter 9 Valerie O'Brien sets out the dimensions and possibilities of 'relative care' and reviews the many issues it poses. In reality no system of public care is likely to be able to close off any source of potential carers. We would expect therefore that in the future most systems of foster care will comprise a more balanced combination of traditional, kinship and salaried placements.

References

Colton, M. and Williams, M. (1997) *The World of Foster Care.* Aldershot: Arena.

Kelly, G. and Coulter, J. (1997) The Children (NI) Order 1995: A new era for fostering and adoption services. *Adoption and Fostering 21*, 3, 5–13.

Triseliotis, J. (1999) Is permanency through adoption in decline? *Adoption and Fostering 22*, 4.

CHAPTER I

The Survival of Long-Term Foster Care

Greg Kelly

Introduction

Since the mid-1970s in Britain and the USA, the weight of theoretical argument has been that long-term foster care has serious deficiencies and that adoption offers the best care to children permanently separated from their birth families (Rowe and Lambert 1973; Rowe *et al.* 1984; Triseliotis 1983; Festinger 1983). This has led to some growth in the adoption of children from the care system in the UK through the 1980s. This has not been as marked or as extensive as might have been anticipated given the weight of professional opinion. The percentage of those, in England, discharged from care to adoption grew from 4.2 per cent to 7 per cent between 1981 and 1994 and varied greatly between different local authorities; since 1994 it has declined again slightly (Triseliotis 1999). Thus only a small minority of children in long-term care are adopted and most remain in long-term foster care, especially if they are over five at admission (Rowe, Hundleby and Garnett 1989). This chapter explores the reasons, firstly, for the growth of foster care at the expense of residential care and then for its survival. In England foster care grew from providing under a third of placements in 1975 to providing two-thirds in 1998 and residential care declined from providing over three-quarters of placements in 1975 to less than 20 per cent in 1998.

There are a multitude of influences on placement policy and practice in any one country, and a number of histories detail these over time (Heywood 1978; Packman 1975). These influences include social, political and economic factors that set the context for professional debate and decision making but which that debate can usually only influence at the margins. Within these broad contexts, however, the professional community has had considerable latitude in the development of policy and practice for children in care. The growth in adoption – often referred to as the 'permanence movement' – is an example of a policy change being led from within the professional community. Key elements in the professional debate on best practice are the values and the theory used to frame, to inform and to justify policy and practice. Here we will discuss, from a UK perspective, the role of values and attachment theory in particular in the development of policy and practice in relation to children in long-term substitute care. We will then consider key developments in the long-term care of children:

- the decline of residential care and the growth of foster care
- the criticisms of foster care
- the growth of the 'permanence' movement
- the survival of long-term foster care.

The chapter will conclude by considering what these discussions tell us about the core qualities of foster care and its key weaknesses and what they indicate about the way forward for long-term foster care.

Values and theory

Values tell us what we ought to do. Theories seek to provide rational models of explanation of the world as we see and experience it. Despite these apparently very different starting points, they can and do influence each other. Values can have a profound influence on what is studied to develop theory and they may also influence how findings are interpreted and put into practice. The influential British study *Children Who Wait* (Rowe and Lambert 1973) is a good example of both the tendency for values to influence what is studied and how findings are presented (Kelly 1998). The decision to study children 'waiting' for family placements in children's homes was taken by The Association of British Adoption Agencies, an organisation devoted to promoting *adoption* as the preferred placement for children facing long-term separation from their parents. The study's findings stressed the potential of adoption as the placement of choice rather than that of foster care, although most of the social workers questioned nominated foster care as the chosen placement for the children 'who were waiting' (Kelly 1998).

The theoretical work of Bowlby (1953) and Robertson and Robertson (1967/68) on the attachment of infants is an example of theoretical work profoundly influencing values. In the light of their work, child-care professionals no longer believed it good enough to provide children with adequate physical care in clean institutions as they had done for the preceding generations. The new theory taught them that attachment and emotional needs as well as physical ones ought to be provided for in care placements, leading to a new value position.

The distinction between theory and values is a useful one much used in social work education. It enables us to concentrate on different influences on practice. We follow that tradition in what follows but with the warning that the two are often not as far apart as they seem or as those apparently arguing from one perspective or the other would have us believe.

Values

Values are essentially belief systems. They are statements of what we believe *ought* to be done, and when strongly held they can be impervious to arguments for change whether these be theoretical, practical or economic. Since child welfare has as its focus the care of children, the role of the family and the interface between the state and the family, it is particularly prone to its practitioners adopting strong value positions. Everyone has an emotional investment in their experience of family life. No-one can pretend to look at issues of child care with anything approaching a scientific objectivity. However, the management culture now current in public services demands that policy and practice are justified on rational and empirical grounds – on outcomes and cost rather than on what we think ought to be done. Practice differences that are, at base, the result of different value stances are often disputed not in terms of the values that are at their root but rather on less emotive theoretical, practical or legal grounds:

> We can all point to examples of literature in which feelings masquerade as reason and in which one senses a powerful need to persuade readers that one side of the story ... is paramount. (Stevenson 1991, p.x)

It is, of course, important that decisions are taken on the basis of what can be shown, 'rationally', to be in the child's best interests. However, if individuals or agencies are 'rationally' resolving all or most of their difficult placement decisions in one direction one should look for an underlying value or belief system that places one solution above another. Some contentions used to justify a particular approach to child placement have the clear ring of value positions. An example of this is the oft-heard view that 'a public authority cannot adequately parent a child' which is used to support the widespread use of adoption as a route out of care. Public care is socially constructed; it is as good as we make it. We can and have in the past made it excellent care for children. To use some evidence of its imperfections to condemn all long-term state care can be seen as a value-laden judgement.

Shifting values

Value systems lived out by people and institutions can appear rigid and impervious to rational argument, but across and within societies they do change over time. In British child care in the 1960s and 1970s the service was based on an ethos of support for families and a belief that child-care problems were the result, predominantly, of poverty. In the aftermath of the child-abuse scandals of the 1970s and 1980s this value base largely gave way to a preoccupation with the harm that parents may be inflicting on their children, and an attitude of suspicion towards families in need. These and other changes in dominant value positions have been likened to the swing of a pendulum, moving to one side and then the other of some apparently unattainable central norm. The engine of change pushing the pendulum in either direction often appears to be the spectacular individual case that, through frequently lurid media coverage, has a profound influence on public opinion and professional attitudes. The inquiry into the death of Maria Colwell (DHSS 1974) at the hands of her stepfather set the pendulum swinging towards a service dominated by the values of child protection. The Cleveland inquiry (Secretary of State for Social Services 1988) into the widespread diagnosis of child sexual abuse pushed it back towards increased rights for parents and support for families culminating in the Children Act 1989. Setting out different value positions, while useful for descriptive and analytical purposes, has difficulty in taking account of this dynamic in the relationships between the different positions.

A final problem in determining the influence of values is that, while the leading advocates of particular positions, for example British Agencies for Adoption and Fostering (BAAF) and the Family Rights Group (FRG) at the height of the permanence movement debate, may be totally committed to them, those whose practice actually determines what happens to children may be much more flexible. They will often choose pragmatically from a menu of value positions according to their perception of the needs of the

family and child they are working with and other pressures and influences –
the culture of their organisation, the resources available, their perception of
their local court proceedings (Fox Harding 1997) This eclectic approach is
further prompted by the law and research findings often being open to a
variety of interpretations.

The child's best interests

The range of different value positions informing practice and policy making
is often hidden behind the now widely accepted core value of modern child
care: that all decisions and actions should seek to further the 'best interests of
the child', making the child's welfare the 'paramount consideration'. Seeking
'the best interests of the child', sometimes called the 'welfare test', has been
established as the core value in child welfare work in many jurisdictions. It
has been enshrined in the United Nations Convention on the Rights of the
Child, Article 3:

> In all actions concerning children, whether undertaken by public or private
> social welfare institutions, courts of law, administrative authorities or
> legislative bodies, the best interests of the child shall be a primary con-
> sideration.

It is important not to underestimate the importance of the establishment of
the welfare test. Histories of child welfare are largely histories of the struggle
to achieve it and accounts of the dire consequences for the generations of
abandoned and neglected children before its acceptance (Heywood 1978;
Robins 1980). The problem in modern practice is that, in all but the most
extreme circumstances, there can be a variety of sincerely held views as to
what is in a child's best interests in terms of long-term care. In the formula-
tion of government and agency policy, there can be plausible arguments for
quite different approaches to child placement. The advocates of each would
argue that their approach is based on furthering children's best interests. In
day-to-day practice, parents, social workers and other professionals can all
take widely varying views of what should be decided in relation to a particular child. They, too, would all claim to start from the point of the child's best
interests although they may often dispute the others' claim to be doing so!
  'The welfare test [the child's best interests] is not an objective test that can
be impartially implied. At best it should be a constant reminder to all adults
in child welfare services that children and young people must be at the heart
of all that we do' (Ryburn 1993, p.4). In this sense the welfare test is not

prescriptive: it cannot tell us what to do. It is an aspiration, a call to best practice. What we do in practice will be influenced by one or more of a number of different, commonly held value positions all of whose adherents would contend that the pursuit of them would further the best interests of children.

Four value positions in child care

In an attempt to develop understanding of the complexity of the state's role in child care and to get beyond simplistic arguments about 'the child's best interests' Fox Harding (1997) has usefully identified four value positions in child welfare.

1. *Laissez faire.* Proponents of this position argue that the state should have a minimum policing function in relation to the family. Further intervention damages the autonomy of the family. The state's role is to establish children removed from their parents in substitute families and then withdraw, sanctioning minimum interference from outside the newly formed family (Goldstein, Freud and Solnit 1980b). This emphasis on minimum state interference clearly points towards adoption with its finality as the solution for children who cannot return home. Its adherents would discourage the use of foster care with its continued social worker involvement and the child remaining in state care.

2. *State paternalism and child protection.* In this view the state has a major role in policing family life and in intervening to ensure good child care. When care is not good enough, it should intervene to remove children, find them substitute family care and, if necessary, support this alternative care at the expense of the child's links to his/her biological family. Intervention is framed in terms of rescuing the child, usually from its parents. This position, too, would support the development of the use of adoption as the most complete 'rescue' solution for children in long-term care. Foster care, too, has always contained strong elements of this child rescue value base, particularly where it excludes the child's past life and birth family. This has been the dominant value position through most of the history of child care and has been particularly dominant in recent decades when child care has been dominated by child protec-

tion. It is clearly stated in a number of UK child abuse inquiry reports (London Borough of Brent 1985).

3. *The defence of the birth family and parents' rights.* From this perspective, the state has a major role in supporting family life. This view would hold that most child-care problems are caused by the under-resourcing of parents and lack of investment in child care and family life. Resources used to 'police' families would be better used supporting them. For children in substitute family care, their relationships with their biological families should be respected and promoted. These links to 'kith and kin' are important in themselves. Advocates would, therefore, be generally opposed to adoption without parents' consent, and would advocate a foster-care practice that encourages birth parents to remain involved. They would stress the importance of state agencies working in partnership with parents. This position has been most cogently represented in Britain by The Family Rights Group and by Holman (1988).

4. *Children's rights.* Services should empower children and enable them to have a real say in decisions made in relation to them in all aspects of their lives. This would include the type of placement sought for them and the relationships they maintain with their families while in care. Children and young people's groups tend to argue for a diversity of provision and a choice of placement, including residential care. They are often much more concerned than professional groupings about the services they receive to help them leave care and survive afterwards. This position has been given a limited encouragement by the Children Act (Lyon and Parton 1995) and the ratification of the UN Convention on the Rights of the Child.

All positions would stress the importance of the family in society, that it should be supported, that children should only be removed as a last resort, that they should be returned to their families if and as soon as practicable and that children's views on their placement should be heard and be influential. They have, as we have seen, very different views about the emphasis given to these different goals and how best they can be achieved. They would all maintain that their approach was consistent with furthering the best interests of the child.

A number of authors trace developments in the relative importance of these different perspectives in the history of child welfare systems in different countries (Kadushin 1980; Packman 1975; Gilligan 1991).

Values in foster care

Foster care touches most of the dilemmas of child care in general and so contains the range of value positions outlined above. Foster parents, social workers, birth parents, children and agencies all bring their own varied and varying beliefs. Thus in long-term foster care one can find foster parents and social workers who advocate an 'inclusive' approach that tries to keep the placement receptive to influences from social services and birth families, close to position 3 above. Equally one can find those that favour an 'exclusive' approach that concentrates on settling the child in the foster family and sees parents and sometimes social workers as interfering in this process, position 2 above (Holman 1982). There has, however, been evidence of a swing from the latter to the former in recent years and an 'inclusive' approach could now be said to represent the ideal in foster care with the 'exclusive' position more readily occupied by adoption:

> The [foster] carer plays a positive role – with the support of the authority – in encouraging a child or young person in her/his care to maintain family and other contacts as set out in the care plan. (UK Joint Working Party on Foster Care 1998)

A way of conceptualising the values of foster care as a service, as opposed to the child care services as a whole or other placements, is to try to identify what foster care can aspire to that other forms of placement cannot wholly achieve. Foster care can be said to be underpinned by beliefs in:

- family life for children and the unique experience that it can offer
- children's continuing relationship with their birth family
- partnership with birth parents
- a partnership between foster parents and the social services agency
- continued (post-placement) support and supervision from a state or voluntary agency
- recognition of carers' professional contribution to the community through various payment structures.

It is the values of 'openness', 'partnership' and 'participation' as well as a belief in and love for family life that we associate with foster carers and these values provide a general guide to what we are looking for in assessing prospective carers. Individual children will need carers with various elements of this mix in various strengths.

Theory and its application to policy and practice

The knowledge and theory that we use to understand and plan action in relation to family and child-care problems is derived from many sources and disciplines. In the issues surrounding substitute family care the key questions that we need answers to are to do with the nature of children's needs and how these can be met within the placements available to us. Common to all classifications of children's needs is their need for 'love and security' and their need to be 'attached' to at least one consistent, caring and loving adult (Pringle 1975; Fahlberg 1994). Attachment theory has grown to explain children's need for attachments, the process by which they develop these attachments and the consequences if these processes go wrong (Bowlby 1979; Rutter 1980).

For most children their relationships with their parent(s) and their wider family and community provide their principal attachment figures. For children removed into care this most basic of needs is immediately threatened and, indeed, they may have been removed because it was not being adequately met within their families. For these children the responsibility for seeing that this need is met lies with social workers and others in the child welfare field. As societies have become more affluent and children's physical and health needs are more routinely met, meeting children's attachment needs has assumed a central importance in child-care policy and practice. There is now widespread acceptance of Bowlby's view that disrupted attachments without compensating, stabilising experiences in childhood lead to unhappiness and often the development of antisocial behaviour (Rutter 1980; Fahlberg 1994). Thus 'attachment theory' has become the key theoretical perspective informing child-care decision making. This may have helped sharpen the focus in decision making but debates have continued on how best to secure children's attachment relationships both in the development of agency policies on child placement and in individual cases.

Attachment theory

Bowlby's early writing on attachment theory in his book *Child Care and the Growth of Love* (1953):

> ...instantly became the bible of the new child care training courses and established itself as probably the most influential publication ever in the field of child care at both policy and practice levels. (Shaw 1987, p.16)

The basis of attachment theory is that human beings (and most bird/animal species) are born with a predisposition to form attachment relationships:

> Children have a natural propensity to maintain proximity with a mother figure, that leads to an attachment relationship and ... the quality of this relationship in terms of security/insecurity serves as a basis for later relationships. (Rutter 1991, p.341)

For most children the 'mother figure' is their mother but children will readily attach to other sympathetic persons who are available and responsive – including fathers!

The function of this element of our make-up, in our early history as a species, was our protection from danger and predators. It is self-evident that babies and young children remain very vulnerable and in need of protection, nurturing and education through their early years. The denial or the disruption of the relationships which provide this protection and the associated sense of security can cause infants extreme anxiety, separation anxiety. Most parents will have seen evidence of this in their parenting experience. The exploration of this anxiety in children separated from their parents in residential nurseries and hospitals and the comparison with the much-reduced distress when children were cared for by foster parents (Robertson and Robertson 1967/68) during similar separations was of central importance in the development of foster care and the demise of residential care for young children. This reduced distress was seen as a consequence of foster care's capacity to provide alternative attachment figures and the basic conditions in which attachment could flourish over time:

- a small number of consistent caretakers caring for the child continuously
- the potential for a good quality of interaction between carers and child
- the commitment of foster parent to the child

- the understanding of the need to 'foster' attachment relationships between foster parents and the child.

It is a measure of foster care's flexibility that, as well as providing substitute attachment figures, it also has the capacity to help sustain the child's relationships with their birth family/parents. This is of prime importance where the plan is to rehabilitate the child to her family. Foster care can:

- enable the foster parents to be known and accepted by the birth family and the child before placement, and so foster care can be seen as an extension of the child's attachment relationships rather than as a disruption of them

- encourage parents to keep in contact and so prevent the attachments being disrupted

- keep the parent(s) alive for the child in routines and conversation of the foster home

- encourage the child's sense of belonging to their 'own' family.

This use of foster care to diminish the trauma of separation and disrupted relationships for children entering public care is greatly aided by the capacity of children to form attachment relationships with a number of people from the earliest age (Schaffer and Emerson 1964). There is nothing inconsistent with attachment theory in children developing a strong attachment relationship with a foster carer but retaining, through visiting and other contact, a similar relationship with their parents.

The problem for these shared attachments is their long-term viability. They are clearly the ideal when children are coming into care for short periods and all are working towards their rehabilitation. They may also be suitable when children are coming into care at an older age with well-established relationships and a strong sense of identity with their families. When the plan is for long-term or permanent care, particularly for younger children with negligible or less developed relationships with their families, then the motivation and capacity to sustain these relationships can diminish. The UK research shows a consistent trend of children losing touch with their families the longer they remain in care (Rowe *et al.* 1984; Millham *et al.* 1986). The children and their foster carers can be left in a kind of limbo where they do not feel they fully belong to each other. It is this sense of drift for these children, the sense of not really belonging to their foster family or to their birth family, that the 'permanence' movement has focused on in its criticism of long-term foster care (see below).

In the debate between the 'laissez faire' and the 'defence of the birth family' value positions, the continuance or otherwise of parental contact in long-term foster care situations was often the chosen battleground. The latter argued, from attachment theory, for contact to be continued to preserve existing family attachments, the loss of which would leave the child damaged (Family Rights Group 1982). The former argued for contact to be discontinued on the ground that it was interfering with the capacity of 'new' parents and child to commit to each other. Both sides also drew, selectively, on research to support their position:

> Many of the arguments for maintaining contact are concerned with the *rights* of children and birth parents ... but arguments based on rights are frequently bolstered through an appeal to research evidence on the *effects* ... (Quinton *et al.* 1997, p.394)

Following an extensive review of the research, which they maintain gives us only 'rudimentary' knowledge, Quinton *et al.* settle for a middle course:

> We agree with the current emphasis on maintaining links in non-adoptive placements whenever this is possible, not least on the grounds that families remain an important potential source of support for their children ... The evidence on adoptive placements is not yet sufficient to make a choice either way. (p.394)

Remedying the damage of disrupted attachments

What the attachment theorists, led by Bowlby, have shown to the satisfaction of most analysts is that the effects of damaged and disrupted attachments are potentially long-term and serious (Rutter 1991). Bowlby's (1953) dictum from *Child Care and the Growth of Love*: 'mother love in infancy and childhood is as important for mental health as are vitamins and proteins for physical health' has become a central belief of subsequent generations of child-care professionals, although the 'mother love' has been widened to encompass stable attachment relationships in general.

Much of the debate about attachment theory has revolved around the extent to which the harmful effects of deprived and disrupted attachments can be remedied. The early work of Bowlby was pessimistic in this respect but subsequent opinion has been much more optimistic (Clarke and Clarke 1976; Rutter 1980). Much of this optimism is based on studies of children who have come into care, from deprived circumstances, and then been successfully placed in adoptive or foster families (Tizard 1977; Rowe *et al.* 1984). This widespread optimism must be tempered by studies that have shown that children with very deprived early childhoods may retain residual damage into their adolescence and perhaps beyond (Rutter 1991).

In terms of the application of attachment theory to policy and practice, foster care can make a unique contribution to remedying attachment-related problems in broadly two ways:

1. It can provide substitute parenting that will complement and support the attachments between the separated parent and child, by providing additional, consistent attachment figures but not seeking to replace the child's existing attachments. In these, usually short-term, situations the foster care service needs to:

    *   support and encourage parents to visit their children
    *   be committed to a partnership with parents that values them
    *   involve parents in all aspects of their children's care and have foster parents committed to doing the same
    *   have placements that are local and accessible where children and parents can be responsible for their own contact arrangements
    *   be responsive to the changing needs and wants as expressed by children themselves.

2. It can provide long-term substitute attachment figures when parents are unable or are judged unable to care for their children. Here the foster-care service needs to provide conditions that enable new attachments to flourish. These will include:

    *   helping the child to come to terms with the past and feel free to move into the new relationships
    *   trying to achieve the birth parents' support for the new foster family and negotiating continued contact within the context of this support
    *   ensuring that the necessary feelings of permanence and security in both foster parents and child are encouraged and not undermined by the over-bureaucratisation of the service or the continued use of the placement for short-term admissions

- having expertise that can offer practical help to foster parents faced with the emotional crises and the behavioural problems that are often the consequence of disrupted attachments.

In all child care the service's decision-making processes need to be open and to 'hear' children, their parents and their foster parents. Attachment relationships are always two-way, between the child and the adult; healthy relationships are dependent on *both* reacting and interacting appropriately (Fahlberg 1994). In foster care they are even more complex and services need to reflect this complexity with balanced support for all the relationships that are important for the child.

The widespread acceptance of attachment theory in the professional child-care community has been criticised by black workers who often complain that the theory as interpreted by predominantly white professionals is culturally biased. The preoccupation with the nuclear family and maternal attachment does not reflect attachment patterns in black families:

> To black people, the meaning of bonding is very different to that which is held by society in general and social workers in particular. Bonding between black children and parents is seen as multi-dimensional while in the British context it is within the nuclear family. (Pennie and Best 1990, p.2, quoted in Fratter 1996, p.11)

The recent growth of kinship care in the USA has been accompanied by the increasing recognition of different patterns of relationships among different ethnic groups. Taking account of cultural differences, families are children's chief source of attachment figures. If the family, broadly or narrowly defined, fails the child, then the adolescent and the adult that the 'child is father to...' are at risk of serious emotional and psychological trauma. The policy and practice messages from attachment theory for child welfare workers are that we should seek to avoid this damage by preventing family failure or, if this is not possible, minimising damage by finding the child alternative care arrangements that meet his or her attachment needs. Attachment theory has helped narrow the range of placement options by establishing the conditions necessary for the growth and development of attachment relationships (Fahlberg 1994) but it leaves a wide area for debate and discretion. We now discuss how attachment theory and the various value stances have influenced the development of placement policy and practice.

Residential care or foster care?

Children who come into care are clearly at risk of emotional damage through lost or disrupted attachments. There have been two principal placements for such children in the last century: residential care and foster care. It will be immediately obvious that foster care, with its family setting, is more likely to be able to provide the conditions for the growth of alternative attachments than residential care with its institutionalised structures. Under modern conditions residential staff work shifts and change jobs frequently, inhibiting the growth of attachment relationships with children. This 'common sense' view of what is good for children is confirmed by research. Colton (1988) found that foster care was more child-centred in each of four areas:

1. The management of daily events.

2. Children's involvement in community activities.

3. The provision of physical amenities.

4. The techniques used by foster parents and staff to maintain control over the children.

He attributed the differences in care to the 'institutionally-oriented nature of the children's homes' and believed this 'owes much to the bureaucratisation of such provision.'

Residential care has declined as the provider of long-term care in many countries. The direct and powerful application of attachment theory, especially in relation to young children, has been significant in this (Robertson and Robertson 1967/68). This process has been accelerated by wider social changes and pressures. Colton and Hellinckx (1993) suggest three main reasons:

1. Institutions in general are in decline, 'from monasteries to kibbutzim to universities and mental hospitals', a reflection of 'much wider social processes in post-industrial societies.'

2. It has become increasingly difficult and expensive to organise residential care to deliver the conditions in which attachment relationships and normal social relations can flourish.

3. In Britain and Ireland confidence in residential care has been severely shaken by a series of abuse scandals over a fifteen-year period. These scandals have involved physical and sexual abuse in homes run by religious orders and the state agencies.

Thus as we have seen above, the proportion of children in foster care in England doubled in 20 years and those in residential care dropped even more drastically. This pattern was repeated throughout the United Kingdom and in many other countries. However, caution is needed: annual figures often do not include the short-term admissions who come into and leave care through the year, for which residential care is more often used. They may therefore exaggerate the decline in the use and the importance of residential care.

Despite the apparently overwhelming arguments ranged against it, residential care, although reduced, is far from extinct. Important as it is, attachment is only one of a range of needs that children who come into public care have and even where attachment is the prime consideration one means of combating loss of attachment is the provision of local user-friendly residential care. Even where there is a developed fostering service, residential care remains an important part of the provision – for admissions, for short-term stays, for older children and for children who do not need, do not want or cannot manage the attachment relationships that foster care offers. It is also often the placement of choice after foster placement breakdown (Rowe *et al.* 1989).

Adoption or foster care?

As we have seen above, foster care became the dominant long-term placement for the generality of children in the UK in public care from the mid-1980s on. In Britain foster care has long been the preferred placement for young children because it more readily provides them with substitute attachment figures. For older children there is more often a mix between residential care and foster care depending on local traditions and resources. Where return home is the plan, it is the capacity of the placement to maintain the child's relationship with parents to facilitate return home that is of central importance.

It has been the placement of the minority of children – particularly younger children – who do not return home from public care that has been the focus of heated debate. How small a minority this is in any particular jurisdiction is very difficult to ascertain. It is one of the weaknesses of child welfare systems that this kind of basic data is not routinely available. It essentially takes a research project to map children's movements in and out of care. This lack of a flow of basic data is one of the most serious impediments to the development of a firm theoretical base. Imagine an immigration office that could not tell who and how many of last year's visitors had departed the country and how many had applied for permanent residence! Research has helped to fill this gap in basic information systems: in the USA, Katz reports that of the children 'placed' in public care as a result of a Child Protection Services report, '25–30% will never go home' (Katz 1996). In the UK, Millham *et al.* (1981) reported that 38% of the children admitted to care did not go home within 2 years, by which time the rate of return home 'diminishes to a trickle' (Rowe *et al.* 1989).

There has been a continuing debate on the relative merits of long-term foster care or adoption as the placement of choice in these situations where return home is not foreseen. This is a good example of a debate conducted on the basis of the theory and knowledge base but with a strong thread of values running through the arguments on both sides. As will be evident from the discussion above, the 'laissez faire' and elements of the 'child protection' value positions favour adoption, where the child is out of state care and removed from the influence of the birth family who have failed it. 'Only a child who has at least one person whom he can love and who also feels loved, valued and wanted by that person, will develop a healthy self-esteem' (Goldstein, Freud and Solnit 1980a).

Goldstein, Freud and Solnit maintained that the child/foster-parent relationship has 'little likelihood' of achieving the desired 'psychological parent'/'wanted child' relationship because of the intrusion of the state agency, the child's birth parents and, what were said to be, the generally temporary nature of the arrangements:

> ... this serves to explain the frequent breakdown of foster placements, the emotional bonds of the adult to the children will be loose enough to be broken whenever external circumstances make the presence of the foster child in the home inconvenient or irksome. (Goldstein, Freud and Solnit 1980b, p.26)

The 'defence of the birth family and parents' rights' value position favours long-term foster care with its potential for continued birth family involvement. It would also be very opposed to the processes associated with achieving adoption without parents' consent. This may include the reduction or the denial of parents' access to their child in care and bitterly contested court proceedings. The result is an adoption order that completely excludes the birth family and this is anathema to a value position that is predicated on support for the natural family.

As well as the criticisms levelled at foster care from the Goldstein, Freud, Solnit value-laden theoretical perspective, a further source of criticism was the research into the long-term public care of children in general and foster care in particular.

Research and evaluation of long-term foster care

In Britain in the 1960s and 1970s there were basically two main areas of research into foster care:

1. The outcomes of foster care placements. These showed high break-down rates for children in long-term foster care.

2. The capacity of the child-care service to deliver the necessary foster placements. In the United Kingdom this was most notably highlighted by Rowe and Lambert's (1973) work *Children who Wait*.

The conclusion often drawn from these studies was that foster care was having difficulty being successful even on its own terms of providing sufficient stable long-term placements, let alone those set for it by the work of Goldstein, Freud and Solnit.

In terms of the outcomes of long-term foster placements, there were two major and influential studies in the UK in 1960s and 1970s (Parker 1966; George 1970) and they both showed high levels of placement disruption. Studying long-term placements, Parker found that 52 per cent disrupted within five years and George found a rate of 60 per cent of disruptions over the same period. These results have produced the oft-quoted dictum – 'a half of all long-term placements break down'. This figure worsens for older children and improves for younger children. In George's study, for children placed when they were five or over it rose to 78 per cent. The negative impact of these and later studies (Berridge and Cleaver 1987) for foster care was greatly heightened by the comparative figures for adoption of older children in the USA (Kadushin 1970) where success rates in excess of 90 per cent were frequently reported even for school-age children.

Children Who Wait was a particularly influential study (Rowe and Lambert 1973). It provided evidence that large numbers of children were spending their childhoods in public care and in residential care. Public care was not achieving stable long-term family placements for many children who were deemed to need them. Rowe and Lambert argued that the preferred placement for many of these children was adoption, although the great majority of the respondent social workers in the study chose foster care. It too used examples of the American experience of successfully placing older and otherwise 'hard to place' children for adoption (Kelly 1998).

The permanence movement

The various strands of the argument against public care in general and foster care in particular and the associated advocacy of adoption were gathered under a one-word banner: 'Permanence'. And what a word! Who could argue against *permanence* as an ambition for children whose lives have been scarred by abuse and disruption? The permanence banner can be traced to the 'movement's' origins in the United States. There it was a much more broadly based practice development than the narrowly 'pro-adoption' lobby it became associated with in the United Kingdom (Thoburn 1986). The 'opponents' of the permanence movement were never wholly successful in matching the public relations achieved by the clarity and the appeal of the call for 'permanence' for children. In Britain The 'Family Rights' Group has, perhaps, come closest. For many years, however, through the 1980s, when the preoccupation of child welfare was principally child protection, which usually meant protecting children from their parents, the weight of professional opinion strongly favoured the permanence lobby. It will be evident from the earlier material on values that this was (and is), in many respects, a debate between fundamentally different value positions: the 'laissez faire' and the 'child protection' positions as expressed in the permanence movement against 'the defence of the birth family and parents' rights' position as defended by family rights organisations.

The permanence movement developed from an amalgam of a value and a theoretical perspective that leant towards the legal security of adoption as providing for the best interests of children who could not be cared for by their parents. In the climate of fear that accompanied the 'rediscovery' of child abuse in Britain it soon promoted radical changes in law and practice (Kelly 1998). In Britain, the Children Act 1975 made it easier for foster parents to adopt and the Adoption Act 1976 introduced a process to free children for adoption. Agencies developed permanence policies to apply the theory and implement the new legal provisions (Hussell and Monaghan 1982).

The survival of long-term foster care

In the 1970s and 1980s in the UK, and to a greater or lesser extent in many English-speaking countries, there was a wide and formidable array of arguments ranged against long-term foster care:

- the popularity and attractiveness of the Goldstein, Freud and Solnit standpoint and that of other 'permanence' theorists
- the anti-birth family mentality that was a consequence of the preoccupation with child abuse
- the evidence from research of foster care's failings
- the changes in legislation and policy that followed the acceptance of these trends.

In such circumstances it is perhaps surprising that foster care has not become extinct as a long-term placement option. There were some who forecast that it would or should do so (Boswell 1980) and there has been a significant growth in the adoption of children from care, albeit from a tiny base. The number of children adopted from care in England doubled between 1988 and 1996 (Ivaldi 1998). However, foster care was not defenceless in the face of these arguments and, perhaps most significantly in the UK, the legal route to adoption for children in the care system where their parent(s) did not consent has proved a difficult, slow and tortuous one (Lowe 1993; Coulter, Kelly and Switzer 1996). This was, in part, because it has involved a conflict in fundamental values. It asks workers and courts to reject their commitment to support birth families and the child in care's relationship with them in favour of the child's 'permanent' and secure future in an adoptive home. Crossing this threshold has demanded a high level of conviction from agencies and workers and exacting degrees of evidence from the courts. Even in a system dominated by fears of child abuse and so often unsympathetic to birth families, this often proved a step too far. Long-term foster care that has the potential to provide a substitute family without the traumas of protracted and bitter court proceedings against often disadvantaged and impoverished parents has proved an attractive alternative.

Foster care had its 'defences' on the theory side of the argument as well. In relation to the Goldstein, Freud and Solnit call for attachment to be promoted to one set of carers only, there was evidence from the study of attachment that did not support this exclusive position. Children show evidence of multiple attachments, to two parents, to siblings, to extended family and even to neighbours (Schaffer and Emerson 1964) from the earliest age at which they exhibit attachment behaviour. This does not support the contention that children need exclusive attachment figures or that they cannot endure the multiple or shared attachment relationships involved in foster care. This work does emphasise that attachment figures differ in significance and does not undermine the principle of the child's needs for stability of at least one primary attachment figure. Nonetheless, children's capacity for multiple attachments can be used to support long-term fostering (Benians 1982) as a potentially viable option. Children can and do receive adequate care in foster care and have the opportunity to make satisfactory attachment relationships without the exclusivity of traditional adoption (see Chapter 3).

The total severance of the 'blood tie' associated with traditional adoption also came to be questioned as adoption services developed. The numbers of adopted children who subsequently sought their birth parents grew in countries where there were opportunities for them to do so (Feast 1992). Their stories and those of their birth mothers led to a reappraisal of the 'fresh start, clean sheet' approach of traditional adoption. It was increasingly recognised that 'genealogical security' or knowledge of origins was an important component in the welfare of children separated from their birth families (Triseliotis 1983):

> All children are concerned with a sense of belonging and the need to know that they are related to and are like someone else, an extension of another as it were … The need to know who they are remains a potent question translated by the young ones into 'What does she look like? Does she look like me?' and by the older ones 'What does she look like? Do I look like her?' (Harper 1993)

This weakened the case for traditional adoption and strengthened the arguments for long-term foster care, where children can maintain a relationship with their birth families. It has also led to the development of 'adoption with contact' (with birth families) which, when taken with adoption allowance payment schemes, has moved adoption much closer to long-term foster care (Fratter 1996).

In relation to the enormous disparities in the success rates of adoption and fostering in providing stable placements, it was recognised at an early stage in the debate that this was in part accounted for by not comparing like with like (Rowe and Lambert 1973). Adoption services were more formally structured and carefully organised than fostering services. All adoption placements had to be approved by the courts and this imposed a discipline often not present in fostering practice where placements could (and often did) drift from short-term emergency placements to long term quasi-adoption situations. Thus some of the differences in placement success may have been a reflection of these organisational factors rather than the intrinsic superiority of adoption over foster care.

This argument that it may be the capacity of the placement to deliver particular qualities that is more significant in determining outcome rather than its precise legal status was supported by research work on the Oregon Project, the original permanence project. Lahti reported that the child's *sense of* permanence was indeed related to placement success but this did not necessarily equate to *legal* permanence. A sense of permanence could be imparted to the child in foster care as well as adoption, and equally it may be absent in adoption (Lahti 1982).

It also became evident that the success rates for adoption and fostering placements began to converge when:

- agencies took the permanence issue seriously in relation to foster care and implemented appropriate planning and practice measures to eliminate the poor practice that had been a common feature in the past (Rushton, Treseder and Quinton 1988)
- adoption was used more often to place older children and those with special needs, who had been formerly placed in foster care.

One extensive study of over 1000 placements, three-quarters of which were adoption and one-quarter foster care, that were intended to be permanent concluded:

> In view of the fact that the increased risk of breakdown is often given as a reason for placing in adoption rather than foster care and for terminating contact with parents, it is important to note that when age at placement was held constant, there was no significant difference in breakdown rates between adoption or permanent foster placement. (Thoburn 1991, p.53)

It is important to emphasise that the foster-care practice studied here and that in the Lahti study was designed to address the issue of permanence. It was not the temporary open-ended situation that has characterised much foster-care practice in the past and perhaps in the present.

A further important element in the survival of long-term foster care was widespread acceptance in the UK and the USA that it simply did not go away despite the apparent strength of the arguments ranged against it. Adoption, despite its popularity with theorists and policy makers, did not develop as expected. Rowe *et al.*'s major study (1989) of placement patterns was among the first to point this out: they found it 'quite astonishing' that there had been such little use of adoption for older children 'in view of all the emphasis on planning for permanence and on adoption as a resource for older children' (Rowe *et al.* 1989). The same study concluded that 'long-term fostering is certainly not a thing of the past' but its emphasis was changing to the care of teenagers.

The findings on the low and patchy use of adoption were confirmed by a later series of studies across the UK. These reported that the use of 'freeing orders', one of the principal means of moving children from care to adoptive placements, had varied considerably from area to area and the process had been dogged by legal and procedural delay (Lowe 1993; Coulter *et al.* 1996; Lambert *et al.* 1990).

In workshops, Jane Rowe used to report her 1980s English study using the theme: 'Things are often not what they seem' and the conclusion of the published work lists commonly held beliefs about the development of practice that her data overturned, a principal one being the supposed demise of long-term foster care (Rowe *et al.* 1989). Acceptance and acclaim in journals and conferences is, fortunately or unfortunately, no guarantee of lasting impact on child-care practice. Practice, unlike theory, policy or law-making, is subject to the final arbiter: what is feasible in the current situation.

In terms of both the development of theory in relation to the needs of children and of research into its effectiveness, foster care has recovered some of the ground it appeared to have lost to adoption in the mid-1980s. In terms of practice it appears to have retained a high profile as a long-term placement, although perhaps less because of its perceived virtues than the problems with the principal alternative form of substitute family placement, adoption. However, so far as traditional long-term foster care is concerned, this debate has led to recognition of some of its weaknesses and to important developments in practice, particularly in trying to ensure the permanence and stability of these placements (Thoburn 1990). In this respect it is possible to see the benefits of a convergence between long-term foster care and adoption where each 'borrows' virtues from the other to counteract its own deficiencies.

Thus, in planning long-term foster care more attention should be paid to:

- consciously planning the placement to best practice standards to minimise the chances of breakdown
- nurturing the child's need for a sense of permanence
- eliminating or reducing the stigma of being in care
- creating a placement where both the child and the foster parents feel he or she belongs and which will potentially provide lifelong relationships.

All of these are qualities which have usually been more evident in adoption.

In planning the adoption, particularly of an older child, attention should be paid to:

- ways of meeting the child's need to have knowledge of and possibly contact with his or her birth family, including siblings
- the post-placement support offered to the child and adopters
- the funding of the placement to encourage a range of prospective adopters
- giving the child and the birth parents a say in decisions in relation to the planning and development of the placement.

All of these are qualities which have usually been more evident in foster care.

The aim should be not to end up with another rigidly applied formula but rather that placements should be creatively negotiated with the child's needs as paramount but also, as most children would appreciate, the needs of their birth families and substitute parents actively considered. Howe (1998) uses the work of philosopher Isaiah Berlin to support this negotiated route through the 'moral maze' of competing rights and to warn us against 'the appeal of the single truth a dominant fashion or a simple formula' ...

> And yet it is impossible to pursue a single set of values or behavioural probabilities without running into contradictions. We simply have to struggle and debate, trading one value for another, weighing the strength of one set of facts against another – with compassion and humility. (Howe 1998)

Conclusion

This chapter has set out to present an overview of the interplay between values and theory in the development of policy and practice in relation to the placement of children in long-term care. Its core message is to beware of global, prescriptive solutions. They may be more a reflection of the value positions of their advocates than a balanced appraisal of the available theory/knowledge base. In this context the value base informing this book is one of belief of and support for foster care. This belief is based on its potential flexibility. It is not a 'solution' to the problems of the separated child in the way the 'total severance model of adoption' or return home can be seen as potentially a 'once for all' solution. Rather it is a means of continuing to work with the issues and problems. This does not mean that it is the best solution in all circumstances or that there are not principles of practice and priorities that should be followed. In relation to much of the discussion in this chapter, the capacity to create a sense of permanence for the child would be an important standard against which foster-care practice should be judged.

With their emphasis on flexibility, foster care and modern adoption practice fit well into the post-modernist (Howe 1994) world where 'answers' and tidy solutions are distrusted. They provide the possibility of a set of relationships within which solutions can be sought. What these relationships are and how they will progress in caring for the child have to be negotiated in each case. This strength may also be seen as a weakness, and this is how it has been portrayed in recent years. Flexibility has been framed as unwieldy and untidy and dependent too much on the varied judgements of individual practitioners. It is difficult, but not impossible, to control with policies and procedures. It clearly demands high standards of professional practice from practitioners. It is our contention that this flexibility can and should lead to genuinely creative practice, enabling the needs of the individual child, their family and the substitute family to be addressed.

The problem for separated children and families is that the best option for them has either temporarily or permanently been lost and what is second best will vary, literally from individual to individual. The range of options potentially available in foster care (and modern adoption practice) can provide a framework for negotiating and moving towards those individualised solutions.

References

Berridge, D. and Cleaver, H. (1987) *Foster Home Breakdown*. Oxford: Blackwell.

Benians, R. (1982) Preserving parental contact: A factor on promoting healthy growth and development in children. In Family Rights Group, *Fostering Parental Contact*. London: FRG.

Boswell, A. (1980) Alternatives to long term foster care. *Adoption and Fostering 2*, 13–16.

Bowlby, J. (1953) *Child Care and the Growth of Love*. Harmondsworth: Penguin.

Bowlby, J. (1979) *The Making and Breaking of Affectional Bonds*. London: Tavistock.

Clarke, A.M. and Clarke, A.D.B. (1976) *Early Experience: Myth and Evidence*. London: Open Books.

Colton, M. (1988) *Dimensions of Substitute Care: A Comparative Study of Foster and Residential Care Practice*. Aldershot: Avebury.

Colton, M. and Hellinckx, W. (1993) *Child Care in the European Community*. Aldershot: Arena.

Coulter, J., Kelly, G. and Switzer, V. (1996) Freeing children for adoption: A review of the process. *Child Care in Practice 2*, 4, 4–12.

Department of Health and Social Services (1974) *Report of the Committee of Inquiry into the care and Supervision Provided in relation to Maria Colwell*. London: HMSO.

Fahlberg, V. (1994) *A Child's Journey Through Placement*. London: British Agencies for Adoption and Fostering.

Family Rights Group (1982) *Fostering Parental Contact*. London: Family Rights Group.

Feast, L. (1992) Working in the adoption circle – outcomes of section 51 counselling. *Adoption and Fostering 16*, 4.

Festinger, T. (1983) *No One Ever Asked Us*. New York: Columbia.

Fox Harding, L. (1991) *Perspectives in Child Care Policy*. Harlow: Longman.

Fratter, J. (1996) *Adoption with Contact, Implications for Policy and Practice*. London: BAAF.

George, V. (1970) *Foster Care*. London: Routledge and Kegan Paul.

Gilligan, R. (1991) *Irish Child Care Services*. Dublin: Inst. of Public Administration.

Goldstein, J., Freud, A. and Solnit, A. (1980a) *Beyond the Best Interests of the Child* (new edition). London: Burnet.

Goldstein, J., Freud, A. and Solnit, A. (1980b) *Before the Best Interests of the Child*. London: Burnet.

Harding, F. (1997) *Perspectives in Child Care Policy* (Second Edition). London: Longman.

Harper, J. (1993) What does she look like? What children want to know about their birth parents. *Adoption and Fostering 17*, 2, 29–36.

Heywood, J.S. (1978) *Children in Care*. London: Routledge and Kegan Paul.

Holman, R. (1982) Exclusive and inclusive fostering. In Family Rights Group, *Fostering Parental Contact*. London: Family Rights Group.

Holman, R. (1988) *Putting Families First: Prevention and Child Care.* Basingstoke: Macmillan.

Howe, D. (1994) Modernity, post-modernity and social work. *British Journal of Social Work,* 24, 513–532.

Howe, D. (1998) Adoption outcome research and practical judgement. *Adoption and Fostering 22,* 2.

Hussell, C. and Monaghan, B. (1982) Child care planning in Lambeth. *Adoption and Fostering 6,* 2, 21–24.

Ivaldi, G. (1998) *Children Adopted from Care – An Examination of Agency Adoptions in England 1996.* London: BAAF.

Kadushin, A. (1970) *Adopting Older Children.* New York: Columbia University Press.

Kadushin, A. (1980) *Child Welfare Services.* New York: Macmillan.

Katz, L. (1996). Permanency planning through concurrent planning. *Adoption and Fostering 20,* 2, 8–13.

Kelly, G. (1998) The influence of research on child care policy and practice. In Iwaniec, D. and Pinkerton, J. (eds) *Making Research Work.* Chichester: Wiley.

Lahti J. (1982) A follow-up study of foster children in permanent placements. *Social Service Review* (University of Chicago), 556–571.

Lambert, L., Buist, M., Triseliotis, J. and Hill, M. (1990) *Freeing Children for Adoption.* London: BAAF.

London Borough of Brent (1985) *A Child in Trust: Report of the Panel of Inquiry into the Circumstances Surrounding the Death of Jasmine Beckford.* London: Borough of Brent.

Lowe, N. (1993) *Report of the Research into the Use and Practice of the Freeing for Adoption Provisions.* London: HMSO.

Lyon, C. and Parton, N. (1995) Children's Rights and the Children Act 1989. In B. Franklin (ed) *The Handbook of Children's Rights: Comparative Policy and Practice.* London and New York: Routledge.

Millham, S., Bullock, R., Hosie, K. and Haak, M. (1986) *Lost in Care.* Aldershot: Gower.

Packman, J. (1975) *The Child's Generation.* London: Blackwell and Robertson.

Packman, J., with Randall, J. and Jacques, N. (1986) *Who Needs Care? Social Work Decisions About Children.* Oxford: Basil Blackwell.

Parker, R.A. (1966) *Decision in Child Care.* London: Allen and Unwin.

Pennie, P. and Best, F. (1990) *How the Black Family is Pathologised by the Social Services System.* London: Association of Black Social Workers and Allied Professionals.

Pringle, M. Kellmer (1975) *The Needs of Children.* London: Hutchinson.

Quinton, D., Rushton, A., Dance, C. and Mayes, D. (1997) *Clinical Child Psychology and Psychiatry 2,* 3.

Robertson, James and Robertson, Joyce (1967/68) *Young Children in Brief Separation* (Films). London: Tavistock Child Development Research Unit.

Robins, J. (1980) *The Lost Children.* Dublin: The Institute of Public Administration.

Rowe, J. and Lambert, L. (1973) *Children Who Wait.* London: Association of British Adoption Agencies.

Rowe, J., Cain, H., Hundleby, M. and Keane. A. (1984) *Long Term Foster Care.* London: Batsford/BAAF.

Rowe, J., Hundleby, M. and Garnett, L. (1989) *Child Care Now: A Survey of Placement Patterns.* London: BAAF.

Rushton, A., Treseder, J. and Quinton, A. (1988) *New Parents for Older Children.* London: BAAF.

Rutter, M. (1980) *Maternal Deprivation Reassessed* (2nd edition). London: Penguin.

Rutter, M. (1991) A fresh look at maternal deprivation. In P. Bateson (ed) *The Development and Integration of Behaviour.* Cambridge: Cambridge University Press.

Ryburn, M. (1993) Empowering Practice in Family Placement. Paper to International Foster Care Conference: Dublin.

Schaffer, H.R. and Emerson, P.E. (1964) The development of social attachments in infancy. *Monographs of the Society for research in Child Development 29,* 3.

Secretary of State for Social Services (1988) *Report of the Inquiry into Child Abuse in Cleveland 1987.* Cm. 412. London: HMSO.

Shaw, M. (1987) *Family Placement for Children in Care.* London: BAAF.

Stevenson, O. (1991) Preface. In Fox Harding, L. (ed) *Perspectives in Child Care Policy.* Harlow: Longman.

Thoburn, J. (1986) *Permanence in Child Care.* London: Blackwell.

Thoburn, J. (1990) *Success and Failure in Permanent Family Placement.* Aldershot: Gower/Avebury.

Thoburn, J. (1991) Survey findings and conclusions. In Fratter, I., Rowe, J., Sapsford, D. and Thoburn, J. (eds) *Permanent Family Placement: A Decade of Experience.* London: BAAF.

Tizard, B. (1977) *Adoption: A Second Chance.* London: Open Books.

Triseliotis, J. (1983) Identity and security in adoption and long term foster care. *Adoption and Fostering 7,* 1.

Triseliotis, J. (1999) Is permanency through adoption in decline. *Adoption and Fostering 22,* 4.

UK Joint Working Party on Foster Care (1998) *Consultation on National Standards in Foster Care.* London: National Foster Care Association.

CHAPTER 2

The Importance of Listening to the Child in Foster Care

Robbie Gilligan

UN Convention on the Rights of the Child

Article 12

1. State parties shall assure to the child who is capable of forming his or her own views the right to express those views freely in all matters affecting the child, the views of the child being given due weight in accordance with the age and maturity of the child.

2. For this purpose, the child shall in particular be provided the opportunity to be heard in any judicial and administrative proceedings affecting the child, either directly, or through a representative or an appropriate body, in a manner consistent with the procedural rules of national law.

Inspired by the above excerpts from the United Nations Convention on the Rights of the Child, this chapter explores why it is important to listen to the voice and experience of the child in foster care. It also considers some of the key themes emerging from what children in foster care have said to researchers who have sought their views on the experience of living in foster care. The reader will find, no doubt, that the children's own words make a powerful impact.

Article 12 of the UN Convention on the Rights of the Child sends out a very strong message about the importance of listening to the child's voice, whether listening as parent, foster carer, social worker, court or public body. This message is echoed and anticipated in the legislation of many states which have ratified the Convention, certainly in relation to the obligations of public bodies to discern and consider the wishes of the child. The Convention expects that the child should be free to express their views. It is not that the child's views must be acted on but that they be given 'due weight' in matters affecting them. The spirit of the Convention strives for balance between protecting children and encouraging their independent development. As Lücker-Babel (1995, p.404) puts it, 'it is not a question of right only, but also of the attitudes of all those who act, in one way or other, for children and in their names'. Cooper also argues for a balanced approach:

> An effective children's rights policy … needs to be based on a view of children as individuals with certain inalienable protection needs, a right to opportunities for full intellectual and social development, and the expectation that, as they mature, they will have more say in their lives. (Cooper 1998, p.84)

There are very strong reasons for giving a much more central place to the voice of the child in our decision making and service planning. There are *pragmatic* reasons: plans/decisions are more likely to be better informed and more likely to stick if the child feels heard and has had their views genuinely considered. As one Australian young person puts it:

> Having a say is good because it gets your point across to other people, what you're feeling. If you don't put your point across then they make the decision and you don't like the decision it just blows up in your face and in their face too, and causes more trouble. It's better to have a say when it's needed. (Quoted in Spall, Testro and Matchett 1998)

There are also *therapeutic* reasons for involving and listening to young people: it is good for children's recovery from adversity, and for their self-esteem and sense of self-efficacy now and in future to be consulted/involved in influencing their destiny. There are *ethical* reasons: involvement helps to reduce the power imbalance between adults and the child and the risks of harm which may flow from that. There are *philosophical* reasons: consistency requires that if one values a child's welfare and interests, then one also should value their views and voice. There are reasons to do with good practice in *management* terms: any service is likely to function better if to some degree at least it is accountable to end-users. There are *legal* reasons: heeding the voice of children is a requirement of the UN Convention on the Rights of the Child and of many national child welfare statutes, e.g. the Children Act 1989 in England and Wales and the Child Care Act 1991 in Ireland.

The Dutch child care expert Micha de Winter argues that involving young people and promoting their participation can be positive in two ways:

- [It] may be a way to strengthen the social influence and power of young people (empowerment)
- [It] may be instrumental in giving young people a chance to develop into competent, independent and responsible fellow citizens (education in democratic citizenship). (de Winter 1997, p.42)

Thus, attending to the voice of young people in care may strengthen their capacity to function both in social relationships and as full citizens in society. These are important goals and presumably very close to those which the care system would set itself. They are also goals which most social workers and care givers are likely to espouse. In the views of at least one young person this is a crucial issue:

> I've been in care for a long time and I never get a say in what I would like. It's always what other people would like and I'm fed up with it. (Young person quoted in Shaw 1998, p.34)

Listening to children not only respects their rights and dignity, encourages their capacity for self-expression and promotes their development, it also provides important evidence for assessing the impact and value of services provided. Listening to health services users in order to evaluate needs and priorities in health care is increasingly seen as important (Jordan *et al.* 1998). As health and social service users, children are entitled to have their views heard in such processes, and not just as relayed by their parents (Hart and Chesson 1998). Given the intense involvement of social services in the lives of children in state care and the rhetoric of rights which usually wins easy acceptance in principle in social services, there seem strong grounds for emphasising the views of children in care in seeking to understand the experience and impact of being in care. It is not a perspective which must absolutely be acted upon, but it is certainly, surely, a perspective which cannot be ignored. In assessing the quality and impact of care, the views and experiences of children are an important source of evidence. As Bush, Gordon and LeBailly (1977) observe, a child's approval of a placement is a necessary if not sufficient gauge of the quality of arrangements. More recently Hart and Chesson (1998) decry the relative neglect of children as consumers in evaluating the impact and quality of health care generally.

There are daunting methodological and ethical challenges involved in trying to research the views of children (Hill 1998). These become even more complex when researching the views of children living in public care. There are issues of getting consent – from the child, the care giver, the social worker and agency, and possibly the biological parents. There are issues of trust – is the child willing to disclose their true views or will they merely say what they think is expected? There are issues of emotional and cognitive development – has the child the emotional and intellectual capacity to reflect on and articulate responses to the questions posed? There are issues of sensitivity – the researcher cannot barge into the child's life, stir deep emotions and disappear. Nevertheless, there is increasing willingness to confront these challenges because the ultimate aim of discerning children's views is so important. Researchers in different fields have begun to devise approaches which are sensitive, age appropriate and effective (Hill 1997; Hogan and Gilligan 1998; Hart and Chesson 1998). Some of these are engaging with the special circumstance of children in state care (McTeigue 1998; McAuley 1996; McAuley 1998).

While there are surprisingly few studies which seek children's views of their care experiences *while they are in care* (partly for the reasons outlined above and partly because of a historic neglect of the child's views), the striking feature of those studies is the frequent consistency of the themes and views which emerge. In what follows a number of key themes are reviewed and the voices of children are relayed

Preoccupation with biological parents and siblings

Children in care are not easily parted emotionally from their family of origin. As I have observed elsewhere, 'you may take the child out of the family but you cannot take the family out of the child' (Gilligan 1995):

> Nobody understands how much I miss my family, however bad living at home was. People can't understand that a foster family are nothing like a real family and that I feel so alone. (Sixteen-year-old girl quoted in Fletcher 1993, p.80)

In McTeigue's study all ten respondents thought it was 'desirable to know about their birth family and to maintain contact with parents and siblings'.

All but three of the 59 children in Johnson, Yoken and Voss (1994) study reported missing their families, with 56 per cent saying they 'missed their parents most of the time'. Buchanan's finding emphasised for her that young people had clear views about contact with their families, which did not always tally with the views of those responsible for the young people's care. But young people sometimes have ways of getting around such obstacles. As one young person put it:

> You should be allowed to go and see your family unless you are in danger. At the moment my social worker is saying no, but I am still going behind her back and going to see them. (Young person quoted in Buchanan 1995)

Parents

In Rowe *et al.*'s study (1984, p.95), only 21 per cent had had contact with a parent in the previous year. Yet from other parts of the same study it was clear that parents remained an important concern for the young people (see Figure 2.1).

- What the parents look like. (Only one child in five had a photograph of even one of their parents.)
- Where they live now.
- Their present well-being.
- What their circumstances were at the time of reception into care.
- Why they could not care for them.
- Their present attitude to them.
- Whether they have any other children.

Figure 2.1 Foster Children's Curiosities about Parents in Order of Importance (Rowe et al. 1984, pp.133–4)

A child in care may value contact but not want to return to live with the parent. 'Ciara' saw her mother every two weeks:

> I don't want to go back and live with her, but I want to go back and visit ... why ... because she's my ma. (In McTeigue 1998)

Even where a child's parent has died, they may remain extremely important to the child. This may require a lot of sensitive work on the part of carers and social workers, which sadly may not always be promptly undertaken:

> I would like to visit where my mum was buried. For me to move on, I have to see for myself if she's really dead or if I'm dreaming. (Baldry and Kemmis 1998, p.37)

It should of course be borne in mind that each child's experiences, circumstances and preferences are different. That is why it is so important to listen very carefully to a child in all the ways that they communicate and disclose their inner worries and preferences. Not all children may value contact with their parents, or at least both parents. The same child may go through different stages in their view of contact with parents or relatives. In McTeigue's (1998) albeit small study she found differences by age in the outlook of the children. Younger children seemed to find contact with parents almost as a tiresome chore or duty. Yet it would be a mistake on the basis of such an impression, according to McTeigue's work, to sever links between child and parent, since the older young people in her study clearly saw contact with parents as an important issue in their lives. A major finding of McAuley's (1996, p.158) in-depth study of 19 children in foster care was the children's 'preoccupation and identification' with their birth families over time despite many difficulties in the home situation. She describes the children's relationship with their birth parents as 'complex' and points to evidence of their 'worrying about their parents' welfare'. These are among the wishes expressed by the children at two years into their placements (when they were aged 10–13):

> I wish [to] live with my dad.

> To live with my family and mum.

> I wish that I got seeing my real mummy more often ... I wish that all my real family was all together again and not living separately. (McAuley 1996, p.111)

But the picture is not always so straightforward; for some young people there may be an ambivalence surrounding contact with parents:

> My parents hurt me when I see them. I get nightmares, so my foster parents get angry with me when I want to see them, but they don't stop me. (Seventeen-year-old girl in foster care, from Fletcher 1993, p.37)

What many young people may need is the permission and possibility to love two sets of carers in their lives:

> I like my foster carers and their family very much, but I love my family, my gran, Mum, brothers and sisters. (Shaw 1998, p.7)

Siblings

Parents are not the only relatives of importance for the child in care. Evidence from a number of studies underlines the importance attached by young people in care to contact with siblings. Those placed with siblings are generally positive about this (although it is not that common an experience to be placed with siblings). For those not placed together, contact is important. The commitment of one girl in care to her sisters is vividly captured in this quote from McTeigue's study:

> I give every inch of anything I have in me to S. and J. I'd give my life for them … It doesn't matter how far away I am from them they know that I am always there and all they have to do is pick up the phone.

Another young person reiterates this point about the significance of contact with siblings:

> If a child is fostered who has a brother or sister in care things should be done more about access. (Sixteen-year-old girl quoted in Fletcher 1993, p.82)

However important family contact with parents or siblings (or grandparents) may be, some children may lack the basic prerequisites of contact, at least that which they can easily initiate themselves. For example, one in five (22.5%) of the 71 young people in care in Baldry and Kemmis' (1998, p.38) study said they had 'no contact numbers or addresses for families or friends with whom they wanted to stay in touch'.

Sense of sadness and loss around leaving previous home

The words of one boy whose foster placement of seven years with his sister had broken down are a poignant reminder of the loneliness and pain that children in foster care may suffer:

> When I left the last family I was with my sister ... when I think back some nights I just get upset ... I don't get any warning, tears just keep coming ... I cry myself to sleep most nights. (Boy quoted in McTeigue 1998)

Repeated moves can aggravate the sense of loss and upset. In the words of another young person:

> I am very angry because when I move I always leave my friends. (Shaw 1998, p.25)

Understanding of why they are in care

Another issue which may loom large for youngsters in care is a proper and clear understanding of why they entered and remain in care. Johnson *et al.* (1994) report an American study in which 59 young people in foster care (median age 12) were interviewed. Twenty-four of the children (40%) were confused about the reasons for being in care (including ten who had no idea). Comments by young people in a British study reveal a similar gap in knowledge which they felt had to be filled. As one young person in care put it:

> You can't just leave them with a blank space. You've got to fill in the gaps so they understand. (Masson, Harrison and Pavlovic 1997, p.35)

One Irish boy reflected on how he figured out he wasn't going home:

> I thought I'd be going home but after a while I knew it just wasn't going to happen. (McTeigue 1998, p.49)

Children are likely to be much clearer about the reasons for being in care if they are consulted and involved while the process of planning for reception into care is under way. One British young person in care puts it rather well:

> Children of any age – if they are going to be moved should know 'Why am I going to be moved? Why am I going to do this?' These questions should be answered. I think kids of three and four really think about the situation they are in and they can get depressed by it, and I think they should be consulted ... I think what the child says should be the deciding factor. It shouldn't necessarily be totally what children say they want, they may not always

know what's best for them, but I think it should be one of the major factors considered. (Young person quoted in Page and Clark 1977, p.30)

Stigma of care

Being in care you feel you've got a cross on your back. You feel marked. (Young person quoted in Page and Clark 1977, p.17)

This quote captures vividly the strong feeling of stigma which seems to be felt by many young people in the care system. Young people in Buchanan's study reported the stigma they felt about being in care. Feeling different and being treated differently seems a constant concern for many young people in care. As one young person puts it:

When other kids find out you're in care they tease you by saying things about their families and how great they are. It can be very embarrassing sometimes. (Seventeen-year-old quoted in Fletcher 1993, pp.27–28)

In Rowe *et al.*'s (1984, p.125) study 36 per cent of the young people reported having been teased at some point by peers about their being in care.

Agency policy may aggravate the sense of stigma which young people feel about being in care. A common grievance may be the checking of friends' families when the young person wants to stay there overnight:

We were told in the summer we had to get a police check. Our best friends, or whatever, had to get a police check so we could go over to their house (Female, 14, in Martin and Palmer 1997, p.39)

If you go and stay at friends I would rather not have the parents checked – it feels awful and embarrassing. (Seventeen-year-old girl quoted in Fletcher 1993, p.96)

Shaniqua Sockwell, an American 16-year-old in foster care, reflects on how she has worked at hiding her in-care status, because of the shame and rejection she fears its exposure might bring her:

Hiding my identity, especially from my friends, is difficult, and unless you've been in my shoes, you don't know how difficult. You don't know how many stories and lies I've told people. I've had to lie about why me and my foster sister look nothing alike, about why I never talk about my family much, and about how I suddenly appeared in my home out of nowhere at the age of ten. (Youth Communication/Desetta 1996, p.126)

Reviews

Review meetings to discuss and plan the progress of young people in care are an important element in foster-care systems in many countries. It is increasingly seen as desirable that the young person, especially when older, should have the opportunity to attend and participate. But this may not prove an easy experience for the young person in care:

> I know you have three months to sort of prepare for it … but because you're thrown into the situation you just forget everything you are going to say and you just don't know what to say, so you don't. And you just go in and sit there. (Young person quoted in Horgan and Sinclair 1997, p.102)

Young people may have different reactions to reviews. Some refer to theirs being 'so *boring*' (an 11-year-old in long-term foster care quoted in Horgan and Sinclair 1997, p.103) or 'the biggest load of rubbish' (16-year-old in children's home quoted in Horgan and Sinclair 1997, p.105). On the other hand, in Baldry and Kemmis' study (1998, p.39), eighty per cent of the young people who attended their reviews said they felt comfortable putting forward their views and considered they were listened to.

While children and young people living in foster care were less likely to attend reviews than those in residential care in Horgan and Sinclair's study, they were also more likely to be positive about the value of reviews than their residential counterparts, although this might have been due to a slightly more deferential tone in the foster children's comments generally. Young people in Grimshaw and Sinclair's study tended to be more positive in their comments on the review experience, although they did still register concerns, many of which echoed the Horgan and Sinclair findings. Concerns included the nerve-racking nature of being exposed in front of so many strange adults, the lack of preparation of the young person by the professionals, the ritualistic nature of much of the process (being asked questions the young person knew that adults knew the answers to), the unwillingness to declare deeper and more sensitive concerns in such a public forum (Grimshaw and Sinclair 1997, pp.153–160). One young woman is pretty unambiguous in her comments:

> I just felt silly, sitting there, everyone discussing me. I hated it. So I just sat there and … I feel totally uncomfortable in those sorts of situations. I hated it. (Young woman aged 16 quoted in Packman and Hall 1998, p.250)

Two young people in care quoted in Packman and Hall's British study (1998, p.249) were unimpressed by meetings which they had attended:

> It was like other people deciding what to do with my life for me, and I don't like that. (Young woman aged 16)

> All these people sitting round and saying I need this and I need that. What do they know? (Boy aged 15)

The researchers agreed with the young people's common perception that their views tended to be ignored by the adults at the reviews. They found that young people could be thought to have participated in 16 per cent of decisions made in the 43 reviews which were observed (Horgan and Sinclair 1997, p.108). Overall Horgan and Sinclair (1997, p.112) commented that for most of the young people in care it seems that 'attendance at reviews is either a boring irrelevance or a frustrating and disempowering experience'. This may lead to a point where a young person feels cynical about the reviews process:

> It's just a waste of time ... they are always making decisions aren't they? They are not speaking to you, they are just telling you what to do. (Young person quoted in Buchanan 1995, p.689)

Young people suggested that knowing the agenda in advance and seeing reports beforehand would help improve the review experience from their point of view. Overall improvements are closely tied to adequate preparation of the young person.

Packman and Hall also note the importance of friends to young people in care, and potentially in the review meetings also. They quote a sixteen-year-old young woman:

> I know it sounds silly, but all the people [at the meeting] were grown up. I was the only child. It would have been nice to have someone on my side. (Packman and Hall 1998, p.251)

School

In Buchanan's study, problems at school seemed to loom larger in the minds of the young people than in the social workers', who tended not to see the educational difficulties and broken relationships when new placements meant new schools. Johnson *et al.* (1994) report that half of the children 're-ported that changing schools [because of placement] was difficult: most found it hard to make new friends and get acquainted with new teachers.'

One fifteen-year-old British boy in care echoed this American experience that being in care has impeded progress at school 'because of moving school four times in three years' (Fletcher 1993, p.31). Yet other young people may find the stabilising effect of foster placement and carer support positive factors in school progress:

> Before I came to a foster home I was very mixed up and confused – but now I am in a secure placement I feel my schooling is getting better. (Boy in foster care quoted in Fletcher 1993, p.32)

A girl in foster care spoke warmly of how a relationship with her foster carer helped to rekindle her 'passion for education and I am doing really well' (girl in foster care quoted in Fletcher 1993, p.33). Attitudes of teachers and fellow pupils can be a problem. As one thirteen-year-old puts it:

> The teachers become more nosey when you are in care. (Quoted in Fletcher 1993, p.27)

Teachers may also have lower expectations because of the care 'label' even where this is not warranted:

> Before I went into care I was in top sets and everything. They put me in bottom sets as soon as I moved into care and moved schools. (Sixteen-year-old quoted in Fletcher 1993, p.28)

Some children in care may have very basic educational needs and be very well aware of them:

> I would like help with writing and help with spelling. (Young person in Baldry and Kemmis 1998, p.39)

The future and the prospect of life after care

Young people understandably admit a good deal of apprehension about what faces them in life after care. 'Living on my own would be my biggest worry at the minute' was the view of one young person, quoted by Horgan and Sinclair. In Buchanan's study young people were also concerned about issues such as money and practical survival skills. Two-thirds of the young people interviewed in Whitaker et al.'s study were concerned about the future: in the sense of feeling trapped, or not knowing what the future held, or having contradictory or unrealistic hopes. According to Whitaker et al. 'quite a number of children said that they intended never to marry or to have children themselves' (1984, p.12). While the children in Whitaker *et al.*'s study are living in children's homes, their worries seem relevant to report in this context.

Martin and Palmer (1997, p.54) suggest that the transition facing young people leaving care 'is an intensely personal event that captures the essence of what goes before it and is the foundation for what follows.' They observe that a lot of the ambivalence and anger which can be discerned in young people's response to leaving care is linked to its arbitrarily enforced nature – at a fixed age irrespective of readiness – and the fact the young person thus receives 'poverty as an age-of-majority gift' (p.55) since their circumstances post-care are almost always worse materially and otherwise than before leaving. Prospects emotionally may also be pretty daunting, as young people in care contemplate their future:

> I won't have any friends when I leave care. (Young person cited in Page and Clarke 1977, p.54)

> Social services should seriously think about the life of young people after care. Most of them are left alone and social services should not forget that those young people don't have anything or anyone. (Young person quoted in Shaw 1998, p.66)

Concerns about powerlessness, bullying and other issues

There are other issues which may worry young people in care. One may be how they are treated by their peers, or by the system itself. They may feel inhibited in looking for help. Young people may feel so vulnerable because of their care status that they are slow to register complaints because of the possible fall-out:

> You sometimes feel left out. Sometimes you might not like where you are, but dare not tell anyone because they would have a go at you. (14-year-old girl quoted in Fletcher 1993, p.80)

Young people in Buchanan's study raised a number of important issues about their care experience. One issue was the inequity of systems of discretionary payment systems which meant what young people got often depended on the advocacy of a social worker rather than on their objective needs and circumstances. Finally, two other worrying issues were raised by the young people: the problem of bullying, particularly in residential settings; and the problem of deliberate self-harm – one in four admitted acts of self-harm with a view to ending their life. Young people in care may be bullied by other young people in care, or by young people not in care. While the risk of being bullied by peers in care may be greatest in residential care settings, it should not be assumed that young people in foster care are free from the risk of being bullied whether by peers in care or otherwise. Pressure to find foster placements may mean small groups of young people who are strangers to each other are placed in the same foster home. In such a context the difference between residential care and foster care in matters such as bullying may begin to fade. Young people in care may also experience serious bullying at school. One sad New Zealand eleven-year-old boy who had a very hard time at school reported being called a 'foster faggot' ('Michael' quoted in Smith, Gollop and Taylor 1998, p.15). A British twelve-year-old boy reported a less severe negative reaction. He thought one of the bad things about being in care:

> is getting the mickey taken out of you at school … other kids say where's your mum? (Quoted in Packman and Hall 1998, p.244)

Comments from a study of Canadian young people in care raises an important issue about the meaning and status of files held about young people in care:

> They're not *your* files, it's *their* files about you, though, and so it's like anybody can go into those files. (Female aged 16, quoted in Martin and Palmer 1997, p.49; emphasis in original)

Stability of care experience

Kufeldt, Armstrong and Dorosh (1989) report a Canadian study on 73 children in foster care. One in four of the children had experienced five or more moves in placement since coming into care. In an Australian study of the care experiences of 294 children, 14.9 per cent had experienced five or more placements (including moves in and out of care) (Fernandez 1996, p.155). In both the Australian and Canadian studies, only 30 per cent of the study children had experienced a single placement in their care history. In another Australian study of one hundred 16–18-year-olds leaving care, over three-quarters of the young people had had three or more placements, with an average of 6.9 placements per each young person in the study (Cashmore and Paxman 1996). In Shaw's British study (1998), one in four of 2073 respondents had had just one placement, half (49%) had had between 2 and 5 placements, 17 per cent had had between 6 and 10 placements and 11 per cent had had 11 or more placements. As one young respondent puts it:

I might be only 13 years old but I have been in and out of care for 8 years, 7 months and 14 days. (Young person quoted in Shaw 1998, p.26)

For many young people then foster care (or other forms of alternative care) may not deliver the stability and continuity of care and relationships which was intended by their placement in care. Nevertheless it is important to acknowledge that for all its risks and hazards care is not always perceived negatively by those who rely on it. For example, the young people in the Kufeldt *et al.* (1989) Canadian study, when asked how time in care had affected them, were overwhelmingly positive with 59 per cent claiming care was 'definitely helpful' and a further 30 per cent saying it was 'probably helpful'. Only 4 per cent believed it was 'harmful' (p.365). Where young people view care positively, their favourable perception is undoubtedly linked to positive relationships with key adults in their day-to-day care such as foster carers and social workers.

Children's views of carers and social workers

In the view of a child quoted in Bush, Gordon and LeBailly (1977, p.497) a good foster parent is 'someone that was strict enough so you wouldn't get into any trouble, but lenient so you could have some fun.' In this study the children wanted firm discipline balanced with freedom and independence. They understandably wanted to avoid verbally or physically abusive behaviour by the carers. In Fletcher's study (1993, p.21), 65 per cent of the 217 young people in foster care 'had something positive to say' about their carers. In one British study, one young person was appreciative of their foster care:

My foster mother is very supportive … Our relationship is very close and I feel more protected. The change has been huge, I feel more self confident and secure. (Baldry and Kemmis 1998, p.36)

Young people in care seem to appreciate that foster carers may vary in their qualities:

It all depends what foster parents you get. Cuz I've had the parents that hover over you like real parents do, and then I live with parents now, it's basically, 'Here's your food, here's your allowance at the end of the month, there's your shelter, your heat … your bathroom.' Everything else – that's left to you. (Female aged 15 quoted in Martin and Palmer 1997, p.52)

> Some are in for the money and some cuz they care and really wanna try to help children that are needy. They wanna help. (Female aged 16 quoted in (Martin and Palmer 1997, p.52)

The issue of parity of treatment with a foster carer's own children can arise:

> It was like I was going through Cinderella syndrome … I would do all the housework for my pocket money and [foster carer's daughter] would automatically get hers … see what I mean? (Masson *et al.* 1997)

Some young people may find cultural differences between home and foster care difficult. Packman and Hall (1998, p.241) refer to two young brothers who found their 'vegetarian, ugh!' foster carer hard going:

> I wouldn't recommend her – there were loads of things – just her attitude. (Boy aged 9)

> When we there [in summer] she even had her Christmas cake already made! (Boy aged 7)

Turning to social workers, Michael, an eleven-year-old New Zealand boy in care had a telling view of what he thought social workers did. (He also had thought his social worker might have been his lawyer.)

> Well they usually carry pens and things and write down what you say and um … they usually tell your dogs to go away and tell you off. They usually blabber on about something you've never even heard before [laugh]. (Smith *et al.* 1998, p.13)

The ten children in McTeigue's (1998) study valued the relationship they had with their social worker. They were the person to whom they could go 'to clarify any situation'. Frequent changes of social worker were a problem for some of these children with one girl saying she was 'on her eighth social worker' since coming into care. In Baldry and Kemmis' (1998, p.38) study, three times as many of the 71 young people were positive as were negative about their social workers. The young people:

> …had clear views about what they thought made a good or bad social worker. The qualities most appreciated in a good social worker were genuine interest, being listened to, meeting up with young people as arranged, getting things done as agreed, being open and honest, and maintaining links with young people's families. (Baldry and Kemmis 1998, p.38)

In Freeman *et al.*'s study, social workers who failed to follow through on plans on time or who didn't keep promises were criticised (Freeman *et al.* 1996, p.236)

One in ten (11.5%) of the young people in foster care in Fletcher's study 'said there were no good things about their social workers' (1993, p.16). A clear majority however were satisfied to varying degrees, including 25 per cent who claimed 'there were no bad things about their social workers' (1993, p.20).

Conclusion

The words of the young people bring to life their lived experience and illuminate for the adults in their lives the tensions, dilemmas and pain that is often their lot. There is much also that is encouraging in what they say which reflects their own resilience and the care and concern they often experience from the adults around them. Nevertheless, the sympathetic reader cannot help but be moved by many of the burdens they carry, burdens of multiple adversities, of ruptured relationships, of uncertainties about their future, of being stigmatised and bullied and more. If adult carers and social services are to have any hope of meeting the needs of children in foster care then they must, among other things, listen very closely to the lived experience of children in foster care, through the medium of research and the participation of young people in policy and decision-making fora. For systems of foster care in every country the United Nations Convention on the Rights of the Child sets a demanding but essential standard in this regard.

References

Baldry, S. and Kemmis, J. (1998) The quality of child care in one local authority – a user study. *Adoption and Fostering 27*, 3, 34–41.

Buchanan. A. (1995) Young people's views on being looked after in out-of-home-care under the Children Act 1989. *Children and Youth Services Review 17*, 5/6, 681–696.

Bush, M., Gordon, A., and LeBailly, R. (1977) Evaluating child welfare services: A contribution from the clients. *Social Service Review*, September, 491–501.

Cashmore, J. and Paxman, M. (1996) *Longitudinal Study of Wards Leaving Care*. Sydney: NSW Department of Community Services.

Cooper, D. (1998) More law and more rights: Will children benefit? *Child and Family Social Work 3*, 2, 77–86.

Fernandez, E. (1996) *Significant Harm – Unraveling Child Protection Decisions and Substitute Care Careers of Children*. Aldershot: Avebury.

Fletcher, B. (1993) *Not Just a Name – The Views of Young People in Foster and Residential Care*. London: National Consumer Council.

Freeman, I., Morrison, A., Lockhart, F. and Swanson, M. (1996) Consulting service users – the views of young people. In M. Hill and J. Aldgate (eds) *Child Welfare Services – Developments in Law, Policy, Practice and Research*. London: Jessica Kingsley Publishers.

Gilligan, R. (1995) Making a success of fostering – what we want for the children, what we need for the adults. In D. McTeigue (ed) *A Journey Through Fostering: Proceedings of the Eighth International Conference of the International Foster Care Organisation, Dublin, July 1993*, pp.3–22, Dublin: Irish Foster Care Association.

Grimshaw, R. and Sinclair, R. (1997) The participation of young people and their parents at review meetings. Chapter 6 in *Planning to Care: Regulation, Procedure and Practice under the Children Act 1989*. London: National Children's Bureau.

Hart, C. and Chesson, R. (1998) Children as consumers. *British Medical Journal 316*, 1600–1603, 23 May.

Hill, M. (1997) Participatory research with children. *Child and Family Social Work* 2, 3, 171–183.

Hill, M. (1998) Ethical issues in qualitative methodology with children. In D. Hogan and R. Gilligan (eds) *Researching Children's Experience: Qualitative Approaches* (Proceedings of Conference 27.5.97). Dublin: The Children's Research Centre, Trinity College Dublin.

Hogan, D. and Gilligan, R. (eds) (1998) *Researching Children's Experience: Qualitative Approaches* (Proceedings of Conference 27.5.97). Dublin: The Children's Research Centre, Trinity College Dublin.

Horgan, G. and Sinclair, R. (1997) Children and young people's participation in reviews. In G. Horgan and R. Sinclair (eds) *Planning for Children in Care in Northern Ireland*. London: National Children's Bureau.

Johnson, P.R. Yoken, C. and Voss R. (1994) Family foster care placement: The child's perspective. *Child Welfare LXXIV*, 5, 959–974.

Jordan, J., Dowswell, T., Harrison, S., Lilford, R. and Mort, M.(1998) Whose priorities? Listening to users and the public. *British Medical Journal 316*, 1668–1670.

Kufeldt, K., Armstrong, J. and Dorosh, M. (1989) In care, in contact? In J. Hudson and B. Galaway (eds) *The State as Parent – International Research Perspectives on Interventions with Young Persons*. Dordecht: Kluwer Academic Publishers.

Lücker-Babel, M. (1995) The right of the child to express views and to be heard: An attempt to interpret Article 12 of the UN Convention on the Rights of the Child. *The International Journal of Children's Rights 3*, 391–404.

Martin, F. and Palmer, T. (1997) Transitions to adulthood: A child welfare perspective. *Community Alternatives – International Journal of Family Care 9*, 2, 29–60.

Masson, J., Harrison, C. and Pavlovic (1997) *Working with Children and 'Lost' Parents – Putting Partnership into Practice*. York: Joseph Rowntree Foundation.

McAuley, C. (1996) *Children in Long Term Foster Care: Emotional and Social Development.* Aldershot: Avebury.

McAuley, C. (1998) Interviewing children in research: Reflections on a longitudinal study of foster care. In D. Hogan and R. Gilligan (eds) *Researching Children's Experience: Qualitative Approaches* (Proceedings of Conference 27.5.97). Dublin: The Children's Research Centre, Trinity College Dublin.

McTeigue, D. (1998) The use of focus groups in exploring children's experiences of life in care. In D. Hogan and R. Gilligan (eds) *Researching Children's Experience: Qualitative Approaches* (Proceedings of Conference 27.5.97). Dublin: The Children's Research Centre, Trinity College Dublin.

Packman, J. and Hall, C. (1998) *From Care to Accommodation – Support, Protection and Control in Child Care Services.* London: The Stationery Office.

Page, R. and Clarke, G. (1977) *Who Cares? Young People in Care Speak Out.* London: National Children's Bureau.

Rowe, J., Cain, H., Hundleby, M. and Keane, A. (1984) *Long-Term Foster Care.* London: Batsford.

Shaw, C. (1998) *Remember My Messages … The Experiences and Views of 2,000 Children in Public Care in the UK.* London: The Who Cares? Trust.

Smith, A., Gollop, M. and Taylor, N. (1998) Children's Voices in Foster or Kinship Care: Knowledge, Understanding and Participation. Paper presented at the Twelfth International Congress on Child Abuse and Neglect, Auckland, New Zealand, September 9, 1998.

Spall, P., Testro, P. and Matchett, R. (1998) Having a Say – a report on the 'Giving Voice to Children' Project, about children and young people participating in processes and decisions which relate to their care and well being. Sydney: New South Wales Child Protection Council.

Whitaker, D., Cook, J., Dunne, C. and Rocliffe, S. (1984) *The Experience of Residential Care from the Perspectives of Children, Parents, and Care-givers, SSRC Contract No. RB 3312/7 Final Report.* York: Department of Social Policy and Social Work, University of York.

de Winter, M. (1998) *Children as Fellow Citizens – Participation and Commitment.* Abingdon: Radcliffe Medical Press.

Youth Communication/Desetta, A. (ed) (1996) *The Heart Knows Something Different – Teenage Voices from the Foster Care System.* New York: Persea Books.

CHAPTER 3

Outcome Studies of Foster Care

Greg Kelly

Introduction

This chapter discusses the principal issues in the contentious area of measuring outcomes in foster care. It then summarises the current state of our knowledge of the outcomes of short-term foster care and specialist 'professional' schemes. Long-term foster care is discussed in more depth with the consideration of studies of existing placements and those that attempt to measure the ultimate effect of placement by studying how the children of the system have fared as adults.

It is part of a professional's and a profession's responsibility to monitor the effectiveness of their performance and to try to improve it. It is no longer good enough, as it was until relatively recently (the 1960s in Britain), to be seen to be trying to do good. The society that is placing trust in professionals and paying for their service increasingly demands evidence of their effectiveness. 'Social work interventions in the private sphere of family life can only be justified if it is believed that the necessary changes will thereby occur' (Parker *et al.* 1991, p.19). Examining the outcomes of a service – what happens to the people who are its clients? – is a key way of measuring effectiveness. 'Do foster placements last as long as needed or break down?' 'What happens to children who spend time in foster care?' 'Does foster care achieve its aims?' These are the kinds of key questions that it is reasonable to expect a professional foster care service to have answers to.

This chapter will discuss the various 'outcome' studies that have attempted to answer questions of this nature. There is, however, little evidence of the outcomes of foster care being monitored systematically by the professional community to guide the development of policy and practice. The kind of regular monitoring that would be associated with the treatment of children's physical illnesses has never been a routine feature of child welfare practice. There are some very deep-seated reasons for this. While claiming to be professional, social work has been much closer to a religious or humanist tradition where the governing ethic has been the attempt to 'do good' rather than the technical, scientific ethic where effectiveness is the prime goal:

> ...if what was being done in the interests of the child was self-evidently right the question of whether it actually led to desirable outcomes was hardly likely to be asked. (Parker *et al.* 1991, p.1)

Social work also seeks to help the whole child and so the measurement of particular interventions has been seen as more complex than, for example, teaching a child a particular skill or treating an identified illness. While these complexities create real difficulties in measuring outcomes, they have long since ceased to be acceptable reasons for not trying to do so. Research in the field of foster care led the way in the evaluation of child-care practice in the UK. Early studies by Parker (1966) and George (1970) reported high rates of foster care breakdown and 'it could no longer be taken for granted that foster care was inevitably superior to other provisions for disadvantaged children' (Parker *et al.* 1991, p.2).

Issues in outcome measurement

There are issues to be thought through and debated at every point in the assessment of the outcomes of foster care:

1. What is the value base that underpins the research?

2. When are outcomes to be assessed?

3. What factors are assessed as measures of outcome, of success or failure?

4. Who or what should the outcomes be compared with?

These will be discussed in turn.

Values

Underlying value problems are often ignored in research, as they are in practice, under the assumption that working for the 'best interests of the child' answers all value questions. As we have seen in Chapter 1, there are competing views as to what is in children's best interests and disagreement about who should decide. Fundamental value questions pervade research into practice as they pervade practice itself. Outcome research in a service that has differing and competing views as to what its goals should be is 'like putting the cart before the horse' (Festinger in Mech and Rycraft 1995, p.97).

The child-care service is not unique in this respect; but in other services such as health and education, while there are value issues to be thought through, they do not often involve the very basics of the service in the way they routinely do in child care. Are children better off in an adoptive home that provides them with a legally secure family but cuts them off from their birth family, or in a foster home that may keep that family alive for them but does not provide the same degree of legal security? What level of support and service should be offered to try to save a failing family? Answers to these questions are not the purely technical questions they would be in a publicly funded health service were we discussing saving a child's leg. In child-care practice, decisions are loaded with morality, politics and values. Does the family impoverished by parental alcohol abuse 'deserve' our help; would the child be better off in a substitute family; should permanence be the ultimate goal of a long-term placement? These questions lack the clarity of issues in treating a child's physical illnesses, where there is a general acceptance that the best available treatment should be deployed with the 'simple' aim of restoring the child to health. Varying views on value issues pervade research and evaluation as they do decision making in practice. Thus we need to consider the political and value base of the research and not see research and researchers as somehow above the fundamental problems that often divide practitioners and policy makers. This is a tall order for busy practitioners, who have enormous difficulty in keeping abreast of research at all. Essentially it is asking them to apply the same healthy scepticism to research and researchers as they would to the policies and pronouncements of their agencies and government.

An example of a value position colouring the presentation of research findings is the adverse comment that foster care often receives in commentaries. In an era when the values associated with 'permanence' and adoption have been dominant in policy and practice, foster family care gets routinely poor comment in American and British professional and research literature. This, despite the fact that most of the research that has looked at the outcomes of fostered children as adults has reported predominantly positive results. Maluccio and Fein, summarising 12 studies, report that despite the

> ...widespread perception that placement in foster care has short term as well as long term adverse effects on children ... researchers have consistently reported that foster care graduates function well, or that no negative effect of foster care on the child's adjustment is detected. (Quoted in Thoburn 1990, p.20)

In American literature 'foster care' usually refers to all state care – residential care as well as 'foster family care'. Most children usually experience a range of placements during the course of a care career. In these studies the dominant placement was foster family care.

One American study was not totally prepared to believe its own finding that an extended period in foster care was not 'in itself harmful to children' and felt the need to add:

> However, we feel that our measures of adjustment are not without problems, and we are not sure that our procedures have captured the potential feelings of pain and impaired self image that can be created by impermanent status in foster care. (Fanshel and Shinn 1978, p.479)

Jane Rowe, concluding her study that reported that 'three out of four foster homes [were] rated by social workers as providing an "excellent" or "good" home for the child' (DHSS 1985, p.31) comments:

> The inescapable conclusion of our findings is that many long term foster children would be better off if they were adopted by their foster parents, not because foster care is so bad but because it is not quite good enough. (Rowe et al. 1984, p.224)

Concluding her study, Festinger, addressing this 'bad press', remarks:

> The assumptions and expectations that abound concerning the dire fate of foster care children seem to have little validity. The products of foster care – the young adults whom we followed in this study – did not measure down to such dire predictions ... Overall they were not so different from others of their age in what they were doing, in the feelings they expressed, and in their hopes about the future. (Festinger 1983, p.294)

Thus the recent evaluation of foster care and its outcomes have been taking place in an era when the conventional wisdom has been that it is not as good a solution to the problem of children's long-term separation from their families as adoption. The argument is not that this has affected the results of the research but that it may have had an impact on the way these results have been viewed and commented on. The values of the researchers and current thinking have led to standards from adoption practice being selectively applied to foster care. This has had the effect of making its successes almost look like failures. We shall return to this, 'compared to what', problem below.

When are outcomes assessed?

It is theoretically possible to measure the outcome of a decision or action at any time after it has been taken and for the outcome to be different on each occasion. This can leave any outcome research open to the criticism that it is being conducted too early or too late. A reasonable approach is to make short-term assessments of the outcomes of courses of action that are designed to have an effect in the short term and use longer timescales for those that are expected to have long-term impacts. Thus short-term or intermediate-length placements would normally be best assessed in their immediate aftermath. Long-term placements can usefully be assessed either at a suitable time in their duration when their long-term viability can be gauged, or, if they have been intended as the child's family for life, at a time, perhaps in early adulthood, when an assessment can be made of how the child has made out as an adult. As we shall see below, studies of long-term foster care fall roughly into these two types:

1. Those conducted during the planned life of placements or shortly after their ending; these either follow a cohort of placements for a period of time after they have been made (e.g. Thoburn, Murdoch and O'Brien 1986; Kelly 1995; Fanshel and Shinn 1978) or take a cross-sectional look at a sample or population of placements at one or more particular points in time (Rowe, Hundleby and Garnett, 1989; Rowe et al. 1984; Berridge and Cleaver 1987). These are by far the most common type of study. They might be called 'current practice studies'.

2. Those conducted when the placements are over and the children are adults (Festinger 1983; Zimmerman 1982; Triseliotis 1983). These are rarer, and rely heavily on the testimony of the former

foster children. They are harder to carry out for a range of methodological reasons, principally the difficulty in getting access to
subjects. These are sometimes called 'follow-up studies'.

These two types of studies yield very different information about foster care
and their advantages and disadvantages are fairly self-evident. The 'current
practice studies' can give us detailed information about how the system is
currently functioning but it does not allow us to say what the longer-term
effects of our interventions are. Children unhappy in the course of a placement may settle and subsequently make a 'success' of their adult life.
Children apparently settled in placement may hit crises in adolescence that
persist into their adult life. The 'follow-up studies' do tell us what the
long-term effects of placements are but the placements may have been so
long ago that the relevance of the findings to current practice may be questioned. It may also be difficult to be sure of the degree to which the 'success'
or 'failure' that is measured is attributable to the placement and not to other
subsequent life events. These latter studies must also, of necessity, rely very
heavily on the testimony of the former foster children themselves, and only
those who are available to the researcher. It is therefore difficult to obtain a
broadly based and scientifically selected sample (Festinger 1983).

What are assessed as outcomes?

In some respects the timescale taken for the measurement of outcome in a
study sets boundaries around what can be assessed as an outcome. Thus, the
early studies that measured breakdown of placement within five years as a
principal outcome measure were framed within this timespan and could not
measure the long-term effects of placement. But within different timescales
there are a wide range of outcomes that can be measured and all have their
competing claims to attention. They can be divided into two main areas:

- Different outcomes for the child. The possibilities are numerous,
  but in broad terms: how has the placement affected the child's
  health, welfare, education; has it delivered stability and
  permanence; has it facilitated the child's return home; has it
  equipped the child for adulthood?

- Outcomes as viewed by the different participants in the foster care
  process: the child, the foster parents, the child's birth parents, the
  social worker, the placing agency.

One major study to grapple with these issues in relation to current practice, *Child Care Now* (Rowe *et al.* 1989), set out the dilemmas and the solution they developed:

> ...we continually felt the need to have some simple classification which would make comparisons easier and might give social workers and managers some sense of what proportion of their placements 'turn out all right'.

> We experimented with various ways of combining our outcomes data and finally decided that the simplest was the best. If a placement lasted as long as the child needed it and met the stated aim in at least most respects it could be called 'successful'. If it did not last as long as the child needed it and the aim was met only partially or not at all, it should be considered 'unsuccessful'. (pp.64, 65).

Rowe was conscious of relying on the opinions of social workers to assess both these outcome criteria. This single-perspective approach is a major weakness of much foster care outcome research. It is usually justified in terms of the logistics of the research and the resources available, and these are critical considerations. In addition, a powerful influence in any research is the agenda of the funder. As most child-care research is funded by government or agency interests their criteria and agenda inevitably dominate. They usually want measures of outcome that reflect their view of the problems. It is reasonable to expect this view to be significantly different in important respects from that of the other participants in foster care who have a heavy personal investment in the outcome – the child, the foster parents, the birth parents.

Thus, when we judge a placement a success or a failure we are invariably making this judgement in a relative or a comparative sense and usually only from the professionals' point of view rather than as an absolute, fully rounded judgement taking account of all the participants' views. The problem from the researchers' perspective is that achieving the fully rounded judgement is much more resource-intensive. For example, if a researcher has the resources to conduct 100 interviews then they can study 100 cases from one perspective, the social workers', or 25 each from 4 perspectives (child, social worker, foster parents, birth parents). The former study has the breadth in terms of sample size that lends it credibility; the latter has depth but will often be dismissed as not generalisable because of its small numbers. There is now, however, a recognition that we need more of the latter, the qualitative, type of study. 'It is hoped that future investigations will often include contact with foster carers and children' (Berridge 1997, p.41).

Outcomes: compared to what?

All foster placements are made as a result of a decision. At the decision point a number of other alternative decisions could, at least theoretically, have been taken. The fostered child could have been returned home, placed in residential care, or made the subject of adoption proceedings. It would be of the greatest use to practitioners and policy makers to have some guidance on which of these or other possibilities are likely to prove most 'successful' for which children. We have seen in Chapter 2 that the growth in foster care was largely a consequence of its being judged more successful in meeting children's long-term needs than residential care and that subsequently adoption became favoured as the permanent placement of choice because it was seen to meet more of children's needs for a 'stable, normal family life' than foster care. Thus even in studies that judge foster care as mostly successful it is not seen as quite good enough. Many of the major studies in the area agree substantially with Fanshel and Shinn's (1978, p.480) conclusion that:

> It is no longer considered sufficient that a child be afforded a placement situation in which his basic needs are being cared for … It is not enough that he might be placed in a foster family home that offers him family-like care. If he cannot regard the people he is living with as *his* family on a permanent basis, his situation is increasingly regarded as reflecting something less than an adequate resolution of his life situation.

Those involved in foster care have every right to complain of a serious case of the 'goal posts being shifted'! They succeed to a greater or lesser degree in delivering the service to an agreed set of values and aims and then are judged according to a new set of standards developed in the meantime. At one level this is 'progress'; if we are buying a 10-year-old car we judge it by today's standards and find it wanting. It is not that it was a bad car 'in its day'. However, to extend the analogy with the car a little further: a car manufacturer would complain loudly were his model to be compared with one that that was not in the same price bracket – one that was of a higher specification and cost substantially more. What is ignored in the comparisons between foster care and adoption is that in all jurisdictions adoption is much harder to achieve than foster care – the price is higher. This 'higher price' is directly linked to the perceived benefits of adoption over foster care – its 'higher specification'. *Because* it seeks to deliver permanence in a substitute family and transfer parental rights from birth to adoptive parents:

1. The demands of the legal processes are much more exacting.

2. The consequent and necessary level of investment of resources, both legal and social work, to achieve adoption is much greater.

3. Children's contact with their birth families is most often terminated, a 'price' the children have to pay.

4. Birth parents (usually mothers) are left to grieve their lost child.

Thus to compare foster care outcomes to those of adoption without recognising its 'higher price' is unhelpful.

The first point above may appear paltry when set beside 'seeking the best interests of the child' and providing a permanent substitute family. However, because the legal processes are so complex, and the standards required of evidence that much higher, achieving adoption can be subject to inordinate delays (Coulter, Kelly and Switzer 1996; Lowe 1993; Lambert *et al.* 1990; Katz 1996). This can lead to damaging delay to the child's placement in any long-term family situation. The process and the delays discourage workers from pursuing this option (Lowe 1993). Despite it being the widely recommended best option for children in long-term care, adoption is only achieved for a small minority of children: 'adoption was the permanency planning goal for only 14% and only 11% were actually adopted ... it is an unrealistic hope for the vast majority of children in care' (Fein and Maluccio 1992, p.341).

Resources are always an issue in a publicly accountable service. It can be argued that adoption usually represents good value for money, in the long term, in that the child is discharged from public care and thus from further years of state support and professional inputs. There are, however, often real obstacles to a broadly based service resourcing the depth, complexity and intensity of the expertise needed to achieve adoption, particularly where it is against the parents' wishes.

The issues surrounding the birth family are complex in that most research reports that, in all forms of substitute care, children's contact with their birth families tends to diminish over time and studies of long-term foster care show very low levels of contact. Rowe *et al.*'s (1984) study of children with at least three years in long-term placements found only 21 per cent 'who had even casual contact with a parent during the previous year' and 'half the children no longer had direct contact with any member of their original family ...' (p.95). These findings are not untypical in Britain, although there has been little research completed on the effects of the Children Act 1989 which, in various ways, strengthens the position of parents in relation to their children in care. Assuming that contact does diminish over time, the question then becomes whether we allow it to take its 'natural' course with the child ending up, at best in foster care, arguably, not being a complete part of any family; or whether we, by various means, test parents' commitment, force the issue and proceed to adoption. However viewed, the loss of birth family is more likely to be complete in adoption.

In summary, it is misleading to criticise foster care outcomes using the standards developed in adoption practice *unless* the whole cost of adoption is fully taken into consideration, and, most crucially, the difficulty in all jurisdictions of achieving adoption for children who have living parents. This is never done. Foster care is adversely compared to adoption as if they were simply interchangeable choices. They are not. The difficulties in achieving adoption have led to various developments in adoption practice in the United Kingdom that have brought it closer to foster care – payment of allowances, encouraging foster parents to adopt and openness to birth family contact (Fratter 1996). This has been accompanied by fostering practice developing to take account of the central criticism of much research and commentary – the need for children to have a greater sense of permanence. Thoburn (1996) describes these developments as 'having our cake and eating it':

> ...the art of child placement lies in both meeting the child's needs for a sense of permanency and his or her need for a sense of personal identity and for that identity to be respected by the substitute parents. (p.134).

Foster care and adoption have roles to play in providing a range of placement types that will allow a choice to meet the needs of the range of children who need long-term substitute family placement. They should not be compared to each other as if they were simply interchangeable.

Outcome studies

During children's childhood

As we have indicated above, outcome studies of foster care come in two main forms: firstly, those conducted during the foster placement or shortly afterwards – during the children's childhood; and secondly, those that consider the effect of foster care, how its 'graduates' fare in adulthood.

There are, perhaps surprisingly, no truly longitudinal studies that follow placed children through their careers in foster care and into adulthood so all the existing studies suffer from fundamental weaknesses. Those conducted during childhood cannot tell us the consequences of the placements for the ultimate adult functioning of the child; those that look back from adulthood make it very difficult to relate adult functioning to particular qualities of the foster placement(s). The strength of studies close to the time of or during placement is that they give us immediate knowledge about current practice, its effects on children as children and how it is perceived by the principals involved.

A further important organisational issue is the type of placement for which outcome is being considered. There are foster placements to meet an immense range of needs from one or two days respite for a hard-pressed lone parent to a permanent substitute family, lasting from placement in childhood to adulthood. Most research effort has been concentrated on long-term foster care but in recent years there has been interesting work done in the development and assessment of 'professional' or 'treatment' foster care, often associated with the payment of foster parents in the form of fees or salaries.

This review summarises the studies of short-term placements and professional schemes. It considers the issues in relation to long-term foster care in more depth. The outcome studies of kinship placements are reviewed in Chapter 9.

A cautionary note. Foster-care systems differ from country to country and within countries between different agencies and authorities. All findings need to be critically reviewed in this light. To what extent these findings are likely to be 'true for us' is a question that should be posed in relation to all research findings. Generally, however, researchers and authors do try to study the elements of foster care common to most practice and it is these that we concentrate on in what follows.

SHORT-TERM FOSTER CARE

There have been few studies of short-term foster care. The principal and most comprehensive in Britain was Rowe et al.'s (1989) work that looked at a broad range of placements. We have seen above how they developed a two-pronged approach to assessing outcome – did the placement last as long as needed, and to what extent were the initial aims met? Short-term foster

care, in the main, has less complex aims than intermediate or long-term fostering and therefore, as one would expect, its aims are more frequently met.
Rowe found that it was successful in meeting the aims of temporary or emergency care, 'at least in most respects', for 88 per cent of the sample. This was
virtually the same across all age groups. On the other criterion, over 80 per
cent of these short-term placements lasted as long as needed, although for
emergency placements for adolescents this dropped to 70 per cent.

Berridge and Cleaver (1987) also reported high levels of success. Only 10
per cent of short-term placements ended in breakdown within their
two-month, 'short-term' timespan. A bigger problem was that in close to 40
per cent of all the placements they lasted 'too long' and a higher proportion
(24%) of this group ended in breakdown. In total 19 per cent 'planned
short-term placements broke down in so far as children were removed in a
manner that was inconsistent with the social work plan' (pp.112–113). As
with long-term foster care – see below – the children's behaviour was a major
cause of breakdown and older and more experienced foster parents tended to
have fewer disruptions.

Millham *et al.* (1986), who reported not dissimilar results for short stays
(only 8% of initial fosterings 'broke down under crisis conditions'), were
nonetheless concerned: 'Many of the children who move are very young and
social workers express concern at the distress experienced by them as a result
of these changes' (p.129). These early moves can become part of a pattern.
Nonetheless, on this, admittedly limited evidence, short-term foster care is a
very successful form of placement for children, a fact often lost sight of in
discussions of foster care that concentrate on the more problematic area of
long-term placements.

'SPECIALIST', 'PROFESSIONAL' OR 'TREATMENT' FOSTERING, USUALLY FOR ADOLESCENTS

The use of 'professional' or fee-paid foster parents in 'specialist' schemes to
try to meet the needs of adolescents in care has been one of the major innova-
tions of the last 20 years. The foster parents are usually recruited specifically
for this task and given specialist training. Despite the success and the public-
ity surrounding the pioneer project in the United Kingdom (Hazel 1981),
there has not been universal replication. A survey by Shaw and Hipgrave in
1982 indicated that there were about 50 schemes in Great Britain (Shaw and
Hipgrave 1983), and Hill *et al.* (1993) had responses from a similar number

from a population of 230 agencies surveyed and twice as many responded that they had no such provision.

In Rowe's *et al.*'s (1989) study, 2 of the 6 authorities had specialist schemes. The study is particularly interesting because it enabled comparison between adolescents fostered in the specialist schemes and those in ordinary foster homes. The specialist schemes placed a higher proportion of boys, and placed more older adolescents and more with severe behavioural problems. The specialist schemes were mostly working at the tougher end of the market. When it came to the aims of the placement, only 18 per cent were temporary/short-term compared with 38 per cent of the ordinary adolescent placements. Almost a third of the specialist placements were seen as a 'bridge to independence'.

Fifty-three per cent of the specialist placements ended sooner than *planned* but 51 per cent lasted as long as *needed*. The 50/50 split was also evident in the achievement of aims – 50 per cent of the placements were said to have 'fully' or 'in most respects' achieved their aims. Rowe concluded: 'Sustaining specialist fostering placements is evidently difficult' (Rowe *et al.* 1989, p.102). The results in the Hill *et al.* (1993) study are not dissimilar, with 44 per cent of the UK placements and 47 per cent of the USA/Canada sample achieving 'treatment goals'. Rowe admits that these are 'disappointing' figures 'for a type of placement about which there has been considerable optimism and enthusiasm' (Rowe 1989, p.102). She does, however, point to the extreme difficulty in working with many of these young people. It may be that the tight criteria of success which she uses may underestimate the usefulness of the placements.

The task in working with adolescents is often minimising the damage they do to themselves and others, on their way, hopefully, to a more settled phase of their lives. A more realistic standard for these placements might be – have they been helpful in this process? Rowe asked about helpfulness and 75 per cent of the placements were thought to have been 'very helpful' or 'helpful' – 'which must surely be considered a satisfactory result for any social work intervention'. An American survey of 'treatment' fostering (Snodgrass and Bryant 1989) used, as a measure of a programme's success, 'the extent to which it is possible to return the child (average age 12–15) to less restrictive settings when they leave' – 77 per cent were so discharged 'and thus may have been considered to have been diverted from group home or institutional care, at least in the short term' (pp.46, 47).

LONG-TERM FOSTER CARE

Most research effort in foster care has been concentrated on long-term placements where children are expected to remain in the placement for the foreseeable future and usually for the remainder of their childhood. Historically these studies have concentrated on measuring the rate of 'breakdown' and the factors that appeared to be associated with this 'failure' or with the survival of placements: their 'success'. Some more recent studies have looked in more depth at the quality of the placements as perceived by the foster carers, social workers and the children. This section will summarise the older studies of success and failure and look in more depth at some of the more recent work.

In the United Kingdom the studies of Parker (1966) and George (1970) led to the most widely known and quoted foster-care outcome statistic: approximately 50 per cent of long-term placements break down or, in Rowe's later term, do not 'last as long as needed'. American studies also deal with the issues of placement instability (Fanshel and Shinn 1978). There appear to be few studies from other countries summarised in the English language literature. In Colton and Williams (1997), *The World of Foster Care*, a country-by-country survey, the research section, where completed for each country, is dominated by comments on the paucity of research of any kind.

The main areas of agreement in the studies of Parker (1966) and George (1970) have been summarised by Berridge and Cleaver (1987):

- Approximately a half of long-term foster placements fail

- The older children are at placement, the more likely is placement failure

- The presence of foster parent's own children near in age to the foster child makes breakdown more likely.

Subsequent studies have supported these findings. The rates of placement disruption have varied from study to study and according to the timescales considered but all large-scale studies have found rates heading towards 50 per cent breakdown within 5 years, especially for older children. The findings in relation to age at placement have been confirmed in relation to adoption placements. Kadushin found 'a statistically significant relationship between the age of the child at placement and outcome' (Thoburn 1990). Berridge and Cleaver (1987), confirming the finding in relation to foster parents' own children, were exasperated to find so many placements where the unequivocal messages from previous research had apparently been ignored.

'If we continue to place children in these circumstances, therefore, it is not because advice is unavailable but because we choose to ignore it' (p.180). This finding was also confirmed by Kelly (1995) but that study noted, as others have, that social workers rarely perceive themselves as having a number of alternative placements to choose from – the choice as seen by the social worker often was: this placement with this associated risk factor or no placement at all.

The rate of placement disruption is a critical issue for long-term foster care. Chapter 1 discusses how the Parker (1966) and George (1970) findings were instrumental in the disillusionment with foster care of an earlier generation of child-care professionals. A crude and depressing reading of the more recent study findings (Berridge and Cleaver 1987) would be that practice had not improved in 25 years. Rowe et al. (1989) disputed this:

> It was only when we looked at the ages of the children in these key research reports that the amazing difference in the population under study became evident … Even after taking account of the shorter period of project placements, the improvement in the breakdown rate for young children is quite dramatic. (p.116)

In the Rowe study, only 4 per cent of the pre-school children's placements broke down in up to two years compared with 30–47 per cent in the earlier studies over a three-to-five year period: 'Today's social workers are placing adolescents as successfully as their predecessors placed pre-schoolers.' So we need to avoid a simplistic reading of research on foster home breakdown. Crucially we need to consider the ages of the children being placed and the difficulty of the aims of the placement.

Studies of more recent vintage have tried to shed further light on factors affecting the success and failure of placements and to broaden and deepen the discussion of outcomes. The Rowe et al. (1989), Berridge and Cleaver (1987), Cliffe and Berridge (1991) and Kelly (1995) studies will be used to develop these themes.

As we discussed earlier in this chapter, the Rowe et al. (1989) study developed the additional criteria to judge the success of placements – whether the aims of the placement were 'met, at least in most respects'. This enabled them to conclude that 'two-thirds of the long-term foster placements that ended were successful.' Of the long-term placements made during the study, 27 per cent had broken down during the first year; this varied from 4 per cent of the under-4s to 38 per cent of 14–15-year-olds.

This study ranged across a number of different authorities with different rates of children in foster care and different 'success' rates and encourages caution in the use of the type of league-table comparisons that have become fashionable in the public services in Britain. It will already be evident that the success rate of placements in a particular area will be related to the degree of difficulty of the aims of the placements being made. Agencies taking risks with older children and teenagers are likely to have more unfavourable outcomes than those 'playing safe' with younger children. A corollary of this is that attempts to increase radically the proportion of children in foster care is likely, at least in the short term, to lead to more breakdowns as children previously thought unsuitable for fostering are placed. This analysis has led to calls for a balanced service that is based on the assessment of children's needs rather than a zealous commitment to developing one type of placement at the expense of others and, crucially, a balance between residential care and foster care. Cliffe and Berridge (1991), summarising their research into an authority that closed all its children's homes, comment: '…we have urged other authorities to think long and hard if they have contemplated repeating what Warwickshire did' (p.233).

Berridge and Cleaver's (1987) study of foster home breakdown confirms many of the central findings of the earlier studies in relation to the breakdown of long-term foster care. It is particularly interesting because it highlights aspects of placement neglected by other studies. It takes a rounder, more holistic, view of the child in placement. Previous studies have concentrated almost exclusively on the child, the foster family and the relationship between them. This can be seen as mirroring practice which as we have seen in Chapter 1 drew heavily on the relatively narrow confines of attachment theory. Social workers were preoccupied with the relationships within the foster family and tended to neglect the range of other experiences that are important to children. Berridge and Cleaver reported a range of novel and interesting findings that ran counter to the preoccupation with adult/foster-child relationships:

There were fewer breakdowns where:

- children who had siblings in care had some of these living with them
- children did not change school when placed
- there were other unrelated foster children in the foster home – even if these children were close in age to the foster child.

They comment:

> Peer support – for example from siblings or school friends – would seem to be valuable in helping children cope with adversity; it is also likely to be of benefit in the longer term if such relationships are maintained. (p.85)

These findings lend strength to the importance of trying to promote resilience in children in care (see Chapter 5).

In a small longitudinal study of 19 planned long-term foster care placements of 4–11-year-olds Kelly (1995) and McAuley (1996) found a breakdown rate of 26 per cent over two years; four (21%) broke down in the first year. These rates are similar to those in the Rowe *et al.* and Berridge and Cleaver studies: Rowe *et al.* (1989) – 23 per cent in two years for primary-school children; and Berridge and Cleaver (1987) – 17 per cent of all placements in year one and 37 per cent in three years for 6–11-year-olds. All the studies point to the vulnerability of placements to breakdown in the first year. In the Northern Ireland study (Kelly 1995) foster parents and social workers argued that these placements should never have been made – that either the children were not committed to the placement or the child's behaviour problems were such that it was unreasonable to expect foster parents to be able to cope. The child's behaviour was seen as critical by the social workers and foster parents. Interviewed at four months into placement, the social workers, in four of the five breakdown placements, identified behaviour problems at home and at school that 'threatened the stability of the placement'. In effect, they predicted 80 per cent of the breakdowns and made no false predictions. Berridge and Cleaver also found that there was a 'statistically significant relationship between social workers' estimation of foster placements and subsequent outcome' (p.61). These findings should encourage social workers to trust their judgement about vulnerable placements, and their managers to take them seriously. They also point to the need for staff with competence in working with behaviour problems (see Chapter 7).

It is interesting (and encouraging!) that a numerically small sample produces findings that are validated by much bigger samples. Kelly (1995) found that the foster mothers of the 'failed' placements tended to be younger (mostly under 40) than the remainder of the sample (mostly over 40), thus agreeing with the findings of Berridge and Cleaver (1987) and earlier studies. In all the breakdown placements in Kelly (1995) the foster parents had a child of their own who was near in age to the foster child. This occurred in under half of the surviving placements. In one situation the foster parents' own child became involved in the sexualised behaviour of the foster child – the foster mother commented: 'We expected buttons and bows and look what we got.' In another the foster parents' own child developed a psychosomatic illness that led to her staying at her grandmother's: 'When she was away, I thought this is all wrong ... sending our own child out of the home...' (because of the problems created by the foster child).

The major study of long-term foster care in Britain remains Rowe *et al.*'s *Long Term Foster Care* (1984). This was not an 'outcome' study in the sense of those discussed above in that it considered only placements that had survived for a minimum of three years. Thus in terms of lasting as long as needed, the traditional preoccupation of foster care research, they were all 'successes', at least at the time of research. That outcome was assured by the focus of the study. However, a variety of outcomes for the participants of a placement can be measured at any point along its course or in their lives thereafter. This work confirms an oft-stated truism about foster care – 'when it works, it works'. If children can be settled in long-term placements and disruptions avoided, broadly speaking foster care can deliver good homes for separated children:

> The overall picture was encouraging with three out of four foster homes being rated by social workers as providing an 'excellent' or 'good' home for the child. Most of the children were very positive about their foster homes and stressed the importance of having a family, but there were disturbing pockets of unhappiness, fears and worries many of which could have been alleviated by better social work practice. (DHSS 1985, p.31)

The 'pockets of unhappiness' were reflected in a rate of behaviour problems higher than samples of adopted children or those drawn from the general population. Much of this unhappiness is attributed to the status of being a foster child – in what were mostly quasi-adoption placements. Only 16.5 per cent of the children in non-relative placements had visiting contact with a parent. On this basis Rowe *et al.* concluded that many of the children would have been better off adopted because fostering is 'not quite good enough'. This takes us back to the 'compared to what' debate above, but they do recognise that adoption is not a panacea. Many foster parents and foster children (not to mention natural parents) would not want it: 'It would be a serious mistake to assume that *all* long-term foster children could or should be adopted' (p.226). In this study of stable long-term placements only 27.5 per cent of the foster parents actually wanted to adopt.

On the basis of these studies we can conclude:

- Long-term foster care remains a placement with a high risk of breakdown

- It is harder to place older children and those with behaviour problems successfully

- Situations where foster parents have a child of their own close in age to the foster child are best avoided

- The 'whole child' is important; we need to look beyond the foster family and maximise support and minimise stress for the foster children in other areas, e.g. education, sibling and peer support.

CONTACT WITH BIRTH FAMILY

The effect of the continued contact of foster children with their birth families has long been an area of contention in foster care. It has been an area where pro and anti arguments have been developed from value positions, using attachment theory and research findings (see Chapter 1). The essence of the issue, in terms of outcomes, is whether children are more likely to prosper in substitute care if they retain contact and a relationship with their birth families or whether is it better for them to have a 'fresh start' and commit themselves wholly to their foster parents. There is a related, although less frequently discussed issue: to what extent is an exclusive parent/child relationship with children necessary for foster parents to develop the commitment they need to make placements work?

The issue does not arise in short-term foster care. If the intention is for the child to return home then continued parental contact is essential. This 'common sense', practice wisdom is supported by research findings (Fanshel and Shinn 1978). Millham *et al.* (1986) commented:

> Even after controlling for other variables, we find that a weakening of parental links is strongly associated with declining chances for the child of returning home. Naturally parental links are not a sufficient condition to ensure exit from care ... [but they are] a necessary condition for exit. (Quoted in DHSS 1985, p.11)

In permanent or long-term foster care the issue is more complex. In an exhaustive review of the research, Quinton *et al.* (1997) report that the only recent study of long-term foster care with data on contact and breakdown (Berridge and Cleaver 1987) shows similar breakdown rates for children

with no contact and those with little contact, and the small group with frequent (at least fortnightly) contact had fewer breakdowns but 'the
differences were not statistically significant'. Studies that have looked at contact in permanent placements – either adoption or fostering – have produced
mixed results. Barth and Berry (1988) found no significant difference in disruption rates between closed placements with no contact and those with
contact. However, Fratter and colleagues (1991) in a study of over 1000
placements found that:

> ...when other variables are held constant continued contact with birth
> parent(s) is a protective factor, that is, it is associated with successful
> outcomes. (p.51)

Quinton and colleagues (1997) could find no evidence in the studies
reviewed that contact improved the adjustment or the intellectual attainment
of children in long-term care. They conclude that, in encouraging parental
contact in permanent placements we are engaged in a 'social experiment'
rather than evidence-based practice. In this respect this area of practice is like
many others, it is driven by value changes in social work and the wider society, by legislation, and by policy changes with, at best, an uncertain research
base. In recent years the child-rescue-driven practice of the 'fresh start' has
become less achievable. Whether the developing openness and continued
contact produces better long-term results for children is still an open question. However, small-scale studies in adoption are encouraging in terms of
openness in that the arrangements, carefully negotiated, appear workable
(Fratter 1996).

Most children who come into public care go home again quite soon
(Millham *et al.* 1986). Many of those who remain in care until they are
eighteen return to their homes on discharge (see Chapter 4). For these
pragmatic reasons and because the law (in the UK), following the logic of
these findings, has made parental access to their children in care a right, the
arguments to stop contact have to be very persuasive.

Retrospective studies

As most of the studies of foster care outcomes during childhood were in the
British literature, so most of the significant retrospective studies are American. These studies are, in the main, conducted on samples of adults who have
spent the greater part of their childhood in foster care (foster family care in
American literature), and have usually 'aged out' of the placement. The

research is usually a mixture of measures of how they have 'made out' as adults, comparing them with the wider population, and their views, reflecting back on their experiences of placement. These studies are important because of the long perspective they give. We know from our own reflections on childhood and adolescence that there were problems that appeared mountainous and made us very unhappy at the time yet we would not now feel that they have adversely affected us in the long term. On the other hand there are hurts which remain with us and affect our confidence and our relationships. These studies are helpful in enabling us to put the foster-care experience in its long-term context and consider the extent to which it is meeting the ultimate goal of all child welfare: equipping children for the adult world.

Overall, the messages from these follow-up studies are encouraging for foster care as illustrated by the following summing-up quotes from the studies and reviews of the studies:

> They (the ex-foster children) were not what might be described as problem ridden when they were discharged nor did they become so in subsequent years; there was no support for the generational repetition of foster care (foster children's children coming into care), there was no evidence of undue dependence on public support, and their records of arrest were not excessive. Overall they were not so different from others of their age in what they were doing, in the feelings they expressed, and in their hopes about the future. (Festinger 1983, p.294)

Festinger reported that 80 per cent were satisfied with the experience of being brought up in foster care; 90 per cent felt themselves lucky to have been placed in foster care.

> The first and most important conclusion is that long-term foster care in and of itself was not injurious to the youngsters in the study. When judged by the criteria of the current adjustment of the former foster children long term foster care provided a better environment for rearing the majority of children than did natural homes. (Zimmerman 1982, p.105)

> Asked about their satisfactions in life, over 9 out of 10 of those adopted, and over 7 out of ten of those fostered said they were 'fairly' or 'very' satisfied with the way things turned out for them. (Triseliotis 1983)

Triseliotis researched the relative merits of foster care and adoption and his conclusion that foster care is adequate but has shortcomings when compared with adoption is a feature of the conclusions of most of the studies. It takes us back to the 'compared to what?' issues discussed above. The aspects of foster care that the former foster children had most problems with were those that distinguished foster care from other forms of family care (Festinger 1983):

- not using their foster parents' name
- visits from social workers
- having their lives controlled by an 'agency'.

Foster sounds like a disease ... It's very hard growing up with a different name ... children make fun of you ... it's a lot of heartache. (Festinger 1983, pp.273, 274)

Zimmerman, however, found that the status of foster child did not necessarily make the children feel different; it was being 'treated differently, primarily by their foster parents' that was most difficult.

Foster care did not, for the most part, deliver on its potential to keep foster children in touch with their birth families (Triseliotis 1983; Festinger 1983; Zimmerman 1982). Festinger did not find that presence or absence of contact with parents affected their view of themselves; they identified heavily with their foster families (Festinger 1983). 'What matters most ... and what is most strongly missed in its absence is acceptance and inclusion in the foster home' (Zimmerman 1982, p.110).

Festinger found that other factors in the careers of those with high levels of satisfaction were:

- those whose placement had been shifted less frequently
- those who were younger at the start of placement
- those who had remained longest in their longest placement
- those who used their foster family's last name
- those who were more comfortable talking about their placement.

In these factors there are strong elements of what we can see as constituting a sense of permanence and belonging.

Recent studies of children in state care have focused on the disadvantages they suffer in relation to their education (Aldgate 1990). These retrospective studies confirm the disadvantage that the children suffer and its long-term consequences:

On the whole, those who fell behind in school while in care still lagged behind years later despite general educational gains. (Festinger 1983, p.158)

Different education systems make exact interpretation of the findings difficult but the broad message is clear:

The overall school dropout rate of 56% is an indictment of the school system, families and the foster care agencies alike for failing to meet the educational needs of the youngsters. (Zimmerman 1982, p.107)

Despite the disadvantages associated with poor educational backgrounds, the former foster children were doing better in employment status and economic terms than their families of origin (Triseliotis 1983; Zimmerman 1982).

The retrospective studies are valuable for the long view they give us of the experience of foster care. They are encouraging in that, for the most part, they show that stable foster placements have been successful in equipping children for adult life and that it is not producing a disproportionate number of unhappy individuals disabled by the deprivations of their childhood. Whether this would be true with today's population of children remains to be tested. In the UK and the USA at least, they have more often come into care as a result of serious abuse and neglect.

The retrospective studies do point us towards a practice that emphasises permanence and stability, enabling children to feel a real part of their substitute families. They also give support to those (Aldgate 1990) who have highlighted the necessity of having greater regard to the disadvantageous effects of a childhood in care on children's education and therefore their chances in the adult world.

Conclusion

A number of concluding points emerge from this consideration of the research into the outcomes of foster care:

1. Short-term placements are predominantly successful, that is, they last as long as needed and achieve most of the aims set for them.

2. Long-term placements are at high risk of breakdown especially if the children are in their middle childhood or older when placed and also have behaviour problems.

3. The successful placement of adolescents, even in specialist professional schemes, is fraught with difficulty.

4. The factors associated with breakdown have remained fairly stable through 30 years of research and insufficient account is taken of them when placements are being made.

5. Recent research has indicated that social workers may be good judges of the placements most at risk of breakdown.

6. There are indications that a more holistic approach to the choice of and support for placements may be more productive than the traditional, exclusive concentration on the relationships between foster children and foster parents.

7. 'When it works – it works.' Those who experience stable long-term placements in foster care predominantly emerge as adequately functioning members of adult society although they often have painful memories of being 'different'.

8. Researchers and commentators who compare foster care unfavourably with adoption do not take sufficient (or any) account of the 'higher price' that has to be paid for adoption in terms of the professional expertise, the legal threshold and by birth parents who do not want to lose their parental rights.

Finally, in reading and trying to apply research to practice one must proceed with caution. Different practice, administrative and legislative systems will create different conditions from those in which the research was carried out. One must be continually and critically asking the question – 'True for us?' It is important, as well, to recognise that researchers and writers in the field of child care generally, and foster care and adoption in particular, come with their own values and pressures. The research role, in particular, calls for the ideal of 'objectivity'. However, if researchers are to be knowledgeable they will usually have been involved in the field in some capacity or other so they will be bringing their 'baggage' in much the same way as experienced practitioners do. Research and commentary should be read with a weather eye to the values that inform or appear to inform it – and to our own values and prejudices as readers.

References

Aldgate, J. (1990) Foster children at school: Success or failure? *Adoption and Fostering 14*, 4, 38–49.

Barth, R.P. And Berry, M. (1988) *Adoption and Disruption Rates, Risks and Responses.* New York: Aldine de Gruyter.

Berridge, D. (1997) *A Research Review.* London: The Stationery Office.

Berridge, D. and Cleaver, H. (1987) *Foster Home Breakdown.* Oxford: Blackwell.

Cliffe, D. and Berridge, D. (1991) *Closing Children's Homes: An End to Residential Care.* London: National Children's Homes.

Colton, M. and Williams, M. (1997) *The World of Foster Care.* Aldershot: Arena.

Coulter, J., Kelly, G. and Switzer, V. (1996) Freeing children for adoption: A review of the process, 1989–1996. *Child Care in Practice 2*, 3.

Department of Health and Social Services (DHSS) (1985) *Social Work Decisions in Child Care.* London: HMSO.

Fanshel, D. and Shinn, E.B. (1978) *Children in Foster Care: A Longitudinal Study.* New York: Columbia University Press.

Fein, E. and Maluccio, A.N. (1992) Permanency planning: Another remedy in jeopardy. *Social Services Review*, September 1992.

Festinger, T. (1983) *No One Ever Asked Us.* New York: Columbia.

Fratter, J. (1996) *Adoption with Contact, Implications for Policy and Practice.* London: British Agencies for Adoption and Fostering.

Fratter, J., Rowe, J., Sapsford, D. And Thoburn, J. (1991) *Permanent Family Placement: A Decade of Experience.* London: British Agencies for Adoption and Fostering.

George, V. (1970) *Foster Care: Theory and Practice.* London: Routledge and Kegan Paul.

Hazel, N. (1981) *A Bridge to Independence: The Kent Family Placement Project.* Oxford: Blackwell.

Hill, M., Nutter, R., Giltinan, D., Hudson, J. and Galaway, B. (1993) A comparative survey of specialist fostering in the UK and North America. *Adoption and Fostering 17*, 2, 17–22.

Katz, L. (1996) Permanence action through concurrent planning. *Adoption and Fostering 20*, 2.

Kelly, G. (1995) Foster parents and long-term placements: Key findings from a Northern Ireland study. *Children and Society 9*, 2, 19–29.

Lambert, L., Buist, M., Triseliotis, J. and Hill, M. (1990) *Freeing Children for Adoption.* London: BAAF.

Lowe, N. (1993) *Report of the Research into the Use and Practice of the Freeing for Adoption Provisions.* London: HMSO.

McAuley, C. (1996) *Children in Long Term Foster Care: Emotional and Social Development.* Aldershot: Avebury.

Mech, E.V. and Rycraft J.R. (eds) (1995) *Preparing Foster Youths for Adult Living.* Washington: Child Welfare League of America.

Millham, S., Bullock, R., Hosie, K. and Haak, M. (1986) *Lost in Care.* London: Gower.

Parker, R. (1966) *Decision in Child Care: A Study of Prediction in Fostering.* London: Allen and Unwin.

Parker, R., Ward, H., Jackson, S., Aldgate, J. and Wedge, P. (1991) *Assessing Outcomes in Child Care.* London: HMSO.

Quinton, D., Rushton, A., Dance, C. and Hayes, D. (1997) Contact between children placed away from home and their birth parents: Research issues and evidence. *Clinical Child Psychology and Psychiatry 2,* 3, 393–414.

Rowe, J., Cain, H., Hundleby, M. and Keane. A. (1984) *Long Term Foster Care.* London: Batsford/BAAF.

√ Rowe, J., Hundleby, M. and Garnett, L. (1989) *Child Care Now: A Survey of Placement Patterns.* London: BAAF.

Shaw, M. and Hipgrave, T. (1983) *Specialist Fostering.* London: Batsford/BAAF.

Snodgrass, R.D. and Bryant, B. (1989) Therapeutic foster care: A national program survey. In R.P. Hawkins and J. Breiling (eds) *Therapeutic Foster Care Critical Issues.* Washington, DC: Child Welfare League of America.

Thoburn, J. (1990) *Success and Failure in Permanent Family Placement.* Aldershot: Avebury.

Thoburn, J. (1996) Psychological parenting and child placement: But we want to have our cake and eat it. In D. Howe (ed) *Attachment and Loss in Child and Family Social Work.* Aldershot: Avebury.

Thoburn, J., Murdoch, A. and O'Brien, A. (1986) *Permanence in Child Care.* Oxford: Blackwell.

Triseliotis, J. (1983) Identity and security in adoption and long term foster care. *Adoption and Fostering 7,* 1, 22–31.

Zimmerman, R.B. (1982) *Foster Care in Retrospect.* Tulane: Tulane Studies in Social Welfare.

CHAPTER 4

Leaving Care and Fostering

John Pinkerton

Introduction

The last placement for a significant proportion of young people leaving care will be foster care. In making that move those young people face the challenge of how to make the transition from the role of young person in care to that of adult out of care. This is a transition to full social citizenship that is made in a variety of ways by all young people. It involves growing out of the world of childhood, through youth, to adulthood. Childhood is characterised by largely prescribed dependency, on family, school, friends and neighbourhood. Adulthood means making choices about relationships, family and friendships, where to live, developing leisure pursuits, dealing with employment or unemployment, making a commitment to a partner, becoming a householder, becoming a parent. These choices, from which adult rights and responsibilities flow, are not easily made and they are not taken in a vacuum. They are heavily influenced by the opportunities and constraints of socio-economic status, ethnicity, gender and disability. The period of preparing to make the choices of adulthood is challenging for all young people. They need to be able to draw on a wide range of formal and informal supports and they need time. For care leavers both of those resources may be in short supply. Making the transition to adulthood is often much harder for them than for their peers. Everyone involved in leaving care from a foster placement needs to recognise that.

Although this is not a new message (Maluccio, Kreiger and Pine 1990; Wade 1997) there is still a need to stress it. Berridge, in his valuable review of the last twenty years of foster care research identified leaving care as one of a number of key areas that stand out as having lacked attention (Berridge 1997, p.85). Coming at the subject from the other direction, Stein, in his comprehensive review of 'what works' in leaving care, noted that young people leaving foster care are one of the groups that least is known about (Stein 1997, p.32). Even taking into account that both foster care and leaving care are relatively under-researched areas, this gap seems strange. The one thing that all the various forms of foster care, like all families, share is that their children will leave them. Stein has drawn attention to how belief rather than research-based evidence has driven practice to date in leaving care. So perhaps what has prevented interest in this area is just the belief that young people's needs on leaving foster care are somehow met as part of them being 'absorbed within their foster families' (Berridge 1997, p.24). Or perhaps it is that interest in endings in foster care has tended to exclusively focus on 'breakdowns' and 'disruptions'. Both these views are particularly likely for adolescents as there is evidence to suggest that their foster care placements include a high proportion of very successful and very unsuccessful results (Triseliotis *et al.* cited in Berridge 1997, p.27)

Whatever the reason for the limited attention to date to leaving care from foster care, the aim of this chapter is to draw attention to the subject based on material from the United Kingdom (UK). However, it is important to note that this is an issue that has been raised in a number of other countries (USA: Maluccio *et al.* 1990; Australia: Cashmore and Paxman 1996; Ireland: Kelleher and Kelleher 1998) and needs to be addressed wherever there is foster care. The chapter starts by drawing attention to the growing recognition of the importance of leaving care and its legislative mandate within the UK. This is followed by a review of research on leaving care, which includes both small-scale qualitative studies and large-scale surveys. The review highlights the one piece of research that focused solely on fostering and leaving care. A way of thinking about the goals that should be pursued for care leavers is then proposed based around the idea of 'coping'. That leads on to suggestions about developing leaving and after-care services based on 'through-care plans'. The place of foster care in this is given particular attention. The chapter ends by setting out a number of immediate action points for ensuring that the importance of the relationship between fostering and leaving care is recognised.

Campaigning and legislation

Leaving care is more firmly on the child-care agenda in the UK than it has ever been before and interest is growing (National Children's Bureau 1992; Broad 1998). The government has identified the experience of care leavers as a key indicator to the quality of local authority personal social services. This situation has come about because of long-term campaigning, going back as far as the mid-1970s. Not only has it taken a long time, but it has required the involvement of a broad range of interested parties – young care leavers themselves, social services practitioners and managers, voluntary agencies, researchers, campaigners and pressure groups (Stein 1983; Collins and Stein 1989; Stein 1999).

Whilst foster carers, individually and through the National Foster Care Association, have made their contribution, they have not played a leading role. At least in part this is because there has always been a tendency, not yet completely gone, of seeing leaving care as an issue about eighteen-year-olds without families being discharged from large residential institutions in which they had spent most of their lives. Also for many of the early campaigners concern for care leavers came from involvement with youth homelessness (Stein 1999). However, as the issue became better understood, it also became clear that care leavers were far from being a homogeneous group. Rather they were a mixture of young people from different types of backgrounds who had come into care for a variety of reasons across a wide age range. They spent different lengths of time in care, they experienced all types of placements and they received both good and bad substitute care. They left care for varied reasons, at different ages and from different placements. Most importantly it was recognised that these differences meant that there needed to be a variety of leaving and after-care options and there needed to be legislative backing to ensure these options were made available.

As the momentum for reform of child care legislation across the UK built up during the 1980s, the opportunity emerged to ensure fuller responsibilities towards young people leaving care were enshrined in legislation. Early on in the process of developing new legislation it was clear that the efforts of those committed to pushing leaving care up the child-care agenda were having an impact. The Social Services Committee Report on Children in Care (Short Report 1984) included recommendations on 'Continuing Care' which subsequently formed the basis of the relevant sections of the Children Act 1989 for England and Wales. These sections of the Act relate to both preparation for leaving care and after-care support, financial assistance and accommodation. Similar sections appear in both the Children Act Scotland 1995 and the Children (NI) Order 1995 (Tisdall, Lavery and McCrystal 1998).

These legislative developments not only provided an opportunity for ensuring that leaving care received a statutory mandate but also set out key child-care principles which underpin the legislation as a whole. The first of these is the paramountcy of the welfare of the child. It is the cornerstone of the legislation. A second principle is that a child with a disability is a child first and foremost. A third principle of anti-discrimination is expressed in the recognition that a child's cultural background must be respected and protected. Participation by children and young people as active subjects is a fourth principle which in particular underlies those sections dealing with representation and complaints. A fifth principle is interagency working on behalf of children and young people. Social services departments are empowered to request the help of other public agencies, such as education, housing and health, and those agencies are obliged to assist insofar as is compatible with their own statutory duties. All five underlying principles are essential underpinnings to those sections of the legislation dealing with leaving care.

The sections that deal explicitly with leaving care start with preparation. Section 24 in England and Wales, Section 29 in Scotland and Article 35 in Northern Ireland, place a duty on local authorities to 'advise, assist and befriend' young people in their care with a view to promoting their welfare after they leave care. Any young people who were looked after by the local authority beyond the age of sixteen have the right on leaving care to be 'advised, assisted and befriended' until they are twenty-one (nineteen in Scotland) by the local authority in whose care they were. Local authorities are also given the power to advise and befriend other young people who were cared for away from home after age sixteen. Where a young person leaves some other form of accommodation (e.g. under the auspices of a voluntary agency), those responsible for the accommodation have a duty to inform the local authority. Similarly a local authority has a duty to inform another local authority when a young person they have been advising and befriending moves elsewhere. As regards material support, local authorities have the power to provide assistance in cash or in kind to any young person who qualifies for advice. Local authorities also have the power to provide financial assistance connected with the young person's education, employment or training and such grants may continue beyond age 21 to allow for completion of education or training (Section 24 in England, Section 30 in Scotland, Article 36 in Northern Ireland). Whilst these powers tend to be permissive rather than obligatory they represent a major advance in providing a legislative mandate for work with care leavers.

Messages from research

The role played by research in shaping the new legislation is well recognised and this was certainly the case for leaving care (Stein 1991; 1993; 1999). Throughout the 1980s, although there was no large-scale research into leaving care, a body of very useful small-scale qualitative work was building up (for a very useful brief summary table see the Appendix in Garnett 1992). This qualitative work is well represented by the seminal work of Stein and Carey (1986). It documented the experiences of forty-five young people who left the care of a local authority in the north of England in 1982. It was very much based on the young people's own accounts and evaluations of what it was like to leave care from residential settings, foster homes and home in care placements, how that was affected by their experiences when in care and how they were coping with their new circumstances outside of the care system.

The Stein and Carey study drew attention to a range of issues that were to appear again and again in later research: the impact of care on personal identity; mixed experiences of care; the role of social workers; the decision-making process; the importance of informal support networks of family and friends; the practicalities of managing finance; finding suitable accommodation; sorting out education, training and employment; handling getting into trouble with the law; and dealing with a variety of statutory agencies. From within this recurring set of issues a number of key messages emerged about the general experience of care leavers whilst they were in care, as they moved out of care and when they had left care.

First, young people tended to leave care not from the security of a stable placement but having experienced a lot of movement and disruption whilst in care. One study found that over half of the young people had experienced between seven and twelve placements by the time they were sixteen years of age and the average for the sample was six per young person (Stein 1990). The Department of Health in summarising findings from a number of child-care research studies completed during the 1980s concluded: 'The instability of "in care" placements is hammered home to the reader of these research studies by the depressing similarity of their findings' (Department of Health 1991). This lack of placement continuity was reflected in the range of placements that they had experienced. Although residential care was generally the final placement from which they left care, many of the young people had also had experience of foster care, children's homes, assessment centres and periods at home in care.

Stein and Carey (1986) found that a change of placement following, for example, a fostering breakdown or a trial period at home not working out usually meant an abrupt end of 'care relationships and a sense of failure, followed by a whole new set of difficulties to deal with and adjustments to make – new foster carers or residential staff, a strange neighbourhood, different friends and a new school. Whilst placement breakdowns are undoubtedly part of the reason for the extent of movement experienced by young people when in care, it also has to be recognised that the routine management and administration of care as part of a formal, statutory child welfare system also generates movement. There is, for example, the need to use both preliminary assessment placements and planned moves during a care career to ensure that children and young people have their needs matched with appropriate services.

The stability required to successfully face the demands of the transition to adulthood is not just about place. It is also about having a secure personal identity. In relation to that, too, the research had a worrying message to give. Young people in care, particularly those who had been in the system a long time and those who were black or had mixed parentage, on leaving were forced to confront difficult issues of identity. Many of these young people lacked sufficient knowledge and understanding about their past, their family, the reasons for coming into care, why they were moved in care and why they were separated from their brothers and sisters. A study by one leaving care organisation (First Key 1987) highlighted the cultural identity problems faced by black and mixed parentage young people brought up in a pre-dominantly white care system. It found that many black young people expressed confusion about their cultural identity. This was particularly the case if they had been fostered long-term with white foster parents.

Although primarily drawing attention to the negative and challenging features of leaving care, the qualitative research also showed there was another side to the picture. Young people themselves identified not only negative but also positive aspects to their experience. The negative included the stigma of being in care, the weakening of family links, the dependency created by care and the poor practical preparation for leaving. But even with something as clear-cut as practical skills, young people reported in the detail a more varied experience. In one study they reported that they had learned some practical skills, cleaning, washing, ironing, but not others, budgeting, shopping and paying bills (Stein 1990). There is also a suggestion that young women are better prepared in practical skills than young men (Keegan 1993). Positive evaluations of care included getting away from problems at home, becoming involved in positive activities, gaining personal attention and friendship, and receiving help with coping and building self-confidence.

Perhaps above all else what comes through from these studies is a the sense of vulnerability combined with possibility:

> When I moved in here – total chaos – I didn't know what was happening, but I've learnt by my mistakes. There was no one to tell me what to get in or out, so I just picked up things and it worked out. (Stein and Carey 1986, p.51)

> Excited, frightened and sad. I couldn't wait to get away but I didn't want to go. To be independent, I wanted to leave. But not to be on my own. I didn't want to leave. (Coyle and Conway 1991, p.12)

Profiling care leavers

Whilst qualitative studies can provide unique insights into the world of care leavers there is always the danger that the picture is a narrow and unrepresentative one. However, the 1990s saw a number of large surveys (Garnett 1992; Biehal et al. 1992; Broad 1994; Cheung and Heath 1994; Pinkerton and McCrea 1999) which all seemed to confirm the rather bleak picture that had been building up. It is also the case that greater confidence can be placed in research findings when a similar approach has been used in different contexts and produced consistent results (Pinkerton and Stein 1995). That was the case for the surveys carried out by researchers from Leeds University and from Queens University Belfast. The Leeds study gathered information on a sample of 183 young people aged 16–19 in three English local authorities using a survey questionnaire which was then used in a modified form for 95 young people leaving care across Northern Ireland. Using material from the England and Northern Ireland surveys it is possible to sketch a very similar, empirically based profile of personal characteristics, care careers and after-care circumstances.

Turning first to general characteristics, the gender balance is much the same in both study samples as in the general population – there were slightly more males than females in the Leeds study whereas the reverse was the case in Northern Ireland. Young people from minority ethnic groups and of mixed race origin made up about an eighth of the Leeds sample, thereby constituting an important subgroup. Young people with special needs made up a similar proportion of the sample. The findings of the Northern Ireland survey contrast in that neither ethnic minority background nor special needs feature significantly as a characteristic of the population. The population was fairly evenly split between Protestants and Catholics with a slight over-representation of the latter. The absence of young people from minority ethnic communities may well reflect their small, though growing, numbers in Northern Ireland. As regards the young people with special needs, their relative absence from the Northern Ireland sample may be because of the very demarcated nature of children's services, which divided off such children from the general child welfare population. Both points emphasise that differences in social and in organisational context need to be recognised as having an effect on the profile of care leavers.

Both studies found that almost two-thirds of care leavers had first entered care in their teenage years. Both studies also found that over four-fifths of the young people had spent more than one year in care. In the English sample just over a third spent more than three years in care and in the Northern Ireland population two-fifths had been in care for over five years. Given these long periods in care it is perhaps not surprising that fewer than ten per cent of the young people in the Leeds study remained in the same placement throughout their time in care and nearly one-third made between four and nine moves and one-tenth moved more than ten times. In the Belfast study just under three-quarters of the young people experienced two or more moves and over a tenth moved more than five times.

In the two studies, despite the promotion of foster care in both jurisdictions, residential placements provided the jumping-off point for the largest proportion of young people – though foster care was the last placement for substantial numbers. The last care placement of over half of the English young people was in the residential sector compared to less than one-third fostering placements. In Northern Ireland it was two-fifths and a quarter respectively. The Leeds University study highlighted the very young age at which care leavers move to independence and contrasts this to the norm of leaving home in early to mid-twenties. UK research (Banks *et al.*

1992) found that less than a tenth of young people in the general population were living away from home at age seventeen or eighteen. By contrast three-fifths of the English care leavers moved to independence at that age. In Northern Ireland there was a very different picture with under a fifth of care leavers moving to independence. It is likely that this difference was at least in part due to a more legalistic definition of leaving care used in the Northern Ireland study (Pinkerton and McCrea 1996).

The Northern Ireland study found that almost two-thirds of the young people initially returned to their families. The importance of birth families to care leavers was also seen in the English study which found a high level of contact between the young people and their families. Some four-fifths were still in touch with family members and, for over half of those who had contact, this contact was at least weekly. This underlines the importance of trying to maintain contact between children in care and their families. The extent of family contact contrasted with that provided by social services. Some contact between social services and the young people usually occurred after they had left care. Indeed, the Leeds study found that social workers were offering support to nearly half the young people and nearly a quarter were being supported by leaving-care schemes. More than a third of the young people were receiving a weekly financial top-up from social services. Contact was reported for three-fifths of the Northern Ireland group, but this did not include regular financial support. However, in both studies the after-care support appeared limited in scope and restricted in duration. Levels of support from foster parents and residential social workers also tended to be low and declined fairly rapidly once the young person had left the placement.

Looking at what happened to the English and Northern Ireland care leavers once they had left care suggests that they were poorly equipped to deal with the demands of the transition they faced. Accommodation for many of the young people was far from the ideal of stable independence. They tended to return to the uncertain welcome of family home, temporary housing or homelessness. In Northern Ireland, where almost two-thirds returned home, within six months of that return less than half were still at home. Just over a fifth of the young people in the Belfast study and under a fifth in the Leeds study were judged to have been homeless at some point. The Leeds researchers found that young people with special needs seemed to be at special risk of homelessness: one-third of homeless young people either had a disability or had previously been classified as educationally and behaviourally disturbed. There was some suggestion in the findings that young women were doing better in terms of housing and finance. That may have been a reflection of the significant proportions of young women in both samples who were also young mothers and accessed services on that basis. The English study clearly identified young parents, generally mothers, as an important subgroup, accounting for about a quarter of the sample. It was a similar picture in Northern Ireland where about a fifth of the care leavers were either pregnant or had been pregnant.

Care has been described as an 'educational hazard' and both surveys bear this out. Two-thirds of the English sample and just under a half of the Northern Ireland population had no qualifications at all. Clearly this had implications for job opportunities, particularly at a time of high youth unemployment. In both studies only about a tenth of the care leavers had employment, with a third of the English sample and a quarter of the Northern Ireland study population registered unemployed. The Leeds University study also found an association between movement in care and poor attainment. Three-quarters of those who had experienced four or more moves in care had no qualifications compared with only half of those who had made no moves. It also found that a higher proportion of young people leaving residential care had no qualifications, around three-quarters, compared with those leaving foster care where the equivalent figure was just over half.

Leaving-care and foster-care research

Whilst both the small qualitative and the large survey research included to some degree the experience of young people leaving foster care, there has only been one study that looked specifically at that group (Fry 1992). Undertaken by the National Foster Care Association, the research consisted of a survey by questionnaire which was published in *Foster Care Magazine* and got a response from 207 foster families. This was supplemented in a number of ways: by compiling information based on a more detailed monitoring form completed by a small number of foster carers in four English authorities; by drawing together the views from fostering support-group meetings and regional adolescent foster-care groups; and by interviewing six foster carers, selected for their experience in caring for black young people, young people with disabilities and young parents.

The picture that emerged, albeit from what was recognised as possibly an unrepresentative sample of foster carers, was one of continued concern for the young people even though they were no longer in care. Foster carers offered support ranging from continuing to provide a home and a family to being there for the young person at times of lesser or greater crisis:

> General safe house – refuge where he can come for company, support and peace of mind.

> Counselling a young mother to decide to switch off the life support machine and taking it in turns to cuddle her baby till death. (Fry 1992, p.18)

Over a third of the young people were still in contact and one in twenty was currently living with their foster carer. What had been a foster home became an accessible, open door, available at all hours; a safe place to let off steam; a place where there was someone to remember special occasions like birthdays. Support tended to be varied. It generally involved different types of support – practical, emotional and financial; all mixed in together. Foster carers were able to draw on their life experience, local knowledge, social contacts and practical skills to help young people through the 'ups and downs' of making the transition to adulthood.

Despite the depth and range of their contribution to helping care leavers, foster carers reported that they got little support for doing so. What encouragement they got from agencies was either unofficial or limited or their efforts were met with indifference. Foster carers believed that financial help, whether in terms of one-off sessional payments to them or direct financial aid to the young person, would help to make their contribution more effective. More important to them, however, was to have their contribution formally recognised and valued by agencies. Foster carers wanted more recognition by social services for their contribution to all aspects of leaving and after-care – in the planning and review process and in the provision of ongoing support and practical help.

Promoting coping

As recognition has grown of the importance of care leaving and of the preparation and supported after-care that is already being done, not least by foster carers, the question has arisen as to what should be the goals of this work. One way forward is to focus on the idea of 'outcome', which has become such a dominant concern within UK child care (Ward 1996):

Recently, research into modern social conditions, the emergence of theories about prevention, the weakening of confidence in the public care of children following a number of well documented tragedies, the attention given to consumer views and the emphasis on cost-effectiveness have all served to produce a climate in which the development of reliable means of assessing outcome is increasingly seen as a necessity. (Parker *et al.* 1991, p.17)

For all these reasons, in the late 1980s the then DHSS (England and Wales) set up a working party which considered the issues around outcome measures in child care. The result was a framework for assessment of outcomes which was closely aligned with the Children Act 1989 and which was to be developed into the influential Looked After Children materials (Ward 1996). The identified outcome measures cover seven dimensions (Parker *et al.* 1991, p.82):

- Health
- Education (including skills training and employment in older age groups)
- Emotional development and behaviour
- Social, family and peer relationships
- Self-care and competence
- Identity
- Social presentation.

The appeal of outcomes as a way of thinking about leaving care is that it both carries with it the notion of the end of a process, time in care, and the means to unpack the elements that go to make for a successful ending. However, the Working Party recognised that whilst it was easy to ask the general outcome question – how far has the service delivered increased the long-term well-being of the child? – it is very difficult to specify, identify and measure actual outcomes and their relationship to particular aspects of the service. When Stein and his colleagues applied the idea of outcomes to their work on the effectiveness of formal leaving care schemes they found themselves facing that same issue (Biehal *et al.* 1995, pp.249–257). Using a broad definition of outcome as 'the effects or results of a process (for example receiving a service) which can be attributed to that process' (Biehal *et al.* 1995, p.249), they found it very difficult to make a neat connection between process (services) and effects (outcomes):

How can the effects of receiving a service from a leaving care scheme be measured when so many other factors may influence the outcomes for any young person? Outcomes for young people will be influenced by the personal histories and experiences they bring to the process of leaving care (their 'starting points'), which will have helped to shape their interpersonal and practical skills, their abilities and motivation. Outcomes will also be influenced by structural factors affecting all young people, such as labour markets and social security policy. The intervention of a leaving care scheme is just one factor, although potentially a significant one, which helps to shape the outcomes for any young person. (Biehal *et al.* 1995, pp.250–251)

In addition Stein and his colleagues noted that there are a number of types of outcome. They cite the distinction drawn by Knapp in his work on the production of welfare (Knapp 1984) between 'final outcomes' (changes in child welfare defined along dimensions spanned by socially sanctioned objectives for child care or child development which can be taken as measures of quality of life) and 'intermediate outcomes' (measures of the quality of care, desirable both in themselves and for their impact on final outcomes). This they see as similar to the distinction made by Cheetham and her colleagues (1992) between 'client-based outcomes' which measure the effects of services on service users and 'service-based outcomes' which are concerned with the process of delivery and hence the quality of care.

If this distinction is made when considering care leaving, final or client-based outcomes would include such factors as accommodation, employment, the presence of a network of family and friends, the ability to make and sustain relationships and a reasonable sense of self-esteem. Intermediate or service-based outcomes would be such things as a young person having attended a leaving-care group which focused on the information and skills needed to access a range of services, or having learnt to manage difficult relationships through counselling or social skills training, or having obtained qualifications necessary for a certain type of work.

At root, the difficulty in using the idea of outcome as a means of clarifying thinking about leaving care is that it tries to present what is a process as a product. An alternative way of thinking about the goals of leaving care is to use the idea of 'coping'. England, when writing about the essential nature of social work, suggested:

Social workers work not with those people who have problems but with those people who have difficulty coping with their problems ... all coping is a function of the interaction between available subjective resources and external resources, both social and material ... social workers may focus upon either the subjective or external resources of their clients ... according to their judgement of the balance of the 'coping equation'. (England 1986, p.14)

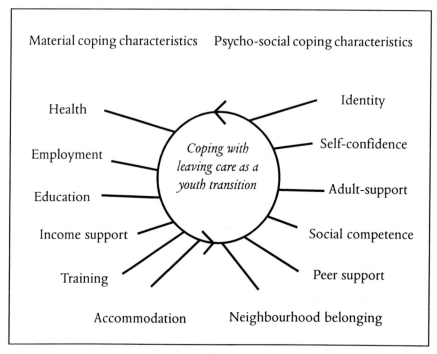

Figure 4.1 Aspects of Coping with Leaving Care

Through combining the seven Bristol dimensions with the work on outcomes done by Stein and his colleagues, it is possible to think about leaving care as a dynamic process which is driven by two sets of interacting characteristics (Figure 4.1). Replacing the rather technical term 'outcome' with the more usable term 'coping' (consider a young person's likely response to being asked 'Have you achieved your outcomes?' compared with 'How are you coping?') recognises that the various aspects of a young person's experience associated with the transition to adulthood are not final attainments but rather indicators of likely capacity to cope with the challenges of that transition. Together they constitute, not a tick list to be worked through in a mechanistic and simplistic fashion, but a set of agenda items which if addressed can allow the coping equation of a young person to be explored at any particular point in time. These agenda items provide the means through which to focus discussion with the relevant people, not least the young people themselves, either about preparation for leaving or about after-care support. It is important to stress that the model, whilst it makes a distinction between material and psycho-social needs, at the same time recognises that coping must be understood as a synthesis allowing for at least some degree of coping with all aspects of the equation.

One result of using the idea of coping is that it makes clear there can be no one right way of meeting the needs of all young people leaving care. Rather, what is required is being clear about the options available and the reasons for trying one rather than another and then reviewing whether or not it has been helpful. Regular reviews of a young person's situation, not only whilst still in care but also afterwards, have rightly been stressed as the key to this (Kelleher and Kelleher 1998; Pinkerton and McCrea 1996; Stein 1997). At the review a 'through-care plan' which addresses the various aspects of coping set out in Figure 4.1 can be used to provide focus to monitoring and planning. As Stein has pointed out:

> The review process prior to the young person leaving care is the foundation upon which good support can be built. It is this meeting or series of meetings which will negotiate the options with the young person, their social worker, their carer and where they exist, representatives from a specialist leaving care team. (Stein 1997, p.50)

Anyone, including foster carers, who is serious about playing an effective role in leaving care has to be a part of this process. This involves contributing to the assessment of needs and to the identification of the means to meet them in a way that allows a young person opportunities to gradually learn skills whilst maintaining the overall stability of a placement. It also requires ensuring there is sufficient support and participation in the necessary discussion, negotiation and risk-taking.

Stein points out that there is a danger of a minimalist approach being taken in through care planning. Expectations of achievement are lowered to levels that would not be accepted by an equivalent young person who was not in care. At the same time, however, there is a need to have realistic expectations; recognising the difficulties and complexities being faced by care leavers over and above that of their peers. Achieving that balance requires attention to detail in both assessment and planning and a capacity to engage the young person in the process. Engagement is one of the most difficult aspects of both preparing for leaving care and providing effective after-care support (Pinkerton and McCrea 1999). Active involvement expresses one of the key principles of the new legislation, as mentioned earlier, and it is also crucial to ensuring the success of a through-care plan. Through-care plans need to be worked up and negotiated directly with young people. This is not only morally right because, as the Voice of Young People in Care have put it, 'It's not just a review but a young person's life' (McAllister 1996), but also because to ensure a through-care plan has a chance of succeeding the young person must be committed to it.

Foster carers are well placed to ensure that the crucial ingredients of attention to detail and engagement are present in planning and delivering through-care. As the exchanges between professionals and foster carers at review meetings so often illustrate, the foster carer's involvement in the mundane routines of a young person's life places them in a position to know the detail of their circumstances, their concerns and their abilities. Planning needs to be flexible and to be able to reflect the changing priorities within the variety of needs which young people have. Truly effective preparation requires attention to what Gilligan has called the 'complex trivia which comprise household and personal organisation' (Gilligan 1991, p.207) which institutional care finds so hard to deliver and which is a major asset of foster-family life. Foster carers are more likely to be close to the complex trivia of a young person's life than any other member of a young person's formal social care network.

This is not to argue that foster carers alone can provide the varied supports required by young people leaving care. In summarising what he and his colleagues found made formal leaving-care schemes work well, Stein (1997) has drawn attention to a number of characteristics. These include some already identified as strong points for foster care, but he also raises others:

- Commitment to the young people for themselves
- Ability to engage young people and involve them in decisions
- Focused targeting of core needs
- Set out clear objectives
- Open communication
- Able to work with other agencies
- Able to influence policy at local level.

Foster carers may be well placed to ensure core needs are attended to and to engage young people but they also need to be able to work with other agencies. Only through foster carers and other interested parties working together is it possible to address the issues in key areas such as accommodation (see Box 1) and training and employment (see Box 2). The two other aspects of successful schemes, being part of a well-developed management and policy framework and being able to influence policy, are remarkably close to what foster carers were asking for in the NFCA survey (Fry 1992). Whilst there are different levels of responsibility for developing policy, managing and providing services, foster carers need to be included in an appropriate and effective manner.

Box 1 Personal planning for accommodation

- Involving young people in planning and decision making

- Assessing needs and preparing young people

- Offering a choice in the type and location of accommodation

- Not moving young people in an unplanned way before they are ready

- Having a contingency plan in case the proposed accommodation breaks down

- Setting up a package of support to go with the accommodation

- Providing information relevant to the type of accommodation.

(Stein 1997, p.47, based on Hutson 1997)

Box 2 Training and employment planning

- Gather detailed information about a young person's achievements and potential

- Carefully assess each young person's capabilities for employment

- Work to increase their employability before they take on the demands of education, training and employment

- Ensure that employment initiatives are flexible

- Look at creative ways of opening up employment opportunities

- Forge links with the local community services

- Provide adequate emotional and financial support for them when taking part in education

- Raise the awareness of social services about the needs of young people in the employment field.

(Smith 1994, pp.86–87)

In addition to working effectively with other agencies, both foster carers and those other agencies need to work with birth parents and family. The research reviewed earlier shows that families are highly likely to be a significant part of the leaving-care experience. Accordingly they need to be given an appropriate and effective role in order to make a positive contribution. Both the birth families and the young people may need help in sorting out what that contribution may be. Again this requires that the other parties involved, such as social services staff and foster carers, have the capacity to engage the families and young people on their own terms. Here again foster carers may have an important contribution to make through their understanding of the birth family and their relationship with the young person. However, it has to be acknowledged that, as Berridge has pointed out, despite the fact that a 'key issue for young people (and parents) was often the relationship with their own family and how accepting the foster carers were prepared to be' (Berridge 1997, p.27), there has generally been limited attention to this relationship with parents (Berridge 1997, p.12). The wider family is even more marginalised. Siblings, grandparents, uncles and aunts, and even estranged fathers, are a hugely under-used resource. There is a need to find new ways of unlocking that resource. For example, one means that has yet to be adequately explored for this work is the use of family group conferencing (Marsh and Crow 1998). Such conferences for children in foster care should also include the foster carers.

Action points for fostering and leaving care

From this chapter it should be clear that leaving care needs to be taken seriously and that foster carers have an important role in ensuring that it is. In part this will depend on foster carers taking on that role as a continuation of their commitment to the young people that have been placed with them. Many already do so, but for their number to increase and for their contribution to be more effective, leaving and after-care must come to be seen as an essential and formal part of all foster placements. The action points below, if implemented, would go a long way to ensuring that this is achieved:

- Every young person should have a through-care plan in which the contribution of foster carers is clear – not just in relation to the period that a young person is in their care, but also after they have left care.

- Foster carers should be involved fully in the process of 'through-care planning' – assessment, action planning, implementation and review.

- The relationship between foster carers and young people who have been in their care should be capitalised on as a major asset for engaging young people in managing their own care leaving.

- Foster carers should recognise their responsibility, and receive support, for drawing parents and extended family into the life of a placement in order to help lay the basis for their contribution to both preparation for leaving care and support on leaving.

- Resources (training, agency staff time, finance) should be provided for supporting and developing the foster-care role in leaving and after-care.

review
changed? working?

- Agencies should make explicit in their policy and in their organisational arrangements that they recognise the crucial role of foster carers in developing effective leaving-care services.

- Foster carers and their organisations should be directly involved in the development of policy making and strategic planning for leaving-care services.

Implementing those action points requires that foster carers, and those they work for and with, review the boundaries of their roles. Defining the foster-care role has never been easy and doing so in relation to leaving and after-care may make it more difficult. But it can be done. 'There are good examples of schemes and past carers working together to offer a package of support, thus maintaining the continuity of care which contributes to positive outcomes' (Stein 1997, p.50). These need to be better understood in order to build on them; and here there is a role for research. There is a need for qualitative studies, similar to those of the early period of leaving-care research, as well as broad-sweep descriptive surveys, such as the NFCA study. In addition there should be rigorous evaluations to explore 'what works' in the contribution of fostering to leaving care.

There is clearly much more work to do in developing and understanding the contribution of foster care to the coping equations of young people leaving care as part of their transition to adulthood. But as a final point, and without wishing to get snared by the difficult debate about the professional status or otherwise of fostering, it is perhaps worth noting that it may well be that it is precisely the 'in-between' status of foster carers that makes them such a crucial resource to young people with that other 'in-between' status – care leaver.

References

Banks. M., Bates. I., Breakwell, G., Brynner, J., Emier, N., Jamieson, L. and Roberts, K. (1992) *Careers and identities.* Buckingham: Open University Press.

Berridge, D. (1997) *Foster Care – A Research Review.* London: HMSO.

Biehal, N., Clayden, J., Stein, M. and Wade, J. (1992) *Prepared for Living.* London: NCB.

Biehal, N., Clayden, J., Stein, M. and Wade, J. (1995) *Moving On – Young people and Leaving Care Schemes.* London: HMSO.

Broad, B. (1994) *Leaving Care in the 1990s.* Kent: Royal Philanthropic Society.

Broad, B. (1998) *Young People Leaving Care: Life After the Children Act 1989.* London: Jessica Kingsley Publishers.

Cashmore, J. and Paxman, M. (1996) *Longitudinal Study of Wards Leaving Care.* New South Wales: Social Policy Research Centre, University of NSW.

Cheetham, J., Fuller, R., Petch, A. and McIvor, S. (1992) *Evaluating Social Work Effectiveness.* Buckingham: Open University Press.

Cheung, Y. and Heath, A. (1994) After Care: The education and occupation of adults who have been in care. *Oxford Review of Education, 20, 3,* 361–374.

Collins, S. and Stein, M. (1989) Users fight back: Collectives in social work. In C. Rojek, G. Peacoock and S. Collins (eds) *The Haunt of Misery: Critical Essays in Social Work and Helping.* London: Routledge.

Coyle, D. and Conway, G. (1991) *Into the Unknown: A Study of Young People Leaving Care.* SSI-DHSS (Northern Ireland): Social Services Inspectorate.

Department of Health (1991) *Patterns and Outcomes in Child Placement.* London: HMSO.

England, H. (1986) *Social Work as Art.* London: Allen Unwin.

First Key (1987) *A Study of Black Young People Leaving Care.* Leeds: First Key.

Fry, E. (1992) *After Care: Making the Most of Foster Care.* London: NFCA.

Garnett, L. (1992) *Leaving Care and After.* London: NCB.

Gilligan, R. (1991) *Irish Child Care Services.* Dublin: IPA.

Hutson, S. (1997) *Supported Housing – The Experience of Young Care Leavers.* Barkingside: Barnardo's.

Keegan, G. (1993) *Analysis and Evaluation of After Care 1985–1992.* Belfast: Barnodo's After Care Project.

Kelleher, P. and Kelleher, C. (1998) *Out On Their Own: Young People Leaving Care in Ireland.* Dublin: Focus Ireland.

Knapp, M. (1984) *The Economics of Social Care.* London: Macmillan.

Maluccio, A.N., Kreiger, R. and Pine, B.A. (eds) (1990) *Preparing Adolescents for Life After Foster Care – The Central Role of Foster Parents.* Washington: Child Welfare League of America.

Marsh, P. and Crow, G. (1998) *Family Group Conferences in Child Welfare.* London: Blackwell Science.

McAllister, K. (1996) Voice of young people in care – review recommendations. *Child Care in Practice 2,* 4.

National Children's Bureau (1992) *Childfacts – Young People Leaving Care.* London: NCB.

Parker, R., Ward, H., Jackson, S., Alsgate, J. and Wedge, P. (eds) (1991) *Looking After Children: Assessing Outcomes in Child Care.* London: HMSO.

Pinkerton, J. and McCrea, R. (1996) *Meeting the Challenge? Young People Leaving the Care of Social Services and Training Schools in Northern Ireland.* Belfast: Queen's University.

Pinkerton, J. and McCrea, R. (1999) *Meeting the Challenge? Young People Leaving Care in Northern Ireland.* Aldershot: Ashgate.

Pinkerton, J. and Stein, M. (1995) Responding to the needs of young people leaving state care: Law, practice and policy in England and Northern Ireland. *Children and Youth Service Review 17, 5/6.*

Short Report, Social Services Committee (HC 360) (1984) *Children in Care.* London: HMSO.

Smith, C. (ed) (1994) *Partnership in Action – Developing Effective Aftercare Projects.* Kent: RPS.

Stein, M. (1983) Protest in care. In B. Jordan and N. Parton (eds) *The Political Dimensions of Social Work.* London: Blackwell.

Stein, M. (1990) *Living Out of Care.* Ilford: Barnardo's.

Stein, M. (1991) *Leaving Care and the 1989 Children Act – The Agenda.* Leeds: First Key.

Stein, M. (1993) *Leaving Care – From Research into Practice.* Leeds: First Key.

Stein, M. (1997) *What Works in Leaving Care.* Barkingside: Barnardo's.

Stein, M. (1991) Leaving care: Reflections and challenges. In O. Stevenson (ed) *Child Welfare in the UK.* Oxford: Blackwell Science.

Stein, M. and Carey, K. (1986) *Leaving Care.* Oxford: Basil Blackwell.

Tisdall, K., Lavery, R. and McCrystal, P. (1998) *Child Care Law – A Comparative Review of New Legislation in Northern Ireland and Scotland: The Children (NI) Order 1995 and the Children Scotland Act 1995.* Belfast: CCCR.

Wade, J. (1997) Developing leaving care services: Tapping the potential of foster carers. *Adoption and Fostering 21, 3.*

Ward, H. (1996) Constructing and implementing measures to assess the outcomes of looking after children away from home. In M. Hill and J. Aldgate (eds) *Child Welfare Services.* London: Jessica Kingsley Publishers.

CHAPTER 5

Promoting Resilience in Children in Foster Care

Robbie Gilligan

Introduction

This chapter examines the concept of children's resilience and how it may work in foster care. It also looks at what foster carers and social workers can do to help a youngster in foster care to be resilient in the face of what has gone wrong in their lives. The chapter begins by discussing some key ideas about what can influence young people's overall development and how seemingly incidental experiences may actually prove important in the longer run. It looks at how development may be said to occur along a pathway which may take different courses depending on what happens along the way. The progress of development may be shaped by the balance of risk and protective factors in the child's life. Building up protective factors may prove very important even where risk factors seem strongly embedded. The reader is reminded that development occurs across a range of contexts and good things happening in one context or domain may have positive ripple effects in others. The chapter then reviews three key qualities with which it is suggested that foster care should try to endow a child, with a view to enhancing the child's resilience. These three qualities are a sense of having a secure base in the world, self-esteem and self-efficacy. The chapter then examines the role of both the foster carer and the social worker/agency in promoting resilience in the foster child.

Developmental pathways, transitions and turning points

As we grow up from birth we follow developmental pathways through the various milestones of development (Bowlby 1988). Our progress is rather like that of a yacht on a deep sea journey. The yacht may be blown off course by unfavourable winds, it may be becalmed, it may be seriously damaged by severe conditions. It may be blown back on course by a fortunate coincidence of wind conditions. Similarly, a child growing up may be blown off course by adverse circumstances. Some who veer off may never recover. Others may be fortunate to reach a positive turning point in the form of a positive event, incident or relationship which brings them back on course (Clausen 1995).

Turning points may occur serendipitously and they certainly underline that change does not necessarily always result from in-depth or enduring experiences or relationships, as reflection on your own experience may remind you. Encounters with a visiting relative, a teacher for one year, a sports coach for a summer scheme, a boss in a short-lived part-time job, a trainer on a short training course may have an impact on a person's career choices or plans or their self-belief out of all proportion to the time spent in contact.

Some turning points in life are normative and can be anticipated – for example, having a baby, going to school, moving from primary to secondary school. Others may arise serendipitously. Rutter *et al.* (1995, p.88) remind us that it is possible to break the links between childhood difficulties and adult adversity 'if the right actions are taken at the right time' along the pathway. Some of those actions may involve key choices made by the growing person, but many will depend on support and help from others. Sometimes turning points may start with something very small. The challenge for foster carers and social workers working with youngsters in foster care is to spot possible turning points as the young person moves along their developmental pathway, and to discreetly help the young person to seize the moment.

Risk and protective factors

Research findings indicate that mounting stressors greatly increase the risk, for example, of developing conduct disorder (Rutter 1989) and reducing IQ over time (Sameroff *et al.* 1993). Happily there is evidence that cumulative protective factors work in the opposite direction – they may have dispropor-tionately positive effects (Runyan *et al.* 1998). The message for child welfare practitioners is to try to build up the number of protective factors in a child's life. For a child in out-of-home care it may be impossible to erase risk factors which have built up over time but it may be possible to assemble some protective factors which can balance, neutralise or outweigh the risk factors. A sense of secure base in the foster home, enhanced self-esteem due to accomplishment in valued activities at school or outside, a strengthened social network all may serve as valuable protective factors which can help to counteract risk factors in the child's life. Thus, adding one more protective factor to a child's profile may prove very important. Measured against the enormity of adversity facing a child, this may seem a modest response. But the evidence does seem to support the proposition that attending to detail and getting even one thing right as a starting point is the right way to proceed. It may also be encouraging for foster carers to realise that the duration of contact may not be vital in terms of enduring impact. Even comparatively brief opportunities or relationships may have long-lasting effects. As two American researchers on human development in adversity, Werner and Smith, observe:

> The life stories of the resilient youngsters now grown into adulthood teach us that competence, confidence and caring can flourish, even under adverse circumstances, if children encounter persons who provide them with the *secure basis* [emphasis added] for the development of trust, autonomy and initiative. (Werner and Smith 1992, p.209)

The word 'encounter' is significant in the above paragraph. It conveys the point that influence does not have to be related to depth or length of relationship. If we think of our own childhood, adolescent and young adult years we can probably think of related and non-related adults who had mentoring roles in our progress. In some cases, some of these influential relationships may well have been relatively short-lived. In workshops on this material in different countries I have been struck by how many professional participants readily concur with this point based on their own experiences. Many acknowledge the influence of a teacher who helped them to appreciate perhaps for the first time their academic potential, or a boss in a short-term position whose praise and support helped them to make key career changes.

'Arenas of comfort' in everyday life

As Masten and Coatsworth, speaking from a North American perspective, observe, children actually live out their lives and grow up through involvement in different contexts. Experiences in these different contexts may help them to transcend adversity:

Successful children remind us that children grow up in multiple contexts – in families, schools, peer groups, baseball teams, religious organisations, and many other groups – and each context is potential source of protective as well as risk factors. These children demonstrate that children are protected not only by the self-righting nature of development, but also by the actions of adults, by their own actions, by the nurturing of their assets, by opportunities to succeed and by the experience of success (1998, p.216).

Young people live out their lives in different domains: home, school, street, sites of leisure activities or part-time work and so on. Some of these domains may prove stressful, others less so, depending on the specific realities of a child's life. A useful concept in supporting young people under stress may be the idea of providing or finding 'arenas of comfort' separate from stressful domains in their lives (Simmons and Blyth 1987, cited in Thiede Call 1996). Where home is stressful the best strategy may be to help the young person find an 'arena of comfort' outside the home which may make home more bearable. School, a work-place, or sites for sport or hobbies, may constitute such 'arenas of comfort'. In the case of foster care the foster home obviously is a potential 'arena of comfort' although carers should be patient in waiting for the home to gradually acquire that status. They should also avoid any sense of resentment if the young person happens to find other 'arenas of comfort' beyond the foster home. Instead they should see this as a positive since it suggests that the young person has a range of back-up in their life to support their development.

A sense of having a 'secure base' in life

Most people have a strong intuitive sense of the importance to the individual of stable relationships with other people, both in childhood and later life. Attachment theory underlines for us the importance of stable attachments for the child growing up. Stable attachments teach the growing child that people and the world are trustworthy and reliable and that the child is lovable. For a toddler that sense of a 'secure base' in the world is cultivated and sustained by reliable care of one or more key care-givers. This sense of secure base helps the toddler or older person to feel safe in exploring the world. This exploration may range from the crawling around the corner out of sight of the toddler, to the slumber party of young teenagers, to the backpacking globe-trotting of some privileged young adults in Western culture.

While primary attachments are necessarily confined to at most a few key people, it is important to note that emotionally meaningful attachments of lesser intensity can also be formed. As the child grows older they may form a series of attachment-type relationships of varying degrees of significance to the child. It may be helpful to think of these as forming a hierarchy of attachment relationships of varying importance (Trinke and Batholomew 1997; Holmes 1993). These attachment figures may form a key part of the growing child's social network. That web of relationships may serve as a secure base within and beyond which the young person may feel safe in exploring the world. This sense of having a secure base in the world may be helped by strong relationships with relatives from within the child's family of origin, with school teachers and other interested adults. A young person's sense of secure base is cultivated by a sense of belonging within supportive social networks, by attachment-type relationships to reliable and responsive people, and by routines and structures in their lives. Most adolescents can normally expect to have a reasonably secure family base with one or both parents, their siblings and perhaps other family members (Byng-Hall 1995). As they get older, these young people may spend increasing time away from their base. But they know they can return – and will do so, especially in times of illness, emotional distress or penury, or, particularly in the case of unattached males, when the clean laundry runs low!

Achieving such a comprehensive and enduring sense of secure base in the world for the young person in foster care is inevitably more challenging and complex. For the young person in foster care, their hierarchy of attachment relationships may thus become more significant and precious. Where relationships with primary attachment figures prove less fulfilling, relationships with figures lower in the attachment hierarchy may inevitably take on greater meaning for the young person. But relations with parents or parent- type figures cannot be overlooked. A sense of mattering to one's parents (and presumably their substitutes) has been found to be important for the well-being of adolescents generally (Rosenberg and McCullough 1981, cited in Sandler et al. 1989). For the young person in foster care, it seems especially important that they feel *cared about* even if not *cared for* by their natural parents. This is a key challenge for carer and social worker: to foster a climate of relations between child and natural parents whereby that message of caring for can authentically be transmitted and received.

Self-esteem / self-worth

Self-esteem is connected to a person's sense of their own worthiness and competence. It comprises many aspects, but generally involves some comparison by the individual between how they would like to be and how they think they actually measure up (Schaffer 1996, pp.164–168). According to research evidence good self-esteem is protective for someone facing adversity in their lives. People will cope better with negative experiences if cushioned by positive self-esteem. According to Rutter (1990), the two types of experience which seem most important in influencing self-esteem positively are: '(a) secure and harmonious love relationships and (b) success in accomplishing tasks that are identified by individuals as central to their interests.' Foster carers can take much heart and inspiration from this message from Rutter. It suggests that even one positive relationship or experience in childhood or adulthood may do much to counter the harm of negative relationships or experiences. Similarly, it implies that success in an endeavour which the person values may do much to combat a sense of failure in other spheres of one's life. Success here is not necessarily based on competition but more on the person's own ambitions and standards. It seems important for foster carers (and social workers) to be alert to the cushioning potential for vulnerable young people's development of even one real taste of success in relationships or fields of endeavour. The foster carer is in a special position to help the young person to find opportunities for affirming relationships or accomplishments.

A sense of self-efficacy

Self-efficacy refers to how proactive and self-directed a person is in relation to the choices and challenges of everyday life. In general, people with higher self-efficacy cope better with the hand that life deals them. Various factors promote self-directedness and self-belief – or *self-efficacy*. They include the parent's belief in the child's own sense of control, responsiveness (since responsive parents show the child that his/her behaviour has an effect), consistency, warmth/praise, support, and encouragement to the child to engage in his/her environment (Sandler *et al.* 1989, pp.296–299). There are clearly many opportunities where foster carers and child welfare professionals can consciously help young people in care to develop a sense of self-efficacy, not least by involving them in the planning process in relation to their own care (and to care services more generally) and by helping them rehearse and develop coping skills and strategies for later life. Endowing children in foster care with an expectation of having a say, of having choices, of having a sense of influence over their future may be a vital part of their recovery from the adversities which have befallen them before coming into and while in care. A sense of purpose, a sense of direction, a sense of where things are leading is very important for young people who are trying to find their way through troubled circumstances (Dowling 1993).

What can the foster carer do to encourage the young person's resilience?

The foster carers can create the conditions in which the child's development can move forward. The child may need help to recover from past hurt and to unfreeze developmental progress halted by different trauma the child may have experienced. The atmosphere in the home and the rapport and trust which may develop gradually between child and carers are important supports to growth and development in all their facets. But it is important for the carers and their social worker and agency to realise that not all of the work or responsibility rests on the shoulders of the carers. There are many natural healing and developmental opportunities in the wider social network and community of both the child and the foster carers. A major contribution of the carers is to assist the child to access the potential support which lies waiting to be tapped in the contexts which constitute and surround their lives together. The school, neighbours, relatives, friends, youth organisations, sporting and cultural organisations, community facilities and many more offer some of the opportunities which may connect with a child's need. If a child makes even one positive connection in the wider set of contexts surrounding the foster home, this may be an important first step and the first movement in a positive spiral of development which may help to reverse what was previously a seemingly irreversible negative spiral.

Foster carers provide physical care, encouragement and emotional support. They can also usefully share enthusiasm they have or encourage and support enthusiasm or talents the young person has. Where these are not immediately obvious, foster carers can usefully expose the child in a sensitive and subtle way to opportunities which may exist in the community. Tasters of different activities and sports may uncover a hidden talent or interest which can release positive energy in the child's life.

The following is a set of specific actions which foster carers might usefully take to foster resilience in the young person in their care.

ENCOURAGE PURPOSEFUL CONTACT WITH FAMILY MEMBERS AND OTHER KEY ADULTS FROM THE CHILD'S PAST

Contact with parents is a major preoccupation for many children in care. Some professionals on the other hand may see contact as carrying possible risks for the child in terms of possible abuse or distress. Contact with grand-parents, siblings, aunts, uncles, previous neighbours or whoever may also be extremely important to a child and not carry any possible 'downside' of parental contact. In the Wisconsin study of young people about to leave care, 75 per cent reported visits with parents in the previous 12 months, compared with 65 per cent with grandparents and 83 per cent with siblings (Courtney, Piliavin and Grogan-Kaylor 1995). This underlines the point that family contact should not be framed as an issue involving parents alone. Similarly, contact does not always have to entail face-to-face encounters: it can involve phone calls, letters, exchanges of photographs, audio tapes, video tapes and so on. All of this helps keep alive potential 'base camps' for the after-care phase in young people's lives.

Certain pointers in managing contact with family can be suggested. Try to have conveyed through this contact a crucial message to the child of being *cared about*, even if not being *cared for* in a day-to-day sense. Try to keep threads of contact alive for the child to past contexts in his or her life. Recognise that positive ties with siblings (Dunn, Slomskowski and Beardsall 1994; Kosonen 1996a, b; Hegar 1988), grandparents (Jenkins and Smith 1990), or even well-functioning neighbourhoods (Brooks-Gunn *et al.* 1993; Reiss 1995) may be very positive for a child or young person in care. Use contact to help the child to see positive aspects of their social heritage, which may in turn help them build a more positive view of their own social identity. Use contact also as a means of rebuilding relationships which may lead to the child's return home (Warsh, Maluccio and Pine 1994). Be imaginative in how the time in contact is spent together. A shared activity may be more rewarding and productive than stilted encounters in the formal settings of offices or clinical settings. Going to a football match together, going on a joint fishing expedition, or going horse-riding together may all be ways of building a bank of shared experience which can help to bond positively relationships between children and important relatives or other adults.

ENCOURAGE POSITIVE SCHOOL EXPERIENCE

It is important not to overlook the contribution that positive school experi-ences can make to general development (Gilligan 1998; Sylva 1994). School offers a rich range of opportunities for social as well as academic develop-ment. It is not just what happens in the classroom that may influence the child's progress. As in the child's life more generally, where the child may thrive in some domains and falter in others, school may usefully be seen as a landscape of different opportunities and contexts. There does not have to be positive outcomes across all of these for the child to gain something. Even if the classroom is not a complete success it is possible that the child may find other contexts within the school experience which may work well for him or her. Remember there is also the school yard or playground, the sports field, the assembly hall, the corridor, the laboratory, the office of pastoral care staff, the school bus, the school play or musical, the walk to or from school, the school outing, the school trip. There are relationships with individual teachers, with peers, with ancillary staff. A young person may happen to strike up a rewarding relationship with the school secretary, or the school gardener, or the school maintenance person, or the school bus driver. All of these relationships and contexts may be potential sources of support and stimulus for the young person's all-round development. It is well also for carers and social workers to appreciate how success at school in the academic, sporting or social sphere may assist recovery from adversity (Romans *et al.* 1995). Success in this sense should be measured not against objective standards but more importantly against the child's own expectations, standards of performance and history. It is the child's sense of accomplishment which must be satisfied for self-esteem to be enhanced, not necessarily some objective measure of achievement.

It is helpful of course to convey high but reasonable expectations to the child about their educational and social progress at school. Ambition by carers about academic progress can be helpful (Borge 1996), a measured degree of which seems desirable for youngsters in care judging by the generally dismal evidence about their educational progress (Aldgate 1990; Jackson 1994). This is a delicate balance since concern about progress can easily tip over into unhelpful 'pushing'. The focus must be on meeting the young person's needs rather than on having the adults' ambitions satisfied by proxy through the child. While bearing this caveat in mind, it is still worth taking active steps to facilitate the educational progress of youngsters in care (Walker 1994) or to coach carers in specific tutorial techniques (Menmuir 1994). There is a very strong case for prioritising educational issues in care planning (Stein 1994).

ENCOURAGE FRIENDSHIPS WITH PEERS

Growing up, the capacity of a young person to build and sustain friendships with own-age peers seems a useful barometer of emotional health (Savin-Williams and Berndt 1990; Schaffer 1996, pp.312–328). Such friendships also contribute potential members of current and future social networks, and thereby vital sources of potential and precious social support. It is important that facilitating continuities in friendship receive adequate attention in care arrangements. In the Wisconsin study of young people about to leave care, the young people scored friends higher than foster family or own family in terms of perceived social support (Courtney, Pilavin and Grogan-Kaylor 1995). It is important that facilitating continuities in friendships receive adequate attention in care arrangements. We should try to ensure three things: first, that placement does not disrupt or sever pro-social friendships which predate the placement; second, that young people have friends; and third, that friendships are not confined to peers who are also in care. Pro-social friendships may help protect young people from bullying (Kochenderfer and Ladd 1997) and help to 'rescue' a youngster at risk from hurtling down a destructive developmental pathway (Fergusson, Lynskey and Horwood 1996).

ACTIVELY FOSTER ANY INTEREST, INVOLVEMENT AND TALENTS IN SPORT, MUSIC, HOBBIES OR CULTURAL PURSUITS

While their importance may seem obvious they may also be easily forgotten, so it is probably worth rehearsing how spare-time activities and interests may enhance resilience (Gilligan 1999). Involvement in cultural and leisure activities serves many valuable preventive functions (Borge 1996; Quinn 1995). These activities can embrace sport, cultural pursuits, the care of animals, volunteering to benefit the community, and even part-time work. In their study of young people in residential care, Sinclair and Gibbs (1996, p.10) found that young people in residential care were happier when they were 'involved in work or proud of something they did in their leisure time'. It is not just that the involvement helps to pass the time constructively; it has many other positive spin-offs. Involvement may help to develop instrumental and social skills. It may give the young person opportunities to learn practical know-how and build up skills in relating more easily to other people. Activities and interests may help to strengthen a young person's social network. Participation in a sports team, or a band, or a scout troop, for example, may introduce a young person to other children who are *not* in care and may help them build relationships which are independent of their in-care status. Involvement may enhance a youngster's sense of self-efficacy and self-esteem. Mastering a skill or successfully performing a skill to a good standard may be valuable in reinforcing a youngster's sense of competence and self-confidence. Involvement in spare-time activities can help:

- to promote a sense of *belonging* to a family or valued social group
- to foster a sense of *mattering* to people who are important to the child
- to encourage a sense of *counting* for something in a context that matters to the child
- to serve as a passport to social contact in new contexts in the future
- to develop physical fitness
- to fill time and provide structure and a precious sense of purpose in daily living.

From the above it seems clear that it is worth carers' while to encourage accomplishment (but without great pressure) in fields of endeavour which appeal to the young person.

Examples of resilience enhancing hobbies and interests

Music: Her ability to play the recorder led to an invitation for a young girl in foster care to play before a Church congregation. Her successful performance and the applause it earned had a distinct effect on the girl's confidence and self-esteem according to her foster carer. An occasion such as this would be an event in any child's life, but for this girl the sense of acceptance and accomplishment earned by the applause was particularly significant.

Swimming: A girl placed in short-term foster care with her siblings was introduced to the sport of synchronised swimming by the foster carers who were devoted swimming enthusiasts. Long after her return home to a materially deprived home, the social worker noticed the girl at the local swimming pool attending the same synchronised swimming club to which she had been introduced by the foster carers. This girl had literally taken something extra from her placement which she did not have beforehand.

Football: Skill in football helped to integrate a boy newly placed in a local foster home into a rural community. While lacking in extensive academic or social skills, his footballing prowess meant that the local team's management saw it as desirable in order to retain his loyalty to help him get a summer job in the local supermarket.

Skiing: A ten-year-old girl with problems of clumsiness and isolation in school was serendipitously found to have an exceptional flair for skiing because her foster carers brought her to a training slope in preparation for a family skiing holiday. School problems receded as the girl's confidence was buoyed by the affirmation of her skiing instructor and foster carers.

Art: A girl in foster care had a talent for drawing and illustration which had her in regular demand for the design of posters, covers for newsletters and so on in the local community. In the view of her foster carer this talent had a great value in building her social confidence and self-esteem.

Care of animals (1): A quite disturbed boy placed with foster carers who were farmers was given a carefully monitored opportunity to hand-rear a baby lamb. This proved a very positive experience for the boy, whose behaviour and engagement with the carers improved. The dependence of the lamb and the trust it invested in the boy proved hugely therapeutic for him.

Care of animals (2): A quiet and withdrawn eleven-year-old boy was placed in a foster home where the foster father had a deep interest in tropical fish. The boy got interested too, to the point where he formed a tropical fish club in school, corresponded with tropical fish enthusiasts abroad and got himself a job in the local pet shop over two summers thanks to his knowledge of tropical fish.

Dance: A teenage boy with many problems but a strong talent for performing dance overcame the mockery of peers in his foster home and his own self-doubt to play a leading role in a public performance. His success led him on to other performing opportunities and significant revision of his own view of himself and his potential. The foster mother had a significant part in counteracting the mockery and challenging and surmounting his self-doubt.

The box above shows some actual case examples of involvement in activities which have proved very beneficial for children in foster care.

HELP THE CHILD TO REHEARSE, OBSERVE AND DISCUSS PROBLEM SOLVING AND COPING SKILLS AND STRATEGIES

Building the coping skills of young people in foster care means taking and creating opportunities that present in everyday living. Certain particular steps suggest themselves. Involve children in discussions about their needs and about their future. Make sure they have the chance to process emotionally the reasons why they are in care and the current plans for their future care and after-care at any given time. It is worth noting that this may take time and patience on the part of foster carers and social workers. The painful and challenging nature of this material emotionally may mean the young person needs help and repetition in order to digest its significance. It is also important to help the young person to contribute to care plans and reviews. This may require arranging if necessary for some suitable adult to accompany them as a supportive companion at the review. There are other relevant messages for carers and social workers in this regard. Give clear information to the young person. Ensure the young person knows about: (i) reasons for entering and remaining in care; (ii) rights while in care; and (iii) future plans and how the young person can influence these. Try to regard young people as resources in the process of seeking solutions in their lives or milieux. Encourage them to make choices and declare preferences in everyday living.

Besides the specific care-related issues, there are everyday issues which can be addressed and used to build coping and survival skills and confidence. Coach young people in how to resolve conflict with peers without recourse to bullying or violence. Explore with key teachers in the child's school opportunities which may be open to the school to help the child to build up skills of negotiation and problem solving. Similarly, it may be worth alerting anyone in a mentoring relationship with the child of the value of such opportunities. These various opportunities and experiences can teach young people in care that their opinions are of value and help them learn some of the skills of influence, negotiation and problem solving.

PROMOTE PRO-SOCIAL QUALITIES IN THE YOUNG PERSON

While resilience may result from and lead onto positive experiences, it should not be assumed that the outcome is always positive. For example, there is a risk that arrogance and selfishness may be associated with resilience as much as altruism or compassion. A young person who is arrogant or selfish may in certain circumstances also prove to be resilient in the face of adversity, but they may not prove to be pro-social in their attitudes or behaviour. In such instances it may be necessary for natural pro-social tendencies of the child or young person to be nurtured or reawakened. Certain behaviours by parents or carers are more closely associated with pro-social behaviour. Foster carers should provide clear rules and principles. Following principles proposed by Schaffer (1996, pp.275–276), they should give messages about expected behaviour with emotional conviction. It is helpful if they frequently tell the child they are 'good', 'generous', etc. (and they will be more likely to live up to the attribution); model, as an adult, the standards desired of the child; and be warm and responsive towards the child. On a more specific point relevant to everyday care, there is evidence that young people who do housework of benefit to others in the home on a routine/self-regulated basis are 'more likely to show spontaneous concern for the welfare of others' (Gruesc, Goodnow and Cohen 1996, p.1004). This gain seems not to apply to self-care tasks but only to those of benefit to others.

The role of the foster carer – getting a difficult balance right

The challenge for the foster carer is to create the living environment for the young person which fits the individual's needs. Depending on their earlier attachment histories, some young people may crave quite intense relationships with their carers, while others may desire a great deal more space and distance in the relationship. By attuning the emotional intensity correctly and by pacing their interest and demands, the carers can assist the young person to move forward at their own speed. The foster carer can contribute by providing structures, routines and rituals which symbolise order, predictability and reliability. This can be done in a low-key way, but the subliminal message will undoubtedly register with the youngster. Attuned and sensitive responsiveness is likely to make the young person feel more secure and may also help them to explore the wider world. The good foster carer might usefully see themselves as a discreet coordinator/'impresario' in the young person's life. In a necessarily subtle way, they will be trying to help the young person make connections outside the home, with friends on the street, in school or in their community of origin. They will also, again discreetly, be trying to help smooth the young person's path in school. They can do this by establishing close links with relevant teachers and making sure that the school is fully briefed and motivated in terms of their part of the care strategy.

The foster carer will also be scanning the horizon for hints of interest in activities which might be helpful for the young person. They will also be alert to the interest of other adults who might be willing to take the young person 'under their wing' in some shared interest or activity. This may mean twisting the arm of a neighbour, teacher, relative, work colleague or relative of the child. The carer will always be trying to expose the young person to opportunities and relationships which may prove helpful in some way or which might blossom into a longer-term commitment which can be a resource to the young person when leaving care or beyond.

Lest the recommendation here be misunderstood, it is essential that the child does not end up feeling like they are living in some kind of 'emotional hot-house' where they are treated like a kind of pressure-grown specimen in some human experiment. The value of helping the young person make connections and networking in a sense on behalf of the child will only work if it is done in very low-key and laid-back way. Over-intrusive and over-enthusiastic parental intervention in the interests and relationships of a young person are frequently counterproductive, as any seasoned parent will tell you. Failure is most often linked to an over-eagerness born of the parent's urge to satisfy a need within themselves rather than within the child. The parent who, for example, tries to live out their failed musical ambitions through a child may find the plan ends in ignominious failure as the child tears up the script. Similarly, many fostering placements have come unstuck as the foster child fails to live up to the educational ambitions held for them by the foster carers. The secret for the foster carers seems to be not to have the arc lamp of concern and anxiety trained on the foster child all the time. The carer should give the young person a lot of space, figuratively, and should make sure that they are not using the young person to fill some gap in their own life. A carer should not use a hobby imposed on the young person to relive a childhood memory or combat a loneliness for companionship in their own lives. If the carer is leading a fairly full and fulfilled life into which they fit a welcoming space for the foster child then the right note may be struck. They should not be so busy that they cannot attend to the child or the child's more subtle communication. But neither should their life be so devoid of other interests that the foster child becomes an all-consuming focus. They should be able to tolerate, and indeed actively seek, sharing the young person with other concerned adults while of course providing a clear emotional anchor for the child's daily life.

The role of the social worker/agency in promoting resilience in the foster child

The social worker and agency obviously play a key part in matching child and carer, and in mediating mutual expectations of child and carer. The agency has a clear role in supplying the requisite level of emotional, material and behavioural management support as and when needed. The social worker will be an important broker and conduit for such support. The social worker will help to interpret for the agency what the specific needs are in a given placement and negotiate with the carer how those needs can best be met. Some of this may involve direct work by the social worker with the carers, while the balance may involve the worker linking the carers into other forms of support.

The agency and social worker can play a key role in facilitating the young person in foster care in terms of their progress through school and in leisure-time interests. The agency must display a strong commitment to encouraging the talents and interest of the young person in care. It must resist some of the defensive instincts of social service bureaucracies in terms of taking risks in, for example, valuing outings and school trips for young people in foster care. If they trust the foster carer to care for the child day-to-day, then they should trust the carer to make judgements about what is prudent in terms of such opportunities for the child. Agencies must fund staff development and supervision in this area. They can place emphasis on these areas of school and out-of-school activities in the recruitment, training and support of carers. They can require an explicit focus on these issues in care planning. They can also ensure the availability of budgets which can encourage youngsters' interests appropriately and which can support mentoring, and the possibility of each young person in care having a number of vouchers to 'spend' on interests and activities.

Conclusion

There are no magic solutions to the problems facing care systems and the young people reliant on them. But however daunting the challenges, foster carers – and social workers (and teachers and other mentors) – should remember that the detail of what they do with youngsters in care counts. Little things can make a difference. Daily or annual routines and rituals may be very precious and consoling for a foster child troubled by broken relationships and by unpredictability in their lives. Something as simple as warm smiles from a caring adult may be appreciated and remembered by a child who has found other adults in their lives indifferent or undermining.

Nurturing talents may sow a seed of interest and accomplishment which may be reaped many times over in the young person's future life. Encouraging and supporting sibling and friendships ties may strengthen the supports an otherwise isolated young person can call on in later life. All of these little things may foster in a child the vital senses of *belonging*, of *mattering*, of *counting*. Any one of these little things we do, these details, may prove decisive turning points in a young person's developmental pathway.

Foster carers are in a pivotal position in relation to much of this detail of caring. Being encouraged to join a swimming club, or learning to play the flute, or having a pet, may each prove to be the turning point in a youngster's life in terms of its impact on self-esteem, social support and self-efficacy. Let us not be distracted or seduced only by the big questions. While, for example, professionals may deliberate at length over whether or when to place a child in a permanent family, and which one, details of what can sustain the positive development of the child *today* may be lost sight of. A focus on longer-term planning may obscure helpful practical things that can be done now – and may thus make the child's problems and long-term planning for them more difficult. This is not to discount the need for a longer-term view, but it is to emphasise that attention to the detail in the present makes the prospects for the future more promising and more attainable. Foster carers can focus on those details that may make a difference. Every child in care certainly needs an investment of adequate resources in terms of their current or future education, health, housing, family support and after-care needs. But they also need an investment of interest and concern by adults personally committed to them. Foster carers can obviously be important among such committed adults. Some of these adults will hopefully have a long-term and consistent involvement. But some adults may only play a shorter-term part. All are important. What we do today may be a turning point in this child's life. What we do today may release healing potential within the child or within their support network.

References

Aldgate, J. (1990) Foster children at school: Success or failure? *Adoption and Fostering 14*, 4, 38–49.

Bowlby, J. (1988) Developmental psychiatry comes of age. *American Journal of Psychiatry 145*, 1, 1–10).

Borge, A. (1996) Developmental pathways of behaviour problems in the young child: Factors associated with continuity and change. *Scandinavian Journal of Psychology 37*, 195–204.

Brooks-Gunn, J., Duncan, G.J., Klebanov, P. and Sealand N. (1993) Do neighbourhoods influence child and adolescent development? *American Journal of Sociology 99*, 353–395.

Byng-Hall, J. (1995) Creating a secure family base: Some implications of attachment theory for family therapy. *Family Process 34*, March, 45–58.

Clausen, J. (1995) Gender, contexts and turning points in adult lives. In P. Moen, G. Elder and K. Lüscher (eds) *Examining Lives in Context – Perspectives on the Ecology of Human Development.* Washington DC: American Psychological Association.

Courtney, M., Piliavin. I. and Grogan-Kaylor, A. (1995) The Wisconsin Study of Youth Aging Out of Out-of-Home-Care – A Portrait of Children About to Leave Care. http://polyart.lss.wisc.edu/socwork/foster/index.html

Dowling, E. (1993) Are family therapists listening to the young? A psychological perspective. *Journal of Family Therapy 15*, 403–411.

Dunn, J., Slomkowski, C. and Beardsall, L. (1994) Sibling relationships from the preschool period through middle childhood and early adolescence. *Developmental Psychology 30*, 3, 315–324.

Fergusson, D., Lynskey, M. and Horwood, J. (1996) Factors associated with continuity and changes in disruptive behavior patterns between childhood and adolescence. *Journal of Abnormal Child Psychology 24*, 5, 533–553.

Gilligan, R. (1998) The importance of schools and teachers in child welfare. *Child and Family Social Work 3*, 1, 13–25.

Gilligan, R. (1999) Enhancing the resilience of children and young people in public care by mentoring their talents and interests. *Child and Family Social Work, 4, 3,* 187–196

Gruesc, J., Goodnow, J. and Cohen, L. (1996) Household work and the development of concern for others. *Developmental Psychology 32*, 6, 999–1007.

Hegar, R. (1988) Sibling relationships and separations: Implications for child placement. *Social Service Review*, September, 446–467.

Holmes, J. (1993) *John Bowlby and Attachment Theory.* London: Routledge.

Jackson, S. (1994) Educating children in residential and foster care. *Oxford Review of Education 20*, 3, 267–279.

Jenkins, J. and Smith, M. (1990) Factors protecting children in disharmonious homes: Maternal reports. *Journal of the American Academy of Child and Adolescent Psychiatry, 29, 1,* 60–69.

Kochenderfer, B. and Ladd, G. (1997) Victimised children's responses to peers' aggression: Behaviors associated with reduced versus continued victimisation. *Development and Psychopathology 9*, 59–73.

Kosonen, M. (1996a) Maintaining sibling relationships – neglected dimension in child care practice. *British Journal of Social Work 26*, 6, 809–822.

Kosonen, M. (1996b) Siblings as providers of support and care during middle childhood: Children's perceptions. *Children and Society 10*, 4, 267–279.

Masten, A. and Coatsworth, D. (1998) The development of competence in favourable and unfavourable environments – lessons from research on successful children. *American Psychologist 53*, 2, 205–220.

Menmuir, R. (1994) Involving residential social workers and foster carers in reading with young people in their care: the PRAISE reading project. *Oxford Review of Education 20*, 3, 329–338.

Quinn, J. (1995) Positive effects of participation in youth organisations. In M. Rutter (ed) *Psychosocial Disturbances in Young People – Challenges for Prevention.* Cambridge: Cambridge University Press.

Reiss, A. (1995) 'Community influences on adolescent behaviour.' In M. Rutter (ed) *Psychosocial Disturbances in Young People – Challenges for Prevention.* Cambridge: Cambridge University Press.

Romans, S., Martin, J., Anderson, J., O'Shea, M. and Mullen, P. (1995) Factors that mediate between child sexual abuse and adult psychological outcome. *Psychological Medicine 25*, 127–142.

Rosenberg, M. and McCullough, B. (1981) Mattering: Inferred significance and mental health among adolescents. *Research in Community and Mental Health 2*, 163–182.

Runyan, D., Hunter, W., Socolar, R., Amaya-Jackson, D., English, D., Landsverk, J., Dubowitz, H., Browne, D., Bangdiwala, S. and Mathew, R. (1998) Children who prosper in unfavourable environments: the relationship to social capital. *Pediatrics 101*, 1, 12–18.

Rutter, M. (1989) Pathways from childhood to adult life. *Journal of Child Psychology and Psychiatry 30*, 23–51.

Rutter, M. (1990) Psychosocial resilience and protective mechanisms. In J. Rolf *et al.* (eds) *Risk and Protective Factors in the Development of Psychopathology.* Cambridge: Cambridge University Press. pp.181–214.

Rutter, M. Champion, L., Quinton, D., Maughan, B. and Pickles, A. (1995) Understanding individual differences in environmental-risk exposure. In P. Moen, G. Elder and K. Lüscher (eds) *Examining Lives in Context – Perspectives on the Ecology of Human Development.* Washington DC: American Psychological Association.

Sameroff, A., Seifer, R., Baldwin, A. and Baldwin, C. (1993) Stability of intelligence from preschool to adolescence: The influence of social and family risk factors. *Child Development 64*, 80–97.

Sandler, I., Miller, P., Short, J. and Wolchik, S. (1989) Social support as a protective factor for children in stress. In D. Belle (ed) *Children's Social Networks and Social Supports.* New York: John Wiley. pp.277–307.

Savin-Williams, R. and Berndt, T. (1990) Friendship and peers relations. In S. Feldman and G. Elliott (eds) *At the Threshold – The Developing Adolescent.* Cambridge, MA: Harvard University Press.

Schaffer, H.R. (1996) *Social Development.* Oxford: Blackwell Publishers.

Simmons, R. and Blyth, D. (1987) *Moving into Adolescence: The Impact of Pubertal Change and School Context.* Hawthorne, NY: Aldine de Gruyter.

Sinclair, I. and Gibbs, I. (1996) *Quality of Care in Children's Homes – A Short Report and Issues Paper.* York: Social Work Research and Development Unit, University of York.

Stein, M. (1994) Leaving care, education and career trajectories. *Oxford Review of Education 20*, 3, 349–360.

Sylva, K. (1994) School influences on children's development. *Journal of Child Psychology and Psychiatry 35*, 1, 135–172.

Thiede Call, K. (1996) Adolescent work as an 'arena of comfort' under conditions of family discomfort. In J. Mortimer and M. Finch (eds) *Adolescents, Work, and Family – An Intergenerational Developmental Analysis.* Thousand Oaks: SAGE.

Trinke, S. and Batholomew, K. (1997) Hierarchies of attachment relationships in young adulthood. *Journal of Social and Personal Relationships 14*, 5, 603–625.

Walker, T. (1994) Educating children in the public care: A strategic approach. *Oxford Review of Education 20*, 3, 339–347.

Warsh, R., Maluccio, A. and Pine, B. (1994) *Teaching Family Reunification.* Washington, DC: Child Welfare League of America.

Werner, E. and Smith, R. (1992) *Overcoming the Odds – High Risk Children from Birth to Adulthood.* Ithaca: Cornell University.

CHAPTER 6

Pathways to Change
The Application of Solution-Focused Brief Therapy to Foster Care

Stan Houston

Introduction

A raft of research (Department of Health 1991; Berridge and Cleaver 1987; Triseliotis, Sellick and Short 1995; Trasler 1960; George 1970) has demonstrated that foster placement breakdown is associated with a diverse and complex range of factors. Some of these factors are child related (e.g. severe behaviour problems) whereas others can be located in the foster home (e.g. unrealistic expectations of carers). Furthermore, outcome studies reveal a concerning (if varied) rate of breakdown – particularly in relation to long-term foster care, where the range falls between 20 and 60 per cent (Triseliotis *et al.* 1995). Clearly, the experience of foster care can be a precarious one for all concerned. As Berridge and Cleaver's (1987) intensive case studies show, the pain and anguish of the child is often shared by the foster parent; and for the social worker, the breakdown can evoke a palpable sense of shame or failure.

When confronted by such difficulties it is understandable that social workers resort to a problem resolution frame of action. A frame is a set of meanings which define, explain and process experience (Goffman 1975). In social work, the frame has been shaped by a humanistic discourse (Rojek, Peacock and Collins 1989). This discourse extols the capacity of human beings to understand and resolve their problems by using reason. Consequently, much practice in social work is problem-centred. But when problems arise in daily practice, an alternative frame – one that is based on solution construction rather than problem resolution – may be more effective in promoting change.

This chapter will expand on this idea by examining the application of Solution-Focused Brief Therapy (SFBT) to foster care. Because of the emphasis placed on 'solution talk' (rather than 'problem talk'), the model offers a positive, constructive and structured response to a range of personal and familial problems – including those encountered in foster care. To examine this application, the chapter will be structured as follows: first, an overview is presented of the background, key assumptions and stages within the model; second, a conceptual frame is set out showing how the model has been adapted to foster care; and third, a case example shows how the conceptual frame has been applied in practice.

Overview

SFBT was developed by De Shazer and his colleagues at the Brief Family Therapy Centre in Milwaukee, Wisconsin (De Shazer 1985, 1988; Gingerich and De Shazer 1991) and has been adapted to a wide range of problem areas such as family work (Berg 1991, 1994), alcohol and substance abuse (Berg and Miller 1992; Berg and Reuss 1997), child protection (Dolan 1991; Walsh 1997) and education in schools (Rhodes and Ajmal 1995). Although used successfully in practice which is enforced by a legal or administrative mandate, the model is more limited in scope where interventions involve serious ethical issues, e.g. work with perpetrators of child abuse.

In relation to foster care, the model can be applied in a variety of circumstances. First, it can be used by foster parents and social workers to tackle troubled and troublesome behaviour in children and young people; second, where there are 'relationship difficulties' within families who foster, or between foster families and outside agencies, it provides a structured approach to reconciliation; third, it can be utilised in training and support forums to guide foster parents in situations which appear hopeless or stuck; and lastly, it can be used at times of crisis to prevent disruption or breakdown in placement.

These applications build on an assumption that the 'narratives' or stories which are used by clients to explain their difficulties are not unchangeable. New narratives, it is contended, can be conjointly created by the practitioner and client using language creatively to reframe experience. This core assumption leads to a number of premises about people, problems in daily life and how solutions can be effected:

- Understanding how a problem has developed is not an essential prerequisite to resolving it

- Change is inevitable; and when helpers and clients recognise this fact (and come to expect it), then it is more likely to occur

- Meaningful change depends on clients articulating their goals or establishing their preferred scenarios

- Problem patterns are rarely as stuck as they appear and there are usually exceptions – or instances when the problem is not present – which can be analysed to determine potential solutions

- Problems do not usually originate in pathological conditions within people; rather, they more often represent unsuccessful attempts to resolve difficulties

- Small changes are sometimes all that is required to set in motion larger, systemic changes

- There are numerous ways to construct a situation, none of which are more correct than others.

These premises are reflected in the key stages of the model (see Figure 6.1).

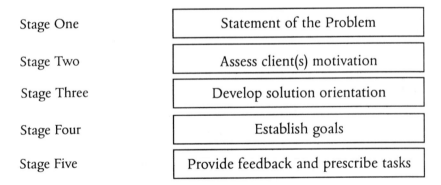

Stage One	Statement of the Problem
Stage Two	Assess client(s) motivation
Stage Three	Develop solution orientation
Stage Four	Establish goals
Stage Five	Provide feedback and prescribe tasks

Figure 6.1 The model of solution-focused brief therapy

The model

Each of the stages is now outlined.

Stage One – Statement of the problem

At the outset, the practitioner will need to make an informed judgement as to whether the family is interviewed together, or whether individuals are interviewed separately. This decision is likely to be a pragmatic one reflecting client interest or motivation. Even if only one family member agrees to participate (and starts to change their behaviour towards finding solutions) this can have a 'snowballing' effect on other family members.

Having considered who to interview, the next step involves defining the problem. Although deep probing into areas of concern is not advised, it may be the case that sufficient exploration of the presenting problem is necessary, as this facilitates a 'therapeutic alliance' between the practitioner and client. At this early stage of intervention the practitioner demonstrates his or her willingness to listen, acknowledge and validate the client's experience (Miller 1998). Creating an empathic understanding is an essential prerequisite to successful outcomes in all therapeutic work (Truax and Carkhuf 1967; Egan 1990). However, a fine balance should be struck between the acknowledgement of client concerns, on the one hand, and the need to focus on solutions, on the other.

Stage Two – Assess client motivation

De Shazer (1988) identified three types of client: 'visitors', 'complainants' and 'customers'. 'Visitors' are usually reluctant and/or resistant clients who present with no complaint and resent any compulsion to accept help. In contrast, 'complainants' are clients who present with a complaint, but are ambivalent about receiving help. 'Customers' are different from the two other types in that they seek out help and are motivated to change. Clearly, client motivation may move over the course of work and the objective is to engage the 'visitor' and 'complainant' so that they will eventually adopt a 'customer' outlook.

De Shazer emphasised that it was important for practitioners to tailor their responses according to the nature of the client's motivation; for instance, treating a 'visitor' as a 'customer' is likely to create resistance, withdrawal or defensiveness. To engage the 'visitor' successfully, a more sensitive and less intrusive response is required which uses positive reinforcement carefully. Similarly, 'complainants' may be made to feel distinctively uncomfortable if change – or 'customer' talk – is introduced too quickly; however, they may be more predisposed to accept help if their ambivalence is accepted without judgement.

As can be seen, one of the key strengths of the model is that it can be used with both voluntary (customers), ambivalent (complainants) and involuntary clients (visitors). In working with the latter, the practitioner can help to reframe client goals around the withdrawal of intervention – or the removal of a legal or administrative mandate (Marsh and Fisher 1992). For example, a primary motivating factor may be the cessation of statutory involvement or the revocation of a Court Order. Once stated, the client's goals can be used to generate solutions and active work can commence.

Stage Three – Develop solution orientation

In this stage the practitioner guides the client to describe any 'exceptions' to the problem (i.e. situations where the problem does not occur). Walsh (1997) underscores the importance of exception-finding in the following terms:

> The simple fact that the problem is sometimes present, and sometimes not (or less of a problem), if amplified by the practitioner, will help to create the expectation that a future is possible which does not include the complaint. The identification of exceptions, and the activity centred around it, is probably one of the most significant strategies in this way of working. (p.6).

In eliciting and amplifying exceptions to the rule, De Shazer (1988) directs the practitioner to extract step-by-step descriptions of the exception: who is involved, what happens, when it occurs, where it takes place and so on. In addition, it is important to find out what works currently, has worked in the past, and might work in the future in extending or creating further periods of exception.

Some examples of exception-oriented, pre-suppositional questions are:

> You have given me a good understanding of the problem, but can you tell me what's happening when the problem does not happen?

> How will you know when the problem is really solved?

> What will have to happen for that (exception) to happen more often?

If clients are unable to identify any exceptions, then the practitioner attempts to elicit hypothetical solutions to the problem: 'If I were to wave a magic wand, how would you want things to change?' Alternatively, if a hypothetical solution cannot be generated, the problem pattern can be scrutinised to highlight any disabling (or habitualised) thoughts, feelings or actions. For example, negative self-talk has been identified as a characteristic of depressed people (Beck 1976). Once recognised, however, it can be counteracted by positive self-talk.

Stage Four – Establish goals

In this stage the practitioner encourages the client to develop a new scenario of what life could be like without the problem. The practitioner's attitude is critical here: he or she should convey an unequivocal belief that change is realisable, expected or inevitable. The essence of goal setting is embodied in De Shazer's (1988) 'miracle' question:

> After you have gone to bed tonight, a miracle happens and the problem that brought you here today is resolved. But you are asleep, so you will not know that the miracle has happened. When you wake up tomorrow morning, what will be different that will tell you?

As can be seen, the language used resonates with the need within us all to be relieved of those burdens which cause us pain. But the question is also carefully constructed so as to elicit concrete differences between the problem and the desired state.

Once the miracle is proclaimed, it can be broken down into specific, measurable and achievable goals. Progress toward these goals can then be measured; this is referred to as 'scaling' and involves the client in ranking – over time – the extent to which the solution has been achieved. This is similar to behavioural approaches which set a baseline against which change can be measured (Herbert 1987).

Stage Five – Provide feedback and prescribe tasks

Having articulated the small steps of change in the preceding stage, positive, complimentary feedback is given to the client. The objective is to convey a strong identification with the client's struggle and to reinforce the solution-focused narrative which has been employed by him. In the therapeutic milieu in which SFBT originated, positive feedback is usually provided after a symbolic break – or planned interruption – in the session. The break allows both the client and the practitioner to gather their thoughts and to reflect on what has taken place.

Following the feedback, the practitioner will (if appropriate) prescribe a task for the client to undertake. A typical task (De Shazer 1988) might be:

Between now and next time we meet, I would like you to observe, so that you can describe it to me next time, what happens in your life that you want to continue to happen.

It is important to note that the task has been worded in such a way that change is taken for granted: a new world has been constructed in which solutions predominate over problems.

The stages described above are typically followed in the first (or second) interviews. Thereafter, subsequent sessions build on these stages: if goals are being met, doing more of the same is advocated; alternatively, if strategies are not working, doing something different (and perhaps unrelated) is advised.

This overview of SFBT will finish with some concluding remarks on the relevance and effectiveness of the model. In terms of relevance, SFBT exemplifies many of the requirements of contemporary social work. First, with its emphasis on goal setting, it is an outcome-led model. Second, by focusing on 'motivational interviewing', it applies to both voluntary and involuntary clients. Third, by promoting short and focused intervention, it is resource-effective. Fourth, by elevating clients to the role of experts, it is empowerment-oriented. Last, because it draws on systems theory, it fits with social work's holistic intent. And for practitioners who may be 'bogged down' in seemingly complex, long-term, intractable and 'impossible cases', the model offers direction, structure and optimism.

There is a danger, however, in presenting the model as a panacea. Despite its unique focus on 'solution construction', many of the model's concepts are found in client-centred (Rogers 1951) and cognitive-behavioural (Sheldon 1995) approaches. A comparison of these approaches – using Whittaker and Tracy's (1989) framework – reveals the main differences and similarities (see Figure 6.2). As can be seen, even though the purpose behind the approaches may differ, the strategies for helping greatly overlap.

Whittaker and Tracy framework	SFBT	Client-centred approach	Behavioural approach
Purpose	To create change through solution-oriented narratives	To facilitate responsibility, problem solving and existential growth	To promote cognitive/behavioural change
Knowledge base	Post-modern perspectives on language and meaning	Humanist and existentialist perspectives	Learning theory
Level of intervention	Client and family focused	Client-focused	Client and family focused
Role of worker	Active and facilitative	Non-directive	Educative and supportive
Strategies of helping	Reframing; motivational interviewing; setting tasks; therapeutic alliance; reinforcing change; use of relationship	Therapeutic alliance; use of relationship; promotion of self-knowledge and congruence	Reframing; reinforcement; shaping behaviour; setting tasks

Figure 6.2 Whittaker and Tracy's (1989) framework for comparing different approaches to client's problems

In relation to the model's effectiveness, The Brief Therapy Practice Group in London have collated a range of client, self-rating effectiveness studies (Iveson 1991; Parslow 1993; MacDonald 1994; De Jong and Hopewood 1996). These studies show significant improvements in originating complaints (e.g. drug dependency and mental illness) in 70–92 per cent of cases. The model has also been favourably evaluated by child protection practitioners (Walsh 1997). What was particularly useful to them was techniques such as goal setting, the miracle question, exception finding, scaling and highlighting positives. However, the practitioners had to adapt the model to the statutory context in which they worked. For example, it was necessary for them to be open about their statutory responsibilities. The next section will consider how the model should be adapted for use in foster care.

Context

In order to make the model applicable to foster care, two main adaptations are required. The first relates to the development of 'explanatory theory' on foster care. The second embraces the limitations imposed by organisational constraints. Each adaptation will be addressed in turn.

Explanatory theory

SFBT can be criticised for exemplifying a post-modern preoccupation with surface rather than depth-oriented practice (Howe 1996). Surface-oriented practice is concerned with questions of 'what' rather than 'why': with process rather than understanding. Explanatory theory (which illuminates our understanding of behaviour) is dismissed as irrelevant; what matters is the here and now – how clients can achieve solutions. But if the model is to be adapted to particular areas of practice – like foster care – then an understanding of context, causation and client situations is important. And it is perhaps disingenuous to suggest that explanatory theory is irrelevant. Rather, it can assist the practitioner to:

- tune in sensitively to client needs
- develop a therapeutic alliance with clients, by facilitating accurate empathy
- set presenting problems and solutions in a meaningful context
- make informed decisions on how the intervention should be planned, organised and progressed
- identify desired outcomes.

Explanatory theory refers to particular ideas or constructs which aid understanding. Three constructs can be developed from the literature on foster care. These constructs are illustrative rather than exhaustive. The first refers to the importance of 'relationship'. Holman (1980) has differentiated relationships in foster care into two main, polar types: 'exclusive' – which attempt to contain the foster child within the foster family while excluding other connections; and 'inclusive' – which are based on a readiness to incorporate significant relationships outside the foster parents and child into daily aspects of living. The former are premised on the notion that the foster child needs to be sheltered from the influence of, or knowledge about, their origins; conversely, the latter are based on the assumption that better outcomes for the child will be achieved if s/he has access to their natural family and knowledge about them. A large body of research (Berridge and Cleaver 1987; Weinstein 1960; Jenkins and Norman 1973; McAuley 1996) has demonstrated a positive correlation between 'inclusivity' and fostering success (even though there are other studies which have not corroborated these findings). These studies have important implications for therapeutic interventions in foster care.

The second construct (which is closely linked to the first) refers to 'need'. Thoburn (1994) postulates that children who are in care have special needs. These are needs for permanence: security, belonging, family life, being loved and loving; and identity: knowing about birth family, past relationships and having contact with significant others. Permanence and identity needs – if fulfilled – lead to self-esteem: the capacity to grow and make new and satisfying relationships as an adult. Knowledge of these major needs dispositions is important when applying the SFBT model, particularly in constructing new scenarios (Stage Four of the model) and setting tasks (Stage Five).

The third construct embraces 'role'. Triseliotis *et al.* (1995) describe, accurately, the complex and often fraught role of the foster carer:

> Foster carers are expected to care and love the child, whilst recognizing that one day he or she will go back to their own family or move to a new one. Carers are also expected to share their family life and affection in a way many people would find difficult. Not only are some of the demands and expectations placed on them contradictory, but they also involve complex and deep human feelings and emotions. (p.2)

One of the key requirements of SFBT is to develop a therapeutic alliance with the complainant (see Stage One). This alliance with foster carers will be significantly hampered if the social worker is unable to empathise accurately with them. Awareness of role tension, ambivalence and ambiguity is also necessary at Stage Two of the model when the worker appraises client motivation.

Organizational context

The second adaptation takes account of the organisational context and there are three dimensions within it. First, all family and child-care practice – and particularly work with 'looked-after' children – takes place in a legal, procedural context where accountability is to the fore (Blom Cooper 1985). Therefore, the worker cannot stick exclusively to a solution frame of reference: problems must be explored, particularly where there is a risk of harm (from whatever source) to the child. And because of these accountability requirements there ought to be openness (when using the model) about the nature of any child-care responsibilities.

Second, SFBT is only one of many forms of intervention in foster care. Practical services – such as affording foster parents relief – must exist alongside therapeutic interventions. As Payne (1996) suggests, social work is embroiled in personal, interpersonal, professional and political issues. What is required, therefore, is an informed eclecticism.

Third, whilst SFBT is traditionally practised in a clinical setting of prearranged sessions, two-way mirrors and therapist consultations, the setting for most social work interventions is more unpredictable and crisis ridden. Accordingly, it may be difficult to enact the model in linear stages. Therefore, the techniques will have to be used flexibly; and certain practices (such as therapist consultation) will have to be reworked to fit with agency constraints.

These theoretical and agency-related adaptations to the model can be presented in the form of a conceptual map (see Figure 6.3).

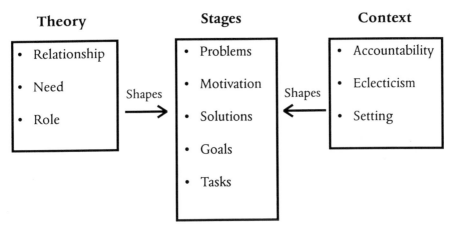

Figure 6.3 A conceptual map: solution-focused brief therapy in foster care

The next section will show how this conceptual map has been applied in practice. The case example (which is drawn from the author's experience) involves a fostering placement facing breakdown.

Case example and application of framework

Background

The case involves Mr and Mrs Smith (foster parents) who are fostering John Jones (14) (see Figure 6.4).

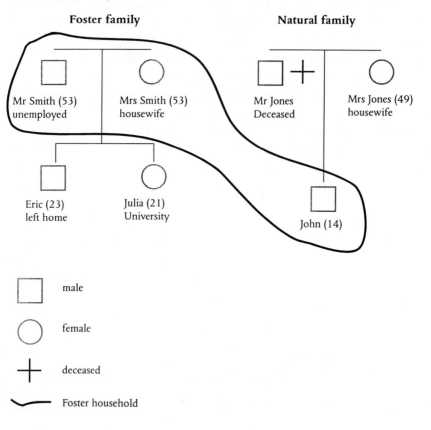

Figure 6.4 Case example genogram

The Jones family first came to the attention of social services when John was 12 years of age. At this time neighbours reported their concerns over Mrs Jones's drinking and her lack of control of John. A preliminary assessment by social services revealed a number of concerns: (1) following the death of Mr Jones (2 years earlier) from cancer, Mrs Jones had resorted to binge drinking; the regularity of her drinking had intensified to the point where John was largely fending for himself; (2) physical conditions in the home were poor; (3) John's attendance at school had been erratic over the preceding year; (4) neighbours had reported seeing John unsupervised very late at night.

After a six-month period of intervention – comprising weekly contact from the social worker, alcohol counselling and support from a family aide – there was little improvement. John's behaviour was increasingly out of control. Episodes of glue-sniffing, non-school-attendance and prolonged absences from the home resulted in an admission to residential care. The experience of care introduced stability into John's life and allowed Mrs Jones to address her feelings of loss following her husband's death.

After six months in care, John was rehabilitated home. But Mrs Jones soon resumed her former pattern of drinking leading to two further short-term admissions to care over the next year. As the placement at home was becoming increasingly precarious, it was decided that John should be placed in long-term foster care with Mr and Mrs Smith. The Smiths had previously been approved as salaried foster parents for young people with challenging behaviour.

The placement

After an initial 'honeymoon' period lasting approximately six months, the problems which John had exhibited while at home began to resurface in the placement. The social worker, Peter Bell, who had been allocated to the case became concerned about the impact of these problems on the Smiths. On Peter's last visit to the foster home, Mr Smith intimated that if the situation did not improve quickly, the placement could end.

Peter had recently attended an intensive training course on SFBT. He had been attracted to the model's emphasis on change and it seemed to offer a coherent framework; nevertheless, he was unsure how it could be adapted to his caseload. But at a hastily convened review meeting, it was decided that Peter would attempt to engage the foster family in an intensive piece of work. Putting his anxieties to one side, he decided to apply the SFBT model. He enlisted the support of the fostering link worker, Sally, who had also attended the course, to help him plan and review the work.

Planning the work

Peter and Sally decided to address the key planning questions of 'who', 'what', 'where', 'when', 'why' and 'how'. They hoped that this approach would assist them to adapt the model to the situation at hand.

DECIDING WHO SHOULD BE INVOLVED

It was decided that Peter would carry out the work by himself because he had established trust with the Smiths. Sally agreed to facilitate debriefing after each session. The early sessions would involve the Smiths and John. Thereafter, it would be important to encourage Mrs Jones' participation. Because of the strong attachment, her *relationship* with John was a pivotal factor in achieving a good outcome. Significant others – such as John's form teacher – might also need to be included later on.

ARTICULATING GOALS

Peter's immediate aim was to avert a breakdown in the placement. Further disruption in John's life was to be avoided: he needed *security*. In addition, John's behaviour was putting himself at risk and Peter was all too aware of his professional *accountability*. John also appeared to have unresolved issues regarding his *identity*: in particular, his father's death and his mother's erratic relationship with him left him feeling confused about events in the past. In articulating these goals, Peter was also conscious of the need to demonstrate empathy with the Smiths. Their *role* was complex and they required a lot of support.

TIMING THE INTERVENTION

Because there was a crisis it was necessary to respond promptly. Therefore, it was agreed that Peter would meet with the Smiths and John, explain how the work would proceed and set a date for the first session. At this meeting Peter would declare his belief that change was possible.

DECIDING ON VENUE

Because of the potential for interruptions within the foster home, it was decided to hold sessions in a local family centre. This would also have the advantage of creating emotional distance from the site of conflict. Peter was aware that any change – even one of location – can break down negativity.

REFLECTING ON HOW THE MODEL SHOULD BE USED

It was decided that three sessions would be offered to the Smiths followed by a review of progress. After each session, Sally would assist Peter to debrief. The sessions would try to work through each of the *stages* in the model. However, Peter would use the model flexibly. He was particularly keen to implement the miracle question, scaling, exception finding and highlighting positives. But an *eclectic* focus was also necessary; for example, the Smiths would be encouraged to attend the local foster-parent support group.

THE FIRST SESSION

Peter was somewhat deflated when approaching the Smiths about the work; while he approved of Peter's intentions, Mr Smith refused to attend the first session, stating he was too distressed by John's behaviour to talk about it. Peter recognised that at this stage Mr Smith was a 'visitor' and that it would be unwise to push the matter further. Mr Smith did agree, though, to reconsider his position if John showed any improvement in his behaviour. Fortunately, Mrs Smith was more willing to engage with the work, as was John after much persuasion.

Peter began the session by asking if there had been any changes in John's behaviour since the work had first been proposed. This provided an opening for Mrs Smith to engage in a long tirade about John: how his behaviour was regressing, how Mr Smith's health was being affected and so on. Throughout this tirade, John sat impassively, showing apparent indifference to Mrs Smith's concerns. Peter attempted to listen attentively to Mrs Smith, occasionally acknowledging the extent of her distress, but this seemed to reinforce her preoccupation with John's behaviour.

Peter's morale began to flag even further when he asked John if there were any changes he would like to see in his life. John replied with responses such as 'don't know' and 'this is stupid'. Totally exasperated, Peter inquired if there were any 'exceptions' to these problems. This produced a negative response from Mrs Smith and John, and it was obvious to Peter that John was now completely disengaged.

In order to retrieve what had been, in Peter's eyes, a disastrous first session, he decided to compliment John on the fact that he had come to the session. He also conveyed to Mrs Smith that she must be doing something right to have kept the placement going for so long. Remarkably, these statements had the effect of introducing a more receptive atmosphere. Following the compliment, John made eye contact with Peter for the first time and Mrs Smith appeared more reflective. Sensing that some success had been achieved, Peter continued by asking Mrs Smith and John to observe times during the next week when the problems were not present. The session ended at this point.

DEBRIEFING

It was clear from the session that John was attending as a 'visitor' and Mrs Smith as a 'complainant'. Through sensitive feedback from Sally, Peter was able to see that his primary mistake was to treat both as 'customers'. In effect, he had not built an alliance with John. This could be remedied in the next session by using some of Selekman's (1993) SFBT techniques for engaging young people. Additionally, it was opined that Mrs Smith might require more time to explore solutions without being pressurised into change.

THE SECOND SESSION

Feeling a little more confident, Peter started the second session by asking for feedback on the observation task. To his surprise, Mrs Smith reported that John had attended school 4 days out of 5; and while there had been quarrels in the home, these had not been as vociferous as in previous weeks.

This positive report enabled Peter to explore in detail what had been different in the household. A key factor seemed to have been the contact which had occurred between John and his mother that week. This contact had been very erratic since the placement started and it was pleasing to Peter to know that his recent encouragement of Mrs Jones had paid off.

Turning to John, Peter implemented Selekman's (1993) technique of 'the adolescent as expert consultant'. (This technique encourages the adolescent to see themselves as the only real problem solver.) Peter framed his question to John as follows: 'It is obvious John that your behaviour has really improved since we last met; can you tell me what you did in the last week to achieve such success?'

Peter now noticed that John was more talkative. He referred, for example, to the fact that contact with his mother had gone well; he also indicated that Mr Smith had not been 'on his back' as much. Drawing on these points, Peter was able to engage Mrs Smith and John in a discussion about what had been positive for them during the week. This led Peter nicely into the 'miracle' question. Responding to this question, Mrs Smith described her miracle in terms of a home environment where John could be happily settled. John described his miracle in terms of more frequent contact with his mother – and 'less hassle' from Mr Smith.

To finish the session, Peter acknowledged the progress which had been made and discussed some small tasks which could be completed before the next session to help the miracles come true. For her part, Mrs Smith agreed to praise John when he attended school. For his part, John agreed to help Mr

Smith with the gardening that week. Moreover, Peter agreed to explore with Mrs Jones what had made the last visit with John so successful.

DEBRIEFING

Peter was delighted with the progress attained, but realised that subsequent sessions might encounter setbacks. Nevertheless, there was evidence of motivational progression towards 'customership'. Various issues were elicited by the session and could be tackled subsequently. First, Peter needed to build up greater trust with John – perhaps through individual sessions with him. Second, it was important to engage Mr Smith in the work, especially as there had been changes in John's behaviour. Third, Peter needed to talk to Mrs Jones to reinforce the need for contact with John.

THE THIRD SESSION

Following the second session, Peter had some success and some disappointment. His arrangement to take John to the local leisure centre had not materialised because of other work commitments. Moreover, Mrs Jones had failed to turn up for a planned visit with John. Peter had tried, unsuccessfully, to contact her to discover the reason, although he suspected that she may have been drinking. More positively, however, Mr Smith had agreed to attend the next session.

Peter opened the session by acknowledging Mr Smith's presence. He also praised John and Mrs Smith for continuing to work so hard to improve relationships. He then asked for feedback on the tasks set in the previous session. Mrs Smith was first to reply. She indicated that while relationships had improved – due in part to John's helpfulness – school attendance had been erratic since the last session. Reacting to these comments, Mr Smith became agitated saying, 'John is going to be expelled' and, 'What will we do then?' These remarks triggered the expression of further concern from Mrs Smith about John's future.

Noticing that John was becoming increasingly disconsolate, Peter decided to refocus on the positives by asking for examples of how John had been helpful. In reply, Mr Smith outlined how John had been of great assistance in the garden. Peter decided to explore what had happened and how everyone had felt in more detail. When the family had enlarged on the events, Peter responded with short verbal reinforcers such as, 'that's incredible' and, 'you must have been so pleased'. John's demeanour became more animated as the significance of his behaviour was amplified. Peter then asked the Smiths to score the improvement out of ten. Both agreed on an improvement from a score of three (pre-intervention score) to six. Peter responded by highlighting that this represented a hundred per cent improvement. Turning to the perceived difficulties at school, Peter asked the Smiths to similarly score this area. Mr Smith said he could only give John four out of ten. Peter remarked, though, that a score of four was positive as it indicated that John was 'just about half-way there'.

To conclude the session, Peter said there were some key messages he wanted to convey to the family based on his observations. Turning to Mr Smith, he applauded his affection and concern for John. Despite his initial hesitance, Mr Smith had co-operated well with the work. Similarly, Mrs Smith, in framing her miracle around John's happiness, had shown how committed she was to him. Lastly, Peter indicated to John that, despite some problems, he had contributed much to the Smith household, particularly at a time when they were missing their own children. At the end of the session it was agreed that Peter would closely monitor progress in the incoming months. For their part, the family agreed to focus on the positives in the situation, by continuing to implement what had worked previously.

DEBRIEFING AND REVIEW

Peter and Sally reflected on the fact that the three sessions had brought some positive changes in the foster home. John was now more responsive to the Smiths and the severity of the identified problem behaviours had lessened. The Smiths had vocalised their commitment to John; and they were now more optimistic about the future: change was in motion. However, there were still some problems to resolve. In particular, Mrs Jones' erratic contact threatened to undermine John's security and identity. Peter would have to work hard to engage Mrs Jones, but he was hopeful that SFBT could be utilised to ameliorate her drinking problem. It was also important to introduce a solution-oriented focus to the discussions with other agencies, such as the school. For the next three months the aim was to meet John's needs by engaging the significant others in his life. The continuing use of techniques such as exception finding, highlighting positives, the miracle question, amplifying change, giving homework and scaling would contribute to the attainment of this aim.

Conclusion

SFBT is not a panacea. As a model of intervention, it has much in common with other social work models. But it is distinctive in offering a solution-orientated approach and a range of practical techniques for keeping this orientation on track. The case example has demonstrated how workers in foster care can move beyond a problem frame – with its connotations of damage limitation – to a new solution-oriented frame. In particular, serious – and apparently intractable – relationship difficulties between foster carers and the foster child, that threaten breakdown, can be reframed into more constructive alternatives for growth and development. Moreover, the model, with its clear structure and range of practical techniques, should be accessible and comprehensible to foster carers, children and professionals. Pathways to change are always attainable in foster care, if only we have the imagination to construct them.

References

Beck, A. (1976) *Cognitive Therapy and the Emotional Disorders*. New York: International Universities Press.

Berg, I. (1991) *Family Preservation: A Brief Therapy Workbook*. London: BT Press.

Berg, I. and Miller, S. (1992) *Working with the Problem Drinker: A Solution-focused Approach*. New York: Norton.

Berg, I. (1994) *Family Based Services: A Solution Focused Approach*. New York: Norton.

Berg, I. and Reuss, N. (1997) *Solutions Step by Step: A Substance Abuse Treatment Manual*. New York: Norton and Wylie.

Berridge, D. and Cleaver, H. (1987) *Foster Home Breakdown*. Oxford: Basil Blackwell.

Blom Cooper, L. (1985) *A Child in Trust*. London: London Borough of Brent.

Department of Health (1991) *Patterns and Outcomes in Child Placement: Messages from Research and their Implications*. London: HMSO.

De Jong, P. and Hopewood, L. (1996) From the home of solution-focused therapy: Outcome research on treatment at the Brief Therapy Centre, 1992–1998. In S. Miller (ed) (1996) *Handbook of Brief Therapy*. San Francisco: Jossey-Bass.

De Shazer, S. (1985) *Keys to Solution in Brief Therapy*. New York: W.W. Norton.

De Shazer, S. (1988) *Clues: Investigating Solutions in Brief Therapy*. New York: W.W. Norton.

Dolan, Y. (1991) *Resolving Sexual Abuse*. New York: Norton.

Egan, G. (1990) *The Skilled Helper*. Pacific Grove, CA: Brooks/Cole.

George, V. (1970) *Foster Care: Theory and Practice*. London: Routledge and Kegan Paul.

Gingerich, W. and De Shazer, S. (1991) The briefer project: Using expert systems as theory construction tools. *Family Process 30*, 241–249.

Goffman, E. (1975) *Frame Analysis: An Essay on the Organization of Experience.* Harmondsworth: Penguin.

Herbert, M. (1987) *Behavioural Treatment of Children with Problems: A Practice Manual.* London: Academic Press.

Holman, R. (1980) Exclusive and inclusive concepts of fostering. In J. Triseliotis (ed) (1980) *New Developments in Foster Care and Adoption.* London: Routledge and Kegan Paul.

Howe, D. (1996) Surface and depth in social work. In N. Parton (ed) *Social Theory, Social Change and Social Work.* London: Routledge.

Iveson, D. (1991) Unpublished thesis on drug dependency. London: Birbeck College.

Jenkins, S. and Norman, E. (1973) *Filial Deprivation and Foster Care.* New York: Russel Sage Foundation.

MacDonald, A. (1994) Brief therapy in adult psychiatry. *Journal of Family Therapy 16*, 415–426.

McAuley, C. (1996) *Children in Long-term Foster Care: Emotional and Social Development.* Aldershot: Avebury.

Marsh, P. and Fisher, M. (1992) *Good Intentions: Developing Partnerships in Social Services.* York: Joseph Rowntree.

Miller, S. (1998) *Solution-focused Brief Therapy with Impossible Cases.* Conference proceedings, Dublin.

Parslow, S. (1993). Unpublished thesis on drug dependency. London: Birbeck College.

Payne, M. (1996) *What is Professional Social Work?* Birmingham: Venture Press.

Rhodes, J. and Ajmal, Y. (1995) *Solution-focused Thinking in Schools.* London: BT Press.

Rogers, C. (1951) *Client-centred Therapy: Its Current Practice, Implications and Theory.* London: Constable.

Rojek, C., Peacock, G. and Collins, S. (1989) *Social Work and Received Ideas.* London: Routledge.

Selekman, M. (1993) *Pathways to Change: Brief Therapy Solutions with Difficult Adolescents.* London: The Guildford Press.

Sheldon, B. (1995) *Cognitive-behavioural Therapy: Research, Practice and Philosophy.* London: Routledge.

Thoburn, J. (1994) *Child Placement: Principles and Practice.* Aldershot: Arena.

Trasler, G. (1960) *In Place of Parents.* London: Routledge and Kegan Paul.

Triseliotis, J., Sellick, C. and Short, R. (1995) *Foster Care: Theory and Practice.* London: BAAF.

Truax, C. and Carkhuf, R. (1967) *Toward Effective Counselling and Psychotherapy: Training and Practice.* Chicago: Aldine.

Walsh, T. (ed) (1997) *Solution Focused Child Protection – Towards a Positive Frame for Social Work Practice.* Occasional paper No. 6, Department of Social Studies, University of Dublin.

Weinstein, E. (1960) *The Self Image of the Foster Child.* New York: Russel Sage Foundation.

Whittaker, J. and Tracy, E. (1989) *Social Treatment: An Introduction to Interpersonal Helping in Social Work Practice.* New York: Aldine de Gruyter.

CHAPTER 7

Managing Children's Behaviour in Foster Care

Ken P. Kerr

Introduction

Managing behaviour often requires more than skills developed from common sense or intuition. All those involved in child care, parents or professionals, can learn from a scientific approach to understanding behaviour. Applied Behaviour Analysis (ABA) is the technology of applying basic principles governing behaviour in everyday situations. It represents a knowledge base of information that can help everyone, including parents and children, lead a fully rewarding life. The purpose of this chapter is two-fold: first, to present an overview of the basic principles of ABA; and second, to illustrate how the principles can be applied in everyday situations involving parent–child interactions. Several examples of problem behaviours will be presented so that readers can readily view the application of the basic principles in changing and maintaining behaviour. The principles described are shown to be easily implemented by foster parents and professionals, therefore allowing successful intervention.

> Thousands of children each day are taken out of their homes for various reasons, but NONE of these reasons are the child's fault, they are just the victims. The amount of children removed from their homes each year due to abuse, neglect, homelessness, drug abuse, and parental incarceration continues to grow at an alarming rate. Imagine one day living life as you know it, when a stranger comes to your door and takes you away from your family … You pull up to a strange house with people you have never met

before, clutching your belongings in one hand … and you are told 'you will be living here for awhile.' (Reprinted with permission of Carl Kuvoic from *Foster Care*; http://members.net/fostercare)

The opening quotation not only describes some of the possible reasons why a child enters foster care but also gives insight into events that may shape certain behavioural problems for the child. Once removed from their natural families, children may still carry the scars of neglect, abandonment and problems relating to attachment. Various problems created by the transition from a natural home to an alien environment may manifest themselves in ways that can have serious implications for the dynamics of the foster family, and may have serious implications for the rest of the child's life. The successful management of behaviour is an essential skill for both foster parents and professionals involved in any aspect of child care. In particular, the management of behaviour in the context of foster care is a crucial area for consideration as behavioural problems are a leading cause of breakdown in foster care placements (see Chapter 3). The application of parenting skills is severely tested within the foster-care system as parents attempt to interact with children who may show inappropriate behaviours learned in a different environment. For this reason, an insight into the skills involved in behavioural management is necessary for both parent and professional alike (see Herbert 1987).

For many parents the management of behaviour is learned from ad hoc sources ranging from folklore and advice from their own parents to the latest fashions in parenting. Whilst there is an unquestionable desire to do the best possible job in child rearing, parents are often let down by their lack of skills. A common-sense approach is often adequate in day-to-day terms but when a day-to-day problem cannot be solved by intuition, what avenues are open?

Behaviour management

Marion Gibson (reported in Dillenburger 1996) described various forms of behavioural problems that children may experience. These included sleep disturbances, separation difficulties, various types of behavioural regression and expressive emotional problems. The aim of this chapter is to enable both professionals and parents to have access to the tools that allow behaviour change in areas of difficulty for adult–child interaction. O'Hagan and Dillenburger (1995) noted the need for access to strategies that allow for the application of brief and effective assessment and interventions in this area:

Childcare workers need a firm base for their practice. They need to know and understand what is going on. They need to be able to *identify* a problem, to *understand* and *describe* it in concrete terms. *They need a good theoretical base for assessment and intervention. They need theories that have been well researched and that are based on scientific study.* They need these theories to provide them with answers to some of their most fundamental questions: ... What causes behaviour in general? How can we change behaviour? ... How can we change the behaviour of a child that is out of control, or in danger of hurting themselves or others? (p.153, italics added)

One type of behaviour management that meets the criterion of a 'firm base of practice' set by O'Hagan and Dillenburger is Applied Behaviour Analysis.

Applied behaviour analysis

Applied behaviour analysis (ABA) is a science that employs empirically validated behaviour-change procedures for assisting individuals in developing meaningful skills with social value. The procedures used in behavioural intervention programmes are drawn from the rich knowledge base of research generated by practitioners.

A range of behaviours including fear and avoidance, language deficits, interpersonal conflict, social skills deficits, attention deficits and separation problems have been successfully managed, in terms of either increasing or decreasing the specific target behaviour, through the application of ABA principles (see Herbert 1987 for a comprehensive list of targeted problem behaviours). ABA provides answers to fundamental questions regarding the 'cause' of human behaviour and offers a variety of techniques to implement positive change. It is a scientific approach that complements the aims of anyone who manages either their own behaviour or the behaviour of others. The principles are equally applicable to everyone, not just children placed in foster care.

From an ABA perspective, behaviour is considered to be lawful in terms of its relation with environmental variables. Accordingly, any behaviour which allows a person greater independence, promotes a sense of security, allows self-fulfilment, and generally increases self-esteem by allowing the person to be an active member of society is considered to be subject to the laws governing behaviour. Similarly, any behaviour that is dangerous, destructive, or impedes the person's ability to interact is subject to the same laws (see Zirpoli and Melloy 1997, p.78ff). Strategies employed in ABA include a variety of techniques to increase appropriate behaviour, decrease inappropriate behaviour, and teach new behaviours (see Deibert and Harmon 1978 and Zirpoli and Melloy 1997 for discussions of behaviour management).

ABA focuses on behaviour in contexts where behaviour is considered changeable only through altering the context in which it occurs, rather than by trying to change the person. Focusing on behaviour, rather than the person, avoids confusion when a child misbehaves. Statements such as 'You are a bad boy' do not identify the inappropriate behaviour. Children should be taught that it is the inappropriate behaviour that is disliked, not the child, as all children engage in both appropriate and inappropriate behaviours. A central tenet of behaviour analysis is that individuals managing behaviour should concentrate on promoting pro-social behaviours as well as decreasing inappropriate behaviour. Clearly targeting such behaviours (i.e. increasing appropriate and reducing inappropriate behaviours) reduces the chances of the person experiencing any form of social exclusion and increases the chances of the individual playing a fully rewarding part in both family and society. In foster-care practice it may reduce the incidence of placement breakdown.

ABA enables both parents and professionals to understand and promote appropriate behaviour and correct any inappropriate behaviour in context (see Sulzer-Azaroff and Mayer 1991). It is proactive in stressing the need for designing an environment where positive consequences are delivered to promote appropriate instances of behaviour. Whilst a complete review of ABA principles is beyond the scope of this chapter, the interested reader is referred to Cooper, Heron and Heward (1987), Miltenberger (1997), Kazdin (1994) and Zirpoli and Melloy (1997).

The remainder of the chapter presents an over view of some of the main principles in ABA. First, the importance of identifying the *context* within which behaviour occurs, the actual *behaviour* itself, and the *consequences* of behaviour are discussed. Procedures to help parents and professionals identify consistent relations between behaviour and environment are introduced. Second, behavioural interventions that promote the occurrence of desired behaviour are discussed. Each principle or procedure is accompanied by a simple example. In addition, an example case study of an ABA programme for a child with a sleep disorder is presented. Emphasis is placed on providing accountability of behavioural management programmes through data-based decision making in bringing about the change of behaviour. The ease with which parents and professionals can learn to apply the behavioural principles is also emphasised.

As simple as ABC

The basic unit of analysis employed in behaviour analysis is the ABC 'contingency'. A contingency is an 'if–then' relationship between *antecedents* (the setting events, or context, that exist before the behaviour occurs), *behaviour* and *consequences* (the events/reactions that happen after the behaviour occurs).

CONSEQUENCES OF BEHAVIOUR

Consequences are considered to be essential in determining whether or not behaviour will occur again in the future. To take a simple example, imagine meeting a person and you say, 'Hi, how are you?' The other person may think that you are quite pleasant and be willing to engage in conversation in the future. The consequences of being polite therefore increase the probability of future interaction. Conversely, had you been rude the other person may be less likely to talk to you in the future. The first step in effectively managing another person's behaviour, or your own behaviour, is realising the powerful role of the consequences of behaviour in determining future behaviour. Following are some examples of arrangement of consequences that may increase the probability of behaviour:

- Arriving home from school, Michael proudly shows his parents a picture he painted at school. Both parents are extremely pleased and deliver hugs and praise. Because of this thoughtful reaction, Michael is more likely to show his work in the future.

- Shauna observes her foster mother tidying the living room. She begins to lift some papers from the floor. Her foster mother is delighted at such help and delivers copious amounts of praise and a comment on how grown-up she is getting. In the future, Shauna helps on a regular basis.

- Michelle is read a bedtime story only if she prepares for bed without a fuss. Consequently, Michelle is motivated to prepare for bed independently so that a story will be read.

These examples highlight the importance of consequences in increasing the probability that certain behaviour will occur in the future. The examples illustrate the delivery of naturally occurring consequences which increase the probability of behaviour occurring in specific contexts. Technically, any consequence that increases the future probability of behaviour occurring is called a 'reinforcer' and any consequence that decreases the probability of behaviour occurring is called a 'punisher'.

Both foster carers and social workers place emphasis on developing meaningful relationships within the foster-care placement. To this extent, an increased awareness of the consequences of behaviour (e.g. reinforcers) can lead to more fulfilling relationships between care giver and child. The foster carer who plans the delivery of reinforcers also adopts the mantle of a more positive role model in nurturing a warm relationship. By arranging consequences to promote socially appropriate behaviour, the foster carer, and indeed the social worker, places emphasis on the importance of identifying positive instances of behaviour rather than solely concentrating on the negative aspects of behaviour.

ANTECEDENTS

An antecedent (or discriminative stimulus) is a stimulus that precedes a response and indicates that reinforcement is likely to be delivered if a response is made. Although rather technical, an example of a discriminative stimulus makes it apparent how stimuli other than consequences affect responding. For example, imagine walking down the street and you see a friend approaching with a beaming smile. Such a cue would suggest that all is well and make it quite appropriate for a jovial greeting. If, on the other hand, you spot your friend approach with a sad face and slightly bent posture you may be right in assuming that all is not well and approach your friend cautiously. We are said to have made a discrimination when we respond differently in different stimulus conditions or in different contexts. Children also discriminate elements in the environment that occasion behaviour. For example, the child who learns to play up when Daddy puts them to bed may behave differently when Mummy does so. Similarly, behavioural problems may become evident at home, but fail to materialise at school. It is possible that the child has learned that each situation contains cues which occasion behaviour that is more likely to be reinforced.

Green, Hardison, and Greene (1984) manipulated such cues when employing an antecedent control procedure to enhance family interactions at a restaurant. It was reasoned that if the children engaged in interesting conversations with their adults or peers that they would be less likely to engage in disruptive behaviour. The researchers introduced educational placemats consisting of pictures and activities relevant to the age of the children in an attempt to cue conversation and improve the dynamics of the family. By manipulating the placemats (i.e. the antecedent) the incidence of meaningful conversation increased (see Risley 1996 for a discussion of positive interventions).

Arranging specific antecedents, consequences, or both, for behaviour can therefore increase (or decrease) the likelihood that the behaviour will happen again. In summary, altering the contingencies (i.e. the ABCs) allows a systematic approach to changing behaviour. Before specific procedures designed to alter contingencies can be discussed, it is necessary for parents and professionals to be empowered with the skills to identify the variables that promote and maintain behaviour (i.e. the contingencies).

Functional assessment: Identifying the ABCs

This section gives an overview of procedures designed to discover the possible causes of behaviour. That is, the contingencies that produce and maintain behaviour are identified through the examination of relationships between the environment (antecedent and consequences) and behaviour. Functional assessment is a general term that describes a set of procedures for defining the physical and social environment in which behaviour occurs (see O'Neill *et al.* 1997 for a comprehensive review of functional assessment and functional analysis techniques). It is a process of discovering both the environmental and physiological factors that contribute to problem behaviours.

One basic functional assessment suitable for parents involves the use of an ABC chart (Figure 7.1). This chart can be used to determine the variables maintaining behaviour (see Miltenberger 1997). Individuals managing behaviour simply record the specific instance of behaviour, what happened just before the behaviour occurred, and what happened just after the behaviour. Once a pattern is established, the information can be used to either redesign the antecedents or alter the consequences of behaviour, as appropriate, to produce the desired change in behaviour. This type of analysis can be employed with minimal instruction resulting in maximum gain. Figure 7.1 shows an ABC chart that suggests that Brian's mother is probably delivering positive consequences (reinforcers) that are maintaining inappropriate behaviours.

ABC Chart				
Individual's name: Brian				
Behaviour: Refuses to get up in the morning				
Date/Time	*Location*	*Antecedent: What happened just before the behaviour?*	*Behaviour: Define the specific behaviour*	*Consequence: What happened just after the behaviour?*
11/8/98 8.35am	Bedroom	Alarm rings	Brian wakes but does not turn off alarm	Mother turns off alarm clock
11/8/98 8.50am	Kitchen/ Bedroom	Mother calls: 'Breakfast ready'	Brian remains in bed	Mother enters room and tells him to get up
11/8/98 9.00am	Bedroom	Mother calls: 'breakfast'	Brain ignores call	Breakfast is brought into the bedroom

Figure 7.1 Example of an ABC chart illustrating the antecedents, behaviour and consequences of Brian's behaviour in the morning

When analysing data from an ABC chart, three basic questions may help focus both professionals and parents. First, what is the target behaviour? Second, how often is the behaviour actually occurring? Third, can a pattern in the occurrences of the antecedents and consequences be identified?

WHAT IS THE TARGET BEHAVIOUR?

When defining behaviour it is important to avoid general terms that do not specify actual measurable behaviour. For example, the summary label 'tantrum' does not refer to an actual behaviour. It refers to a category of behaviours (cf. Grant and Evans 1994). When introducing a behavioural management programme, the target behaviour should be identified and written in clear, concise terms to avoid possible confusion. So, rather than talk about tantrums, it is more productive to consider actual behaviours such as 'crying', 'screaming', 'kicking' and 'shouting'.

HOW OFTEN DOES THE BEHAVIOUR OCCUR?

Collecting information on ABC charts, and related data sheets, avoids any possible confusion or error in terms of how often or where the behaviour occurs. Parents often overestimate the number of instances of inappropriate behaviour due to increased nuisance. Similarly, appropriate behaviour often goes unnoticed. Data collection allows an objective picture of actual behaviour. It also provides a source of accountability in that parents and professionals can view evidence of behavioural change. This allows external validation of the programme and allows clear decisions based on the data to be implemented.

For some parents this may sound a daunting prospect. However, various 'user-friendly' methods of collecting data have been developed. Common methods of recording data include simple pen/paper recording, or using a simple recording device such as an abacus, or transferring coins from one pocket to another depending on the occurrence of the target behaviour. Although this may sound complex, support from external agencies will help a home-based programme run smoothly. For example, professionals trained in ABA would be able to provide support in terms of ready-made and simple-to-understand recording sheets and provide the direction required to develop a proactive programme. Involvement from professionals in empowering parents with the necessary skills to implement a successful programme would not only help parents but would ensure that the behavioural principles are applied in a manner consistent with the discipline.

IS THERE A PATTERN OF ANTECEDENTS AND CONSEQUENCES?

In relation to the consequences of behaviour, four basic types of consequences are usually considered in a functional assessment of behaviour. These are: avoidance of task, attention from adults or peers, gaining a tangible reinforcer and automatic reinforcement. By identifying the pattern of antecedents and consequences from the ABC chart it may be possible to pinpoint the contingencies that are maintaining certain patterns of behaviour (see Cooper *et al.* 1987). For example, the pattern of antecedents and consequences for Brian (Figure 7.1) suggest that his mother is maintaining his inappropriate behaviour by delivering attention and tangible reinforcers (i.e. breakfast in bed).

Although a more complete functional analysis than that allowed by an ABC chart may be merited for more severe behavioural problems, the observation methods highlighted above may suffice for most instances of behaviour. One advantage of using an ABC chart is that it is easy to use. Also, it allows parents to have an active role in identifying the variables that control behaviour. More rigorous functional analytic techniques can also be employed as necessary, without the assessment being an increasing drain on resources (e.g. Northup *et al.* 1991). The information collected is subsequently used to determine what type of intervention can be introduced (Wacker 1989).

Perhaps at this point the appearance of a rigid structure may put foster carers and professionals off implementing a behavioural programme. Two points are worth noting. First, it is important to recognise that the degree of structure is dependent on the type of programme required. For example, a basic knowledge of ABA principles and an awareness of arranging consequences of behaviour may be all that is needed. For more serious problems, a higher degree of structure and related data collection may be needed. Second, if a higher degree of structure is required, this is not incompatible with the emotional bonds between adult and child. In fact a structured and consistent approach to managing behaviour can be more effective in developing positive relations.

The need for increased structure in any foster placement may be seen as adding increased pressure and work on care givers. However, training in behavioural principles is based upon a supportive collaborative triadic model consisting of parents, children and professionals. The model facilitates long-term change and utilises an ever-present resource, namely the immediate care givers. The structuring of parent training through a mix of consultation-based learning (i.e. lectures, videos and demonstrations), individual parent training (i.e. one-to-one training) and behavioural discussion groups led by external agencies can lead to the implementation of successful programmes (see Herbert 1987 for a discussion of family-oriented behavioural work).

Summary

The use of ABA principles has been highlighted as an effective way of man-aging behaviour. At this point, the reader should be aware of the importance of identifying the contingencies that control behaviour. By doing this, a sys-tematic approach to changing behaviour is possible through manipulation of the antecedents and consequences of behaviour. It is possible to create an environment that includes contingencies designed to promote appropriate behaviour. Moving on from this basis, it is now possible to discuss procedures for increasing desirable behaviour.

Establishing and increasing desirable behaviour

By the time that a child enters into the foster care system it is likely that s/he will have been exposed to contingencies that have produced inappropriate behaviours. Foster parents do not have access to the context in which problem behaviours were developed and are left with a child who may engage in problem behaviours from several categories ranging from social withdrawal or attachment disorders to tantrumming. This section introduces several procedures that will help create a stable environment that develops socially appropriate skills and encourages emotional development through the systematic implementation of behavioural principles (see Miltenberger 1997 for a comprehensive list of behavioural procedures).

Establishing behaviour: Shaping

Shaping is a procedure used to develop target behaviour not currently displayed by an individual. The easiest way to learn a complex behaviour is by breaking the complete behaviour into small manageable components or steps (see Dillenburger and Keenan 1993). The shaping process works by training behaviour to a certain criterion and gradually extending the criterion until the target behaviour is produced. By starting with the most basic step and systematically teaching each component it is possible to teach a new or desired behaviour by arranging positive consequences for the occurrence of each step (see Deibert and Harmon 1978).

Consider Vignette 1 where an illustration of the principles involved in shaping highlights the systematic approach to changing behaviour (see Keenan 1997 for the application of a shaping procedure to decrease a child's fear of bathing).

Vignette 1

Shaping behaviour to promote independence and anxiety-free interactions

---

Four-year-old Siobhan had recently begun to show distress when her foster mum, Jane, was absent. More and more, this resulted in Jane rearranging her schedule to avoid any problems.

On direction from a behaviour analyst the following steps were recommended to shape behaviour appropriate to separation:

Days	Breakdown of steps
1, 2, 3, 4	Parents used ABC charts to highlight variables controlling behaviour and to record the baseline number of times Siobhan tantrummed when Jane left home. Results from the ABC chart suggested that attention was contributing to the inappropriate behaviour. It was decided to alter the antecedent (i.e. Jane departing) gradually.
5, 6, 7	Siobhan was engaged in play activity by Jane and Nick in the living room. During the activity Jane took 2 steps away from Nick and Siobhan. Siobhan made no reaction to the increase in distance between Jane and herself. Positive consequences (e.g. hugs, praise) were delivered when Siobhan did not tantrum.
8, 9	Jane stood at the living room door and watched. Siobhan engaged in play activities with Nick.
10, 11, 12	Jane stood at the front door with her coat in her hand and watched activities. Siobhan approached Jane but quickly resumed her games with Nick.
13, 14	Jane stood at the open front door and watched the play activities.
15, 16	Jane went outside during playtime and re-entered the house at various intervals.
17 onwards	Siobhan presented no problem behaviours whenever Jane left home.

It is important to note that both inappropriate and appropriate behaviour can be changed through shaping. Analysis of the contingencies controlling behaviour may well show that initially, due to concern, Siobhan's parents remained at home if Siobhan showed any signs of distress. Across time, the intensity of Siobhan's tantrums increased in order to produce the end goal where both parents always gave in and stayed at home. In other words, Siobhan and her parents reciprocally shaped each other's behaviour (albeit unintentionally), resulting in problems with separation (Brigham 1989a). A knowledge of the principles involved in shaping means that parents can establish behaviour previously not in the individual's repertoire. As Dillenburger and Keenan (1995, p.38) note, the benefit of applying shaping principles correctly is that it 'does not only lead to better behaved children but also to happier and healthier relationships between the adults and children'.

Increasing behaviour I: The use of negotiated contracts

For the older child who understands 'cause and effect' and is capable of displaying the desired behaviour, a behavioural contract provides the least intrusive way to change behaviour. A behavioural contract is a written agreement between two parties in which one or both parties agree to engage in a specified level of a target behaviour or behaviours (see Miltenberger 1997). For some instances of behaviour a *negotiated* contract may suffice in producing behaviour deemed to be appropriate. The contract is effective in producing reciprocal advantages for both parent and child. The contract allows the child ownership of his/her own behaviour and helps develop a sense of independence and responsibility. The contract clearly states the consequence that will be delivered contingent upon the child's behaviour.

COMPONENTS OF A BEHAVIOURAL CONTRACT

The first step in negotiating a contract is clearly identifying specific target behaviour. A strategy for measuring the behaviour must also be developed. The contract should be written so that both the parents and child are aware of how often the behaviour is expected to occur and what the consequences are for occurrence (or non-occurrence) of the target behaviour (Sulzer-Azaroff and Mayer 1991). That is, the proposed contingency should be clearly written. It should also be fair and free from any pressure from either party. The point of the contract is to produce the behaviour through a joined commitment to engage in different behaviours (see Vignette 2).

Vignette 2

An example of a behavioural contract

Cormac had recently shown an interest in a puppy in a local pet shop. For his 13th birthday, his parents decided to buy the puppy. Whilst Cormac looked after the puppy for the first few weeks, it soon became obvious that he had begun to neglect his duties in feeding, caring for, cleaning and walking the dog. His parents decided to arrange a newly agreed set of contingencies by implementing a behavioural contract that required Cormac to walk the dog. (A similar contract would also be written on behalf of the parents who would agree to deliver the consequences as written on completion of Cormac's side of the contract. This contract would clearly state the privileges that could be earned and lost depending on the occurrence of appropriate behaviour.)

Behavioural Contract

I, Cormac, agree to take my puppy, Flip, for a walk once a day at 4 pm between the period of _____ and _____. I will be accompanied by _____.

- On completing each walk I will be given a stamp in my personal diary. If I have 5 or more stamps in the diary I can choose a special prize from the activity menu.

- If I engage in walking Flip every day for a week, I will receive an extra surprise from the agreed list.

- If I do not walk Flip for 2 days, I will have one of my favourite activities removed from the list of activities for the week.

- If I miss 3 or more days in any week I will not be allowed any of the activities on the agreed list.

Signed:

Cormac ———————————————————

Foster Parent ———————————————————

Behavioural contracts work by clearly indicating the contingencies influencing behaviour. Older children benefit from the contract as they play a major role in determining the consequences to be delivered for engaging in appropriate/inappropriate behaviour. The contract also works as a public commitment to engage in the target behaviour and encourages the child to take ownership of his/her behaviours. If the child does not engage in appropriate behaviour a response cost is specified (for example, in Vignette 2 the response cost was that Cormac was not allowed to engage in any activity specified on the agreed list). Contracts have been shown to be successful with children as young as 6 years old in a variety of target areas (see Zirpoli and Melloy 1997). Contracts can be used for a wide variety of behaviours and have been highlighted as an effective tool in dealing with adolescent behaviour (Brigham 1989b). In summary, the contract allows the creation of a supportive environment where reinforcement will be delivered whilst enabling children to accept responsibility for their own behaviour in a positive fashion.

Increasing behaviour II: The use of token economies

A token economy is a system where tokens are delivered to individuals as reinforcers for desirable behaviour (Kazdin 1977). The tokens are later exchanged for back-up reinforcers on an exchange menu (e.g. extra sweets, planning of special activities or more time to play computer games). The token economy, like the behavioural contract, can also be employed to teach and maintain desirable pro-social behaviours. By teaching the importance of the consequences of behaviour it is possible to teach the child to engage in positive social interactions. For example, positive consequences may be arranged for getting up on time, making the bed, washing and dressing, being polite, and doing school homework. The only limit to activities on the token economy is the creativity of the person in charge (see Vignette 3). Certain steps should be followed to ensure that the token economy is successful (see Alberto and Troutman 1995, p.222). These steps include:

- Deciding on the target behaviours. That is, what are the problem behaviours? What behaviour does the child not engage in frequently? What behaviour would benefit the child?

- Deciding what tokens are going to be used. Stars, toy money, stickers, etc. It is extremely important that the tokens cannot be accessed through any other source and that the child cannot manipulate the token board.

- Deciding what back-up reinforcers the tokens can be exchanged for. That is, whilst the tokens are delivered immediately for positive instances of behaviour they have no intrinsic value. It is only when the child is allowed to exchange the tokens for a meaningful object/activity that the tokens have worth.

- Deciding on exchange periods. How often will it be possible to exchange the tokens for the desired items/activities?

Vignette 3

An example of a token economy

David (9 years old) and Michael (10 years old) were frequently in trouble with their foster parents as they often fought over what TV programme to watch, what toys they would play with, and who would get the most attention from their foster parents. Also, the boys had exhibited separate instances of inappropriate behaviour ranging from rough play with the next door neighbour's child to instances of over-dependence on the presence of a family member.

Their foster mum, Jane, decided to introduce a token economy to increase the children's social competence. That is, she decided to arrange contingencies to increase the use of appropriate social skills.

Jane began by listing the general areas of behaviour that she wanted to include in the programme:

- Turn-taking in play activities
- Co-operation in deciding who would watch what TV programme
- Appropriate play behaviour with younger children
- Increased independence (including separation from family members).

Jane then created the tokens to be employed. She bought books of colourful re-usable face stickers, as she knew both boys liked the funny shapes. She also knew that the boys did not have access to similar stickers.

Next, Jane created an exchange menu. She asked the boys to identify some possible reinforcers for the programme. Suggestions included 5 minutes extra watching cartoons, extra time on the computer, a trip to the zoo, a trip to the aquarium, and a new football. Jane awarded a point value (or price) to these activities/objects. The price depended on how frequently the boys currently engaged in each activity, the importance of each to the boys, and the actual cost of each to Jane. She also awarded a point value for the occurrence of each appropriate behaviour, graded from most difficult to least difficult (depending on how often they currently occurred). In this way the boys could earn points for appropriate behaviour, save these points up, and exchange them for items on the exchange menu.

Target list	Points to be earned	Exchange menu	Cost
Turn-taking	2	Favourite desserts	5 pts
Polite behaviour	1	Computer (5 min extra)	5 pts
Agreeing TV schedule	5	New football	5 pts
Appropriate play	5	Edible surprises	10 pts
Tidy appearance	1	Trips to surprise destinations	20 pts
Cleaning up	2	Cartoons (5 min extra)	3pts

Jane also implemented a response cost whereby prearranged consequences for inappropriate behaviour were agreed. For example, any instances of arguing over the TV would cost both boys 5 points, inappropriate play would cost 4 points, and rudeness during mealtime would cost 1 point. These points would be deducted from any points gained.

Next, Jane helped the boys make a chart where they could monitor their own behaviour. The boys both designed a pirate chart. These were posted on the fridge door so the boys were frequently reminded of their progress 'in search of the buried treasure'.

Finally, Jane made it clear that the first tokens could be exchanged for desired items/activities two hours after the economy was implemented and at subsequent designated intervals.

Jane was delighted when David and Michael almost fell over each other in co-operating and being polite to each other in an effort to gain tokens. By positively reinforcing appropriate behaviour Jane noticed a snowball effect (Dillenburger and Keenan 1995) whereby many areas which were not targeted improved, such as a better relationship with parents and improved standing amongst peers.

Certain adjunct behaviours on behalf of parent or care giver may result in a more productive token economy. First, as highlighted in Vignette 3, the economy must be an agreed one. It must be perceived as being fair. Second, the exchange rate must be realistic so that the child can always earn a few tokens to exchange during the designated period. When the child engages in inappropriate behaviour, it is best not to engage in reprimands. Simply comment on the activity and the related response cost. In this way any inadvertent reinforcement (such as increased attention) may be avoided (see Alberto and Troutman 1995 for a complete discussion of token economies).

In bringing together the principles highlighted in this chapter an example case study of a sleep disorder is presented. The study illustrates the strategic planning of a behavioural management programme whereby the following steps are planned:

1. The situation is analysed (including data collection to monitor rate of natural occurrence of behaviour).

2. The contingencies maintaining current behaviour are determined.

3. Desired behaviours are indicated.

4. Contingencies to produce new appropriate behaviour (including data collection to monitor efficacy of intervention) are arranged.

Example case study: Separation at bedtime

Marie was 5 years old when she was placed in foster care. On arriving at her new home, Marie had various problems adjusting to the different lifestyle. The most serious and disruptive of these related to refusal to go to sleep, refusing to stay in bed once there, and frequent night waking. Marie's foster parents were concerned that the situation was worsening and sought help to manage this behavioural problem.

Observations

The bedtime routine was broken down into two specific behaviours:

1. Evening disruptive behaviours – this included tantrums before getting into bed, and getting out of bed and rejoining parents in lounge.

2. Night wakening – this included waking and getting into parents' bed in the middle of the night.

Pre-intervention

Both parents were instructed on how to complete an ABC chart to identify the antecedents and consequences of night-time disruptive behaviour (Figure 7.2). A simple count of how many times the target behaviours occurred across a 14-day period was also recorded. This baseline measure presented a picture of current behaviour under natural conditions before the intervention was introduced (see Figure 7.3).

ABC Chart				
Individual's name: Marie				
Behaviour: Refusal to go to bed and return to lounge/night wakening				
Date/Time	Location	Antecedent: What happened just before the behaviour?	Behaviour: Define the specific behaviour	Consequence: What happened just after the behaviour?
1/5/98 9pm	Living Room	Maries asked to go and put pyjamas on	Marie shouts and cries	Parents repeat instruction and try to calm her down
11/5/98 9.15pm	Bedroom	Bedtime story completed; parent says goodnight	After 5 minute interval Marie returns to lounge	Parents engage Marie in discussion; parent places Marie in bed
1/5/98 9.25pm	Bedroom	Light turned off in room, door closed	Marie gets out of bed	Parent interacts with Marie, gets her a drink, and puts her to bed
2/5/98 12.45am	Bedroom	Unknown	Marie gets into parents' bed	Parents interact with Marie; she is cuddled and put back to bed
2/5/98 1.10am	Bedroom	Unknown	Marie returns to parents' room	Marie is allowed to spend the night in parents' bed

Figure 7.2 ABC chart illustrating the pattern of antecedents and consequences of behaviour for Marie's problem night-time behaviour.

Intervention: Evening disruptive behaviours

Marie was taken to a toyshop and asked to choose a book with stickers. She was told that if she went to bed without engaging in screaming, kicking or refusing she would be read a story (something she really liked) and she would be allowed to put a sticker on her book. Story-telling only occurred if Marie complied with the bedtime routine. If at the end of the week there were 3 stickers in the book, Marie was allowed to choose a special prize from a number that she had listed. The number of stickers was set at 3 so that Marie could manage this number easily and access the special prize. Across subsequent weeks, the number was to be increased.

Intervention: night wakening

After the baseline data showing the number of times Marie woke and went into her parents' room were collected, an intervention consisting of a more systematic bed-time routine was introduced. Each time Marie got out of bed she was taken straight back without any fuss or scolding. If Marie stayed in bed for the previous night's number of wakenings minus 1, she was praised highly in the morning and allowed to put a sticker on her favourite Freddie Dangerously book. In addition, if there were no occurrences of problem behaviour Marie was allowed to eat her breakfast whilst watching her favourite video.

   Both parents kept a record of all instances of inappropriate/appropriate behaviour.

Outcome

Simple frequencies of inappropriate/appropriate behaviours were recorded and graphed (Figure 7.3). The graphical presentation allowed a clear view of

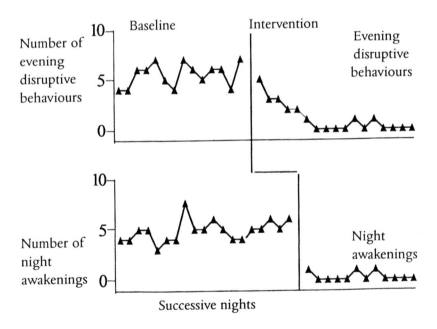

Figure 7.3 Graph showing the observed decrease of Marie's problem night-time behaviour from recorded frequency of natural occurrence (baseline) to frequency after implementation of a new set of contingencies (intervention).

the change in Marie's behaviour. The number of refusals to go to bed and the number of night wakenings reduced considerably. The reinforcers were gradually faded until Marie engaged in appropriate behaviour independently. These results, stemming from a change in the contingencies during the intervention phase, showed that the use of positive consequences can easily promote appropriate behaviour. Marie now engaged in a systematic bed-time routine which eased any family strain and allowed her and her parents to have a better night's sleep.

Conclusion and implications

This chapter has presented an overview of the basic behavioural principles that have proven effective in bringing about and maintaining behaviour change. The most important aspect of managing an individual's behaviour is an understanding of the contingencies that promote and maintain behaviour. Behaviour change is made possible only through altering the contingencies. Various commonly used techniques that produce behaviour change, including shaping, behavioural contracts and token economies, have been described with examples illustrating the application of the principles.

The steps involved in implementing a behavioural management programme were highlighted as

- identifying and clearly defining a target behaviour
- identifying the contingencies maintaining behaviour
- measuring the target behaviour at current level (baseline data collection)
- planning an intervention (i.e. arranging a new set of contingencies to promote the desired behaviour).

The careful planning and implementation of behavioural principles is advocated as providing the least confusing environment to enhance the development of a child. Whilst a certain amount of structure is required in implementing behavioural principles, care givers have a degree of flexibility in designing individualised programmes. The systematic work required is compatible with, and indeed enhances, the developing emotional bonds between carer and child. Professional and foster carers have a responsibility to implement effective procedures that improve the quality of life of children in their care. This chapter advocates the application of behavioural principles from the beginning of placements so that a stable, secure environment may be developed.

Acknowledgement

I would like to thank Fiona Mulhern for helpful comments and review of this chapter.

References

Alberto, P.A. and Troutman, A.C. (1995) *Applied Behavior Analysis for Teachers* (4th edition). New Jersey: Prentice-Hall.

Brigham, T.A. (1989a) *Managing Everyday Problems.* New York: Guildford Press.

Brigham, T.A. (1989b) *Self-Management for Adolescents.* New York: Guildford Press.

Cooper, J.O., Heron, T.E. and Heward, W.I. (1987) *Applied Behavior Analysis.* Columbus, OH: Merrill.

Deibert, A.N. and Harmon, A.J. (1978) *New Tools for Changing Behavior.* Illinois: Research Press.

Dillenburger, K. (1996) Helping children in care deal with trauma. *Child Care in Practice 2,* 40–45.

Dillenburger, K. and Keenan, M. (1993) Mummy don't leave me: The management of brief separation. Practice. *British Association of Social Workers 1,* 66–9.

Dillenburger, K. and Keenan, M. (1995) Dealing with child problem behaviours effectively. *Child Care in Practice 1,* 33–38.

Grant, L. and Evans, A. (1994) *Principles of Behaviour Analysis.* New York: Harper Collins.

Green, R.B., Hardison, W.L. and Greene, B.F. (1984) Turning the table on advice programs for parents: Using placemats to enhance family interactions at restaurants. *Journal of Applied Behavior Analysis 17,* 497–508.

Herbert, M. (1987) *Behavioural Treatment of Children with Problems: A Practice Manual* (Second Edition). New York: Academic Press.

Kazdin, A.E. (1977) *The Token Economy: A Review and Evaluation.* New York: Plenum Press.

Kazdin, A.E. (1994) *Behavior Modification in Applied Settings.* California: Brooks/Cole Publishing Company.

Keenan, M. (1997) Case of 'Michael'. Parents' *Education as Autism Therapists (P.E.A.T).* Newsletter.

Miltenberger, R. (1997) *Behavior Modification: Principles and Procedures.* California: Brooks/Cole Publishing Company.

Northup, J., Wacker, D., Sasso, G., Steege, M., Cigrand, K., Cook, J. and DeRaad, A. (1991) A brief functional analysis of aggressive and alternative behaviour in an outclinic setting. *Journal of Applied Behaviour Analysis 24,* 509–522.

O'Hagan, K. and Dillenburger, K. (1995) *The Abuse Of Women in Social Work.* Buckingham: Open University Press.

O'Neill, R.E., Horner, R.H., Albin, R.W., Sprague, J.R., Storey, K. and Newton, J.S. (1997) *Functional Assessment and Program Development for Problem Behavior.* California: Brooks/Cole Publishing Company.

Risley, T. (1996) Get a life! Positive behavioral intervention for challenging behaviour through life arrangement and life coaching. In L.K. Koegel, R.L. Koegel and G. Dunlap (eds) *Positive Behavioral Support: Including People with Difficult Behavior in the Community.* Baltimore: Paul H. Brookes.

Sulzer-Azaroff, B. and Mayer, G.R. (1991) *Behavior Analysis for Lasting Change.* London: Holt, Rinehart and Winston.

Wacker, D.P. (1989) Introduction to a special feature on measurement issues in supported education: Why measure anything? *Journal of the Association for Persons with Severe Handicaps 14,* 254.

Zirpoli, T.J. and Melloy, K.J. (1997) *Behavior Management: Applications for Teachers and Parents.* New Jersey: Prentice-Hall.

CHAPTER 8

Safe Care, Abuse and Allegations of Abuse in Foster Care

Stephen Nixon

Introduction

Foster care can undoubtedly provide high standard care for many foster children and many foster carers have positive experiences and feel the task is worthwhile. However, there are occasions when things go wrong to such an extent that foster children can be abused, or foster carers may have allegations of abuse made against them which turn out to be unfounded. When such events occur they are traumatic for all involved, whether foster child, birth parent, foster carer, social worker or manager.

The need for a chapter on safe care might be seen as an indictment of a system, an indication that a child in foster care is not necessarily safe. This is a particularly poignant issue when the reason for the child's initial removal from his or her own family is often to secure a safe and caring environment, indeed a place of safety. It is important to examine the nature of abuse in foster care before such problems can be tackled effectively and policy formulated to ensure that best practice is developed, implemented and evaluated.

This chapter considers the nature and extent of reports of abuse in foster care, the impact of such events on the different individuals involved as well as approaches to the investigation of these reports. Ways of seeking to prevent abuse in foster care will be examined, and the implications for practice in each stage will be considered from the first report through the investigation to dealing with the aftermath.

Four brief case studies are included in this chapter and are drawn from interviews with foster carers and foster children. In order to anonymise these cases, certain identifying information has been excluded and some details altered, including the names of the individuals involved.

The extent and nature of unsafe care

Abuse in residential children's homes has been a continuing area of concern for some decades (DoH 1991, 1997). In contrast, abuse in foster care has rarely been highlighted and it is only comparatively recently that this possibility has been discussed to any great extent. Many social workers and foster carers have encountered an allegation of abuse in foster care which has involved someone they know. The popular perception of such incidents is of sexual abuse or allegations of sexual abuse with the male carer allegedly sexually abusing a female foster child. However, the research studies to be discussed below reveal that sexual abuse accounts for under half of such reports. When the overall statistics are examined, a more complex pattern emerges than the anecdotal accounts would suggest. Knowledge based on anecdotes is an insufficient foundation on which to develop policy and practice. Research studies provide important evidence that can assist in providing a broader understanding both of the nature of abuse in foster care and of the impact of allegations on those involved. Studies of abuse and allegations of abuse have so far focused on agency records or foster carers' experiences, largely because it is relatively simpler to access these sources rather than tackle the dilemmas raised by undertaking research with foster children who may have been abused. Hence these studies have their limitations but it is still possible to draw some broad conclusions about the nature and extent of abuse and allegations of abuse in foster care.

Several studies have been undertaken, but each one has used different definitions of abuse and different methodologies of data gathering so that direct comparisons between the findings is difficult (Nixon forthcoming). For example, when comparing figures for the frequency of allegations, it is particularly important to bear in mind the breadth and inclusiveness of the definitions of abuse used in studies. One recent study included only children dealt with under child protection regulations, which is a comparatively narrow definition. In contrast, an earlier study used a very broad definition of abuse and maltreatment, including children about whose care concern had been expressed where ordinarily this would not have warranted classification as a child protection case (Ryan, McFadden and Wiencek 1987). Such a disparity in definitions can dramatically affect the reported incidence of allegations of abuse.

The term 'safe care' suggests that the foster child is secure from abuse or risk of abuse. Hence, correspondingly, unsafe care indicates that the child is thought to be at risk of abuse or maltreatment. However, just where the boundary lies between the two terms may be difficult to define as is demonstrated in another significant variable. This is the threshold at which concern is expressed by agencies and social workers, and action taken in relation to children who allegedly have been maltreated. The thresholds applied have been seen to vary according to the worker making the judgement that abuse may have occurred. In particular, differences have been observed between the children's social workers and the family placement social workers. The threshold for action was apparently lower amongst children's social workers than family placement social workers. Children's social workers were more likely to instigate an investigation into 'less serious' allegations than the foster carers' social worker (Nixon forthcoming).

Thus the frequency of reported allegations varies substantially between studies. This is also influenced by the methods of data collection. One study, a postal survey of agencies relying on formal central records, found the frequency of reports was 4 per cent and after investigation, half of these were substantiated, indicating that 2 per cent of carers had abused children (Nixon and Verity 1996). In contrast, another study examined what was reported to have occurred over the course of a year in each foster home in a sample and revealed that up to 12 per cent of foster carers had been the subject of a report. Subsequent investigation by social workers revealed that there was sufficient evidence to determine that 6 per cent of foster children in this study were subject to some form of maltreatment which had caused concern to a social worker during the course of a year (Nixon forthcoming).

The nature of abuse by foster carers reported has included a wide range of behaviour covering physical, sexual and emotional abuse as well as neglect. The proportions of each type vary substantially between the studies. For example, physical abuse ranges from 24 per cent (Benedict et al. 1996) to 50 per cent (Benedict et al. 1994) while sexual abuse varies from 10 per cent (Benedict et al. 1994) to 48 per cent (Benedict et al. 1996), and neglect from 8 per cent (Verity and Nixon 1995) to 26 per cent (Benedict et al. 1996).

The person reported to be the abuser tends to vary according to the nature of the abuse. In cases of sexual abuse, the alleged perpetrator is most often reported to be the male carer. In contrast, female carers are more frequently the alleged abuser in reports of physical abuse. When all forms of abuse are considered, foster carers are most frequently reported to be the abusers, although other people who have contact with children in the foster home are also reported, including both relatives and friends. For example, in one study ten per cent of reports related to adult males who had regular access to the foster family home, comprising baby-sitters, neighbours, friends and relatives including grandfathers. It is also important to note that, while accounting for a small proportion of reported incidents, foster children can abuse other children in the foster family, including carers' own children, and carers' own children occasionally abuse foster children (Verity and Nixon 1995).

The source of reports and allegations against foster carers provides a further insight. Allegations are not just derived from foster children, but also originate from carers' friends, neighbours, the foster children's birth parents, and from a range of other professionals particularly in the fields of health and education. A higher proportion of these reports turn out to be unfounded than those which derive from foster children themselves.

This brief outline of the nature of reports of abuse is a reminder of aspects of the issue. Not only is a single solution unlikely to be found, but a number of dilemmas are evident. These dilemmas most sharply focus on the ways of protecting the foster child yet at the same time safeguarding foster parents from unfounded accusations. If such a balance cannot be arrived at, foster care itself is in danger. It will lose public confidence if abuse is unchecked and no-one will want to become foster parents if they feel vulnerable to unfounded allegations.

The implications of unsafe care

When abuse occurs, or allegations have been made, the consequences for those involved are immense. In this section, the impact on children in foster homes is considered first, followed by an exploration of the impact on carers, social workers and agency managers.

Foster children

There is little research which has specifically examined the impact on children of abuse in foster care. However, it is likely that the consequences are substantial and that they will aggravate the effects of any previous experiences of abuse. Suffering abuse for the first time is likely to be traumatic; for those children who are re-abused in foster care, the effect may be profoundly so. The impact will be heightened by the child's assumption that placement in the foster home was intended to offer safety and protection. The sense of shock is likely to be considerable and will be combined with a further loss of trust in adults (Morris and Wheatley 1994; Farmer and Owen 1995). Individual children will respond differently, in part according to the nature of the abuse they have suffered. All will, to a greater or lesser extent, be devastated and disturbed both immediately and over the passage of time.

In addition to the damage caused directly by the abuse, a proportion of foster children are likely to be moved to another placement with more disruption, separation and loss. Since social workers do not necessarily have to follow child protection procedures when taking action in relation to foster children, there is a risk of some foster children being moved at any point during an investigation, even though the allegation may turn out to have been unfounded.

JANINE

Janine, a 16-year-old girl in foster care, described part of her experience in the following way: she had been in foster care since the age of 12, in three different foster homes. She viewed herself as quite experienced in the system, which she felt had given her a hard time. She described life in foster care and away from her own family as quite tough. Yet some of the carers she had experienced had not treated her as part of their family. Recalling the physical abuse that she experienced at home she said, 'you get used to it and soon forget it'. She suffered emotional abuse in her second foster home, linked in part to racial abuse and to her parents being called derogatory names. She said it was 'hard to take at the time and it stays with you compared to the pain of physical abuse which soon wears off.'

While actual abuse in foster care is likely to be damaging, even an unfounded allegation of abuse can have a substantial impact on the foster child. The stress experienced by carers is likely to be sensed by foster children in the fraught atmosphere of a foster home undergoing an investigation (Hicks and Nixon 1991).

Foster carers

While comparatively little is known about the precise impact of a report of abuse concerning the foster care household on foster children, there is more evidence about the profound impact on foster carers. A detailed study of foster carers' experiences has indicated that they show a series of emotional responses when first learning of the allegation and experiencing the subsequent investigation. Notable responses amongst foster carers are those of shock, anger, bitterness and isolation (Nixon 1997).

When foster carers are first told of a report of abuse, they face the prospect of a series of losses. These include the possible loss of the foster child, their self-esteem, the loss of a sense of control over their lives during the investigation, and loss of a proportion of their income. Perhaps most characteristically they will experience the common stages of grief and loss (Hicks and Nixon 1991; Carbino 1991b).

GAIL

Something of the nature of the foster carers' experience is conveyed in this brief account. The foster carer was just about to set off to meet Gail from junior school when a phone call from the fostering agency suggested that she should wait at home until the social worker arrived. She was told that Gail was currently being examined by a doctor and seemed to be well. There was no further explanation. The social worker rang off and left Mrs Wendup in a state of puzzlement that grew steadily into something like a state of panic. This was interleaved with feelings of uncertainty and then shock, with the realisation that she was being perceived as a possible abuser. She recalled hearing of something similar happening to another foster carer. Later, she became angry, resentful and tearful, as well as afraid. By the time the social worker arrived, some two and a half hours later, these feelings were intertwined in such a way that she felt her head was 'swimming'. She listened to the social worker in a haze with a mixture of anger, shock, concern and uncertainty combined with physical symptoms of an increased heartbeat and feelings of nausea. It all began as an accident when Gail had hit her head on a protruding electric socket causing the skin just by her eye to become badly bruised within a day. It had now become a case of assumed abuse. However, the following day it was accepted by both doctor and social worker that the bruise was most likely to have been caused by such an accident. The foster mother was highly relieved but by this time she was emotionally and physically exhausted by the implied criticism of her work by the agency and its social workers and by the lack of trust in her by seeking a medical opinion without consulting her.

The immediate reactions of foster parents are often those of shock and denial that this could happen to them. This is followed by feelings of anger, expressed at the person or agency making the allegation or indirectly at the child or relative. Such hostility seems to be linked to great bitterness, particularly towards the social worker involved in informing them of the allegation. Betrayal, isolation and fear also emerge with greater realisation of the potential consequences of the allegation. Foster carers sense that their most obvious source of support, the social worker, is no longer a trustworthy source of help. As these emotions take hold, carers also spend time going over past events seeking to identify what might have been misconstrued as abuse. Irrational conclusions can be drawn about the circumstances or the person who may be perceived as responsible. As a result there can be growing discord within the home, disruption of personal relationships and, in some cases, breakdown of the marital relationship and separation of partners.

Since it can be many weeks before investigations are completed, foster carers can experience a sense of powerlessness as they realise that they have no control over events. This can be associated with anxiety and stress-related illness. When informed that the allegation has not been substantiated, there can be a sense of relief, although almost all foster carers are likely to feel residual anger over the manner in which the allegation and investigation have been handled and the role played by social workers and the police. Foster carers who reach a more reflective and philosophical acceptance of the experience appear to be those whose relationship with the social worker has been sustained through frequent contact in a highly professional, non-judgemental counselling and listening mode.

Though the underlying causes are not fully understood, some carers do abuse foster children. Foster carers can find themselves viewed by their immediate community as having committed the most atrocious of crimes if the reasons for them no longer fostering become known in the locality. It can be hard for neighbours and others to comprehend how foster carers can breach the trust placed in them to care and protect other people's children and then end up maltreating them.

Impact on agencies

A fostering agency is likely to have responsibility for both the maintenance of a pool of foster homes and the supervision of children placed with those foster carers. The identification of actual abuse means that previously approved foster carers have maltreated a child in some way. The agency's duty to protect children is paramount and the implications of the abuse are profound.

These implications will be considered at different stages of investigation and follow-up.

The agency's duty to protect children can, at times, appear to be in conflict with its need to maintain a sufficiently large pool of foster carers to look after children. This can be seen in the sometimes difficult relationships which can arise between the child's social worker involved with the investigation, and the family placement social worker whose key role is to sustain and support foster homes.

A report of abuse in a foster home can also have a substantial impact on the social worker. The individual social worker involved in the initial interviewing and approval of foster carers can experience a loss of personal and professional self-confidence. The social worker may express feelings of guilt about what they consider to be their own failure to identify potential abusers and their role in the placement of a child in what may have been an unsafe foster home. The social worker may fear a loss in professional standing. Social workers therefore clearly need an opportunity to review the unfolding situation in a supportive environment.

Social workers can respond to foster carers in a number of ways when an allegation is made (Nixon 1997). Some social workers can find it painful to work with foster carers who have had an allegation of abuse made against them and may respond by adopting an approach which implies a belief in the foster carers' account of events. For the social worker to offer such an undertaking during an investigation is not sustainable. Any comments about belief in the carers' innocence can only come after the completion of an investigation, much as foster carers themselves want to hear such statements of unconditional support.

In other cases, social workers may be removed from working with foster carers, because of the requirements of an investigation. This can add greatly to foster parents' feelings of lack of support. A minority of foster carers thought social workers had ensured that they were dealt with in a highly professional and non-judgemental way. Such an approach can be greatly assisted by the investigation being carried out by another agency, so that the family placement social worker is not perceived as being closely involved in the active investigation of the allegation. However, foster carers may also see the two social workers, even though from different teams or different agencies, as working together, or at the very least communicating with each other and consequently not to be counted on (Nixon 1997).

The difficulties which confront agency managers at this point can affect other aspects of fostering provision. For, in addition to the maintenance of normal day-to-day services, the agency is seeking to cope with several interrelated situations including foster children who may need to be moved, foster carers who need both to be investigated and to be supported while in addition social workers are being subjected to unexpected pressures. All these circumstances can absorb and deflect resources from normal provision, potentially putting other placements under pressure too.

In addition, there is a longer-term issue related to the recruitment and retention of other foster carers. Once people learn of the possibility of allegations being made against foster carers, they can seriously question the wisdom of remaining as foster carers and potential foster carers can withdraw their applications. Hence unsafe care generates serious problems and pressures, creating an environment of potentially unstable placements which have to be carefully monitored and managed by the agency if foster-care services are to be maintained and the quality and safety of care enhanced.

Avoiding abuse in foster care

This section considers some of the approaches which may help to diminish the possibility of abuse. The evidence about the incidence of abuse in foster care suggests that while a limited proportion may be premeditated and deliberate, usually it is spur-of-the-moment actions which culminate in abuse. There are a number of steps that can be taken to reduce the latter form of abuse although the risk will always remain and vigilance will always be necessary. Differentiating between different forms of abuse is important in seeking explanations for the abuse and for considering ways of dealing with it.

An approach to avoiding or preventing these events is part of a risk management strategy in which risks are considered and ways of minimising the likelihood are developed and used. Within such a framework, it is possible to consider the nature of practice, the nature of the report and the level of risk. Steps can be taken in relation to each of the three main sets of individuals involved.

The foster child

Foster children are initially placed in foster care because the balance of risks suggests that they should be moved from their family of origin. The nature of those risks needs to be considered carefully in relation to the impact of the placement on the child and upon the foster-care household. Consequently, in addition to the individual preparation of the child that has to be undertaken for each specific foster placement, the foster child may require other assistance, guidance and access to people to whom he or she can turn. Such direct work with the child clearly has to include how to seek out and talk to people that the child can trust and how to deal with people who seek to exploit the child's trust. The issue of physical or sexual abuse needs to be explored in a way that emphasises that their bodies are their own and private and that gives them permission to say no to an adult. This is an important element of keeping the child safe (Elliott 1988).

Within the rather closed and private world of a family, extended networks may help in keeping the child safe. A close link with other foster carers may add to this network. Paired arrangements with respite carers, for example, may be a formal way of developing and enhancing such a network which can be encouraged by the agency.

The role of the child's social worker is also crucial. It is important that, within the social worker's relationship with the child, frequent opportunities exist to meet the child and that they are readily accessible to the child at other times. In addition, the role of children's rights officers has emerged recently (Rae 1996). Based in an independent agency, or at least reasonably unconnected to the fostering service, a children's rights officer is someone to whom a child can turn for guidance and support and can become directly involved in taking up a child's concerns or helping a young person to make a complaint. Further extension of this role is now being developed in the UK (DoH 1998b). There is now some evidence that children's rights officers are perceived by some children as a medium through which to express their distress or unhappiness about a placement. The children's knowledge of, and access to, such a person is a further element in the network of adults to whom they can turn. Building up children's knowledge and skills, and their relationships with a network of other adults, are important foundations for creating a protective environment (Boushel 1994). Yet, we always have to be aware that it is likely to be a person in a child's comparatively limited network of adults who may be a future abuser.

Foster carers

It is at the point of recruitment, application and interviewing that the first stage of screening out of some applicants can take place. Access to information about the criminal records of convicted sex offenders would help eliminate known offenders. While such information will be found in relation to a comparatively small proportion of applicants, nevertheless, a single individual incident of abuse thus prevented is important for a child. Beyond this, prevention becomes less certain with the absence of reliable indicators which might predict potential abuse.

Seeking to avoid abuse in foster care involves a number of elements. Preparation of carers in general through induction training is a start, but specific preparation for the placement of each child is also fundamental. This will include an exploration of how the placement will affect individual family members and their relationships. It should also involve consideration of the kinds of behaviour that may arise and possible strategies for handling these and other situations not encountered before. An important component is to help everyone to recognise that they may have limits to their skills or their temper or that they may experience an unexpected sexual attraction to a child. These discussions need to explore how foster carers can be placed under pressure. For example, major behavioural problems exhibited by a foster child may prove beyond the foster carers' experience and skills to handle. They may need the chance to discuss ways of dealing with such critical points – how to react in the situation and to whom they can turn at that moment to help them deal with their own responses and ways of managing the situation.

A range of supports such as additional training and access to a child psychologist may help to prevent foster carers reaching the limit of their skill and tolerance. Otherwise there may be the danger of physical abuse of a foster child occurring through inappropriate punishment. There is also some evidence that overloading of carers by multiple placements can generate pressure and growing stress in carers who eventually reach breaking point (Nixon forthcoming).

In seeking to develop preventive approaches in relation to the risk of sexual abuse in foster care, foster carers should be encouraged to avoid situations which may be open to misinterpretation, for example with bathroom, bedroom and bedtime routines. Such an approach requires careful background preparation of foster carers to ensure that the reasons for such steps are considered and understood, and methods of handling difficult situations developed.

ANNA

One situation where this was not fully considered is illustrated by the placement of a teenage girl, Anna. Sixteen-year-old Anna had told a friend at
school that her foster mother's boyfriend, who visited most Saturdays, had
'touched her up' when greeting her in the kitchen on the previous Saturday
(i.e. sexually assaulting her by inappropriate touching). Upon receiving a
phone call from the social worker, the foster mother was placed in a dilemma.
She had been approved as a foster carer as a single woman and also received a
high level of payment for her willingness to work with particularly demanding and complex placements. Mrs Needham therefore felt that she was
expected to demonstrate high standards all round. She had not wanted to
draw attention to what she perceived to be a limited change in her circumstances when the boyfriend began to visit her at home as she knew he was a
married man living some distance away with his partner and family. She had
therefore not told the agency. At initial interview the boyfriend acknowledged that he may have accidentally touched the young woman's breasts
when greeting her. Investigation revealed furthermore that he had for some
weeks given her some spending money, which she had to obtain by putting
her hand into the pocket of his jeans, and this happened in the kitchen out of
Mrs Needham's vision.

After some days it was eventually agreed that, if Mrs Needham were to be
allowed to continue as a foster carer, the boyfriend could not be allowed to
visit the foster home. Mrs Needham also agreed that in future she would tell
any male visitors about the necessity for police checks as a routine part of
seeking to protect any foster children placed with her. The boyfriend was
eventually dealt with through a police caution on condition that he did not
visit the house again.

Fear of an allegation and sometimes surprise at their own sexual
responses, for example, can drive foster carers, and social workers who
recommend them, to take an increasingly 'defensive' approach to their
interactions with foster children. As part of such a defensive approach foster
carers adjust their caring regimes in an attempt to minimise the perceived
risk. This may include avoiding being alone at any time with the specific
child or young person, indeed avoiding any circumstances or even
interaction in which a possible allegation could be made or abuse considered
to have happened. While this may be understandable, the unintended
consequences need to be considered, including possible undermining of the
potential therapeutic experience of foster care. It is important, however, to

avoid a blanket-coverage approach which is inflexibly adopted. While foster carers may potentially be protected from allegations of abuse, the consequences for foster children may be detrimental. Deprived children may need physical closeness to their carers, including 'hugging' and 'cuddling'. In such circumstances, foster children are potentially left more confused and earlier damaging experiences might be repeated and reinforced.

Swan (1997) gives an example of a teenage girl in foster care for whom the experience may be of a distant uninvolved male who conforms to a stereotype of minimal involvement in a pattern of care and an environment not dissimilar to her experience with the male who abused her in the first place. This study provides important evidence that unintended consequences may occur which can adversely affect foster children. Comprehensive implementation of such an approach will need to be reassessed and other approaches considered.

Investigation of reports of abuse

When a report of possible abuse is received, a sequence of events unfolds in which the basis of the allegation is examined by the agency's staff. Previous sections have outlined how the dynamics of the foster home are disrupted by the allegation. An unexpected investigation of foster carers, who are often seen as close colleagues, can also test to the limit the relationship between foster carers and social workers, both of whom may have experienced shock. Such situations can be exacerbated by a lack of clearly articulated policy and procedures.

An investigation takes place because someone has expressed concern about some aspect of the foster child's care and that the child may be vulnerable in some way. Any report must be taken seriously, particularly when foster children make reports themselves. The child's safety and security are paramount in the investigation. Evidence from the child will be a crucial part of the process. Interviewing the foster child and keeping him/her informed of progress will be key elements in not only gathering information but also demonstrating to the child that the report is being taken seriously.

Experiencing the mechanics of an investigation can be difficult for foster carers. In one study, one-third of the foster carers first learned of an allegation during a telephone conversation with their social worker, even though this is a most traumatic piece of information to receive (Hicks and Nixon 1991). In addition, while investigations can sometimes be completed within two or three days, some investigations can last several weeks and it may even be months before carers learn the outcome of the investigation (Nixon and Verity 1996). The length of time which an investigation takes can feel endless to carers who have had their innocence questioned. Stress levels are accentuated by long investigations.

In conducting investigations, it is important to recognise that carers (and sometimes social workers) have limited knowledge of the existence of written policy and guidelines. In addition there can be limited awareness among agency managers and social workers about the impact of the allegation and investigation when informing carers about the report.

Multi-professional investigations which involve not only social workers but also doctors and police officers can increase the time required to complete an inquiry as well as confuse carers about the processes involved. Close co-operation between those involved in an investigation is important to produce a speedy outcome and to diminish confusion for foster carers.

Investigations can be complex activities. Not only do carers need to know about the possibility of an allegation, but also how an investigation will be conducted. A spoken explanation of this is not sufficient. Carers need to have a copy of the procedures so that they have something to which they can refer during the stressful times of an investigation. In fact, information about the likely timescale and regular progress reports are crucial. The issue of powerlessness felt by carers in these circumstances needs to be handled sensitively. An investigation carried out by a number of officials visiting the family home and looking at the family members from the outside is disempowering and leaves carers feeling a lack of control over their own lives. Understanding what is going on can remove an element of this sense of powerlessness.

The potential for conflicts of interest to arise is a significant issue in the investigation of allegations against foster carers. While this has been recognised to a considerable extent when formal investigations take place, before that stage is reached there is a chance for the interests of agencies, foster carers and foster children to become confused. At one level the conflict can arise when a social worker from an agency carries out an investigation of the agency's own carers while at the same time another member of staff may be seeking to offer support to the carers. Foster carers are usually well aware of this conflict of roles at this point and social workers can lose the trust of foster carers, the foundation of their supportive role, when an investigation begins (Nixon 1997).

More significantly, a further conflict of interest arises when a social worker investigates the report of abuse in relation to the agency's own foster carers and foster child. The foster carers are agents or employees with whom the agency has had an established relationship, perhaps over several years, and who are valuable resources in their own right, being expensive to recruit, train and maintain. In such circumstances it may not always be possible to retain a sufficient level of objectivity in decision making when pressure prevails to ensure maintenance of the existing pool of available foster carers.

In the final decision-making stage of the investigation, having established the safety of the child, which must be the prime concern of those involved, there are other needs to be considered. While problems can readily occur in circumstances which are very sensitive and emotionally charged, it is possible to identify an approach to investigations which emphasises the need for the child's protection *and* long-term emotional well-being. This appears to be increasingly recognised, with decisions being made to allow children to remain in placement in the foster home, despite, for example, some maltreatment having occurred. At one level it may seem inconsistent to allow a child to remain in a foster home when he or she has been subject to some limited degree of maltreatment, since the child is likely to have been placed there for protection. However, the argument which is used to support continuing the placement is that for the foster child, who may otherwise be well settled, a further move to another foster home would result in greater emotional damage through, for example, further experience of separation and loss than if the child were to remain in the foster home. Clearly, such decisions cannot be taken lightly and a careful assessment of the potential risks needs to be undertaken.

Investigations also have to follow legal procedures to ensure, for example, that evidence is not compromised or lost in an attempt to recognise the pain and trauma of the foster carers being investigated. Investigation into a report of abuse in foster care must conform to best practice as applied in the investigation of reports of abuse where children are living with their own parents. The child must be the prime concern of those involved. But foster carers should also be treated with respect and dignity during the investigation in recognition of the trauma which they will be suffering. While this may seem like special treatment for foster carers, it is only the same approach which all carers, whether parents or foster carers, are entitled to expect.

It has been observed during investigations that foster carers can sometimes report feeling that they have been treated in a way that is less than impartial. Some carers have experienced an underlying punitive attitude by social workers towards them. Carers sense that, having been entrusted with the care of other people's children, the social workers consider that they have failed to live up to that trust, and hence should be punished, even before the conclusion of the investigation (Nixon forthcoming).

Follow-up after an investigation of abuse

Following an investigation, one of a number of decisions may be made by social workers, agencies and even the courts. These can range from the decision that the report was *unfounded*, where investigation has revealed there to be no foundation for the allegation; through *unsubstantiated*, where there was not enough evidence to confirm that the alleged events took place; to *substantiated* or founded, where the evidence is sufficient to confirm that abuse or maltreatment has taken place.

The decision is conveyed to foster carers in a number of ways. The information is not always provided in writing and can sometimes be communicated by telephone or during a visit by the social worker. The amount of information given may be very limited. This may be because there is insufficient evidence to confirm or substantiate an allegation. What foster carers are seeking, however, is a clear statement that the allegation was unfounded. Anything other than this is a cause of frustration and distress to carers. When such a statement is not forthcoming, the disappointment and resentment of carers can be substantial. Indeed, it is at this point that some carers may decide to stop being foster carers, even when the report is unfounded, largely as a result of their experience of the report and the investigation (Nixon and Hicks 1987).

A number of possible outcomes for foster children may follow an investigation. Where the foster child has already been removed, he or she may, or may not, be returned to the original foster home. Where the child remained in the foster home during the investigation and the findings of the investigation are to substantiate the report, the child is usually removed.

Nevertheless, even where maltreatment is substantiated, the decision is sometimes made that the child should remain (Nixon forthcoming). While the maltreatment in such cases is generally relatively mild (if maltreatment can ever be described as mild), such decisions have normally been in relation to physical chastisement and the decision includes the proviso that additional support and resources are provided to enable the foster carers to enhance their caring capacity without reaching breaking point again.

After completion of an investigation, a review of the foster home involving social workers, carers and manager ensures that the details of the allegation and investigation are considered within the broader context of any changes, additional pressures and the need for further support and training. Keeping careful records, both by carers and social workers, of any incident in a foster home is important as there is evidence that in some instances a sequence of less serious events in the foster home can be identified prior to an occasion which triggers a formal investigation. Regular reviews of foster homes using such records also provide an opportunity for carers to be involved in discussion about their past and future role as carers. Such reflections on the preceding months enable learning from the events to take place and for decisions to be made about the future which may help to diminish potential abuse in the future.

After an investigation of an allegation, the decision may be that no further placements should be made with the foster carers and that they should be de-registered because the findings indicated some foundation for the allegation. For example, the carers may have abused the child by inappropriate physical chastisement. In such circumstances, the carers may find themselves traumatised and isolated. Yet after a period of several years of useful caring such foster carers will surely feel entitled to the compassion of the agency and continued support as they seek to rebuild their lives (Carbino 1991a).

MR AND MRS WELDEAN

The situation of the Weldeans illustrates this. Mr Weldean, a fifty-year-old male foster carer, had been the subject of what were said to be unsubstantiated allegations of sexual abuse of a 14-year-old girl who had lived in the family for just one year. As a result of an investigation it was deemed that there was insufficient evidence for a court hearing. Sufficient doubt remained, however, for the agency Fostering Panel to make the decision to suspend the foster home from further placements.

Mrs Weldean was described as being totally devastated at the time of the investigation. Some months later the couple had separated. Mrs Weldean had found the whole experience so painful and humiliating as well as feeling let down by her husband's alleged behaviour. Contact with the agency stopped at the point of removal of the child. Mrs Weldean had fostered some twelve children over a period of seven years.

Carers usually accept and recognise when actions are taken in the best interests of the foster child, something which is usually closely related to why they became foster carers in the first place. It is particularly important for sensitive and careful handling of carers in these circumstances. While they are less likely to talk about an allegation of abuse against them in public, they can talk about poor treatment by an agency leaving a negative impression about the agency, which can make initial recruitment of foster carers even more difficult.

CHILDREN

Perhaps the most difficult arena in follow-up work is with children in the foster homes. Where a child has been abused, the need for explanations, support and therapy will be important. These therapeutic needs may be met within the setting of the foster home with a blend of carer, social worker and therapist interventions as a child seeks to make sense of, and deal with, the feelings engendered by abuse in an allegedly caring setting.

A similar approach can also be applied to carers' own children, who can occasionally be subjected to abuse. Carers' own children, whatever their experiences, may have been through difficult times, and they too need to be able to deal with their experiences. Agencies have a clear responsibility towards these children to ensure that therapeutic help is made available for them. Attending a group for children of carers may help the children to deal with their experiences in day-to-day fostering. Such a group may also assist them to come through the experience of a report or allegation of abuse within their family. Carers' own children are affected in multiple ways by the work undertaken by their parents on behalf of agencies (Part 1993; Pugh 1996; Reed 1996). Agencies have a responsibility to ensure that the welfare of these children is not put at risk and to support these children when problems and potential damage occur.

Social workers who have to deal with reports either as the key worker in the selection and approval process, or as the one who failed to detect that anything might be going wrong in the foster home, can experience feelings of guilt and a loss of confidence. While this may seem a lower priority in comparison to the experience of children and of carers, it is nevertheless an area of importance in terms of maintaining a social work workforce in full working condition and ready to learn from and work with similar stressful situations in the future.

Conclusion

A number of dilemmas can be identified which confront those involved in their different roles in foster care. Carers or potential applicants need to be aware of the possibility that allegations of abuse could happen to them. Just how this information and the issues underlying are to be presented and shared are potentially critical points in the recruitment and training of foster carers. Information about abuse and allegations of abuse in foster care has to be conveyed carefully and sensitively as there is anecdotal evidence of carers panicking and withdrawing when first hearing of this possibility. A parallel process of steadily increasing carers' awareness of the information about such problems while at the same time exploring alternative methods of dealing with situations and building skills and confidence to handle such events may help to reduce loss of foster carers.

When children are removed from their own families of origin and placed in foster care because of the risk of abuse, the intention is to provide them with a safe, caring environment. Fostering such children can be a very demanding and stressful task for foster carers. Sufficient carefully defined support and training is an essential for survival. High quality foster care requires high standards of support and supervision; low levels of support *may* be linked to difficulties in foster care (Nixon 1997).

However, as this chapter has outlined, the possibility of abuse in foster care exists. It creates a new perspective when considering foster children's welfare. The question must be asked as to whether children should be removed from their own families in the first place if the alternative care provided cannot be guaranteed to be risk-free. Looking after a child in foster care combined with the necessary support for foster carers requires resources. Consideration must be given to the issue as to whether resources committed to providing foster care which may turn out to be unsafe might have been used more appropriately in supporting and maintaining the child and his or her own family of origin in the first place. This forms part of the continuing debate about the provision of support for birth parents to assist in preserving the family, in contrast with the more procedural child protection investigation and removal approach that has eventually emerged in the UK (Parton 1997).

While the numbers of children abused or maltreated in foster care may not be large, the possibility that this can happen is a vital consideration for foster-care services, child protection systems and those involved in the support of birth families. The various supports for foster carers are essential elements in enabling the task to be undertaken effectively. However, social workers are the key people involved in the provision of support and have a dual responsibility of ensuring that the child is safe and being well cared for. Placing a child in a family is a very private setting where inspection or surveillance is at its most difficult. No inspection system can be foolproof. Social workers support and inspect – a dilemma that is not easily resolved. The nature of the relationship built up between the social worker and the foster carer becomes one of the most critical components in protecting the child. This can be further endangered when a report of abuse is made.

Disquiet about safeguards for children in foster care and children's homes has generated government action in the UK. A broad policy, laid out in a number of documents, seeks to improve standards through measures related to a series of issues in foster care from recruitment, selection, monitoring and review of foster carers and the provision of a range of support elements including training and greater sharing of information. The impact of these provisions will need to be monitored and reviewed, but in theory should sharpen the focus of objectives of fostering services, their management, delivery and evaluation (DoH 1998a, b, c).

The limited available evidence reviewed in this chapter emphasises that safe care for all foster children has so far not been achieved. Indeed, a small percentage of children, perhaps greater than has been assumed, are maltreated and abused while in foster care. It is unlikely that safe care could ever be guaranteed or unfounded allegations of abuse avoided. While comparatively little is known about the origins of such abuse, the result is significant trauma for those children and carers involved.

Hence there are risks, principally for children and foster carers. However, a dilemma exists as to the best way of protecting and supporting foster children yet at the same time safeguarding foster carers from unfounded allegations and supporting them when such allegations are made.

The knowledge that such events can occur emphasises the need for each aspect of foster-care practice to be reviewed with the aim of diminishing the risks for those involved. Indeed, the whole process of risk management, with the foster child as the central, though not exclusive, focus must be a key task in foster-care practice in seeking to reduce the incidence and impact of abuse and allegations of abuse.

References

Benedict, M.I., Zuravin, S., Brandt, D. and Abbey, H. (1994) Types and frequency of child maltreatment by family foster care providers in an urban population. *Child Abuse and Neglect 18*, 7, 577–585.

Benedict, M.I., Zuravin, S., Somerfield, M. and Brandt, D. (1996) The reported health and functioning of children maltreated while in family foster care. *Child Abuse and Neglect 20*, 7, 561–571.

Boushel, M. (1994) Keeping safe: Strengthening the protective environment of children in foster care. *Adoption and Fostering 18*, 1, Spring, 33–39.

Carbino, R. (1991a) Advocacy for foster families in the United States facing child abuse allegations: How social agencies and foster parents are responding to the problem. *Child Welfare LXX*, 2, March/April, 131–149.

Carbino, R. (1991b) *Consequences of Child Abuse Allegations for Foster Families: Report of a Symposium.* University of Wisconsin – Madison: School of Social Work.

Department of Health (1991) *Children in the Public Care: A Review of Residential Child Care.* London: HMSO.

Department of Health (1997) *People Like Us: The Review of the Safeguards for Children Living Away From Home* (Utting Report). London: Stationery Office.

Department of Health (1998a) *Modernising Social Services* (White Paper). London: Stationery Office.

Department of Health (1998b) *Quality Protects.* London: Stationery Office.

Department of Health (1998c) *The Government's Response to the Children's Safeguards Review.* London: Stationery Office.

Elliott, M. (1988) *Keeping Safe. A Practical Guide to Talking with Children.* London: Hodder and Stoughton.

Farmer, E. and Owen, M. (1995) *Child Protection Practice: Private Risks and Public Remedies.* London: HMSO.

Hicks, C. and Nixon, S. (1991) Unfounded allegations of child abuse in the UK: A survey of foster parents' reactions to investigative procedures. *Child and Youth Services 15*, 2, 249–260.

Morris, S. and Wheatley, H. (1994) *Time to Listen.* London: Childline.

Nixon, S. (1997) The limits of support in foster care. *British Journal of Social Work 27*, 913–930.

Nixon, S. (forthcoming) The incidence of reports of abuse in foster care.

Nixon, S. and Hicks, C. (1987) Experiencing accusations of abuse. *Foster Care,* December, 10–11.

Nixon, S. and Verity, P. (1996) Allegations against foster families: Agency procedures and practices. *Foster Care,* January, 11–14.

Part, D. (1993) Fostering as seen by the carers' children. *Adoption and Fostering 17,* 1, 26–31.

Parton, N. (ed) (1997) *Child Protection and Family Support: Tensions, Contradictions and Possibilities.* London: Routledge.

Pugh, G. (1996) Seen but not heard? Addressing the needs of children who foster. *Adoption and Fostering 20,* 1, 35–41.

Rae, R. (1996) Researching Children's Rights Officers. In M. Long (ed) *Children In Our Charge.* London: Jessica Kingsley Publishers.

Reed, J.A. (1996) Fostering children and young people with learning disabilities: The perspectives of birth children and carers. *Adoption and Fostering 20,* 4, 36–41.

Ryan, P., McFadden, E.J. and Wiencek, P. (1987) *Analyzing Abuse in Foster Family Care.* Michigan: Eastern Michigan University.

Verity, P. and Nixon, S. (1995) Allegations against foster families: Carers' expectations and experiences. *Foster Care,* October, 13–16.

CHAPTER 9

Relative Care

A Different Type of Foster Care – Implications for Practice

Valerie O'Brien

Introduction

Stories abound in our families and communities about the rearing of children informally within extended families rather than with their birth families. This represents the efforts made by many families to cope with particular social, economic and political constraints of the time. Relative care, as distinct from informal care within extended families, is a care option now being used increasingly by the state, and involves the formal placement of children unable to live with their parents in their extended family networks. (The terms relative care, relative foster care and kinship care are used interchangeably in the literature to refer to this practice. In this chapter the term relative care is used, as it reflects the common language used to describe family relationships in Ireland and UK. Kinship is the term used predominantly in the American context, as it is deemed more culturally appropriate.)

In this chapter, the emergence of relative care as a growing option in recent years is examined. The known advantages and constraints are discussed and particular attention is drawn to the differences between relative and traditional foster care. Relative care is then considered in the context of five principal issues identified in a review of the literature, and through a research study (O'Brien 1997) undertaken in a child care agency in Ireland. The chapter concludes by putting forward a number of proposals for changing practice in relative care, arising from the research, for optimum use of this care option.

O'Brien's (1997) study, hereafter referred to as the Irish study, which used a combined qualitative and quantitative methodology, examined the evolution of relative care networks following an emergency placement of a child in a relative home. It provided baseline data on a population of ninety-two children. The study traced the processes involved through the decision-making, assessment and post-assessment stages. It examined the ways in which current case management practices, derived primarily from an application of a traditional foster care approach, impact on the evolution of the networks. A process-oriented descriptive account of the evolution of the networks was presented. The multiple perspectives on issues offered by the birth parents, children, relatives and social workers involved was an important feature of the study. A post-Milan systemic framework, drawing principally on the 'fifth province model', was the main theoretical frame used to orientate the study.

The emergence of relative care

In the 1990s, renewed interest has arisen in family and social networks as a placement resource for children in need of formal state care in a context of major shifts in the child welfare system. Several factors account for the change. These include:

- *The shift from residential care to foster care* (Triseliotis 1989; Colton 1989). This shift is associated with the increased awareness of the negative effects of long-term institutionalisation, the importance of a more family-based experience for children, especially those in long-term care, and a concern among service providers with the increased cost of residential care.

- *Demographic trends* resulting in less availability of foster homes (Kusserow 1992; Gilligan 1990) at a time when family-based care is preferred.

- The challenge to the *inter-generational abuse/dysfunctional family theories* that accounted for negativity towards relative placements among practitioners, influenced by the emergence of family therapy, systemic and strength-based approaches.

- The shift towards *partnership* in child care (Thoburn 1994; Ryburn 1993) opened up the previously untapped potential of family and social networks among service providers. As a result greater emphasis was placed in practice on the process of consultation, client participation and consumer satisfaction.

- *Principles of child care* were reappraised as people reared in alternative care began to narrate their stories, and the importance of identity and roots was reinforced. This challenged core premises previously held regarding 'substitute' care. As part of this evolving thinking, many theories central to child care, e.g. the family and social networks, attachment, identity, separation and loss, were re-examined.

- *Outcome studies*, which indicated lower disruption rates and more security for children placed within family networks (Rowe *et al.* 1984; Fein *et al.* 1983; Dubowitz *et al.* 1993; Iglehart 1994). These studies, though small in number, influenced practice at a time when practitioners were dealing with increasing difficulties in foster care, i.e. recruitment, breakdown, etc. (Caution is needed in drawing conclusions from outcome studies to date, as the studies tend to be predominantly American, and lack highly significant representative samples and adequate control groups.)

Arising from the shift in practice, important legal challenges occurred which resulted in the redefinition of relative care. The highly significant *Miller* v. *Youakim* (1979) Supreme Court judgement is cited as an important determinant of subsequent developments in the USA. This case provided that children in statutory care could only be placed with approved foster families. Before this ruling, child welfare agencies had placed many children in statutory care with relatives who were unapproved as foster carers, and who did not receive the standard foster care allowance. Subsequent to the ruling, all relatives caring for children in statutory care had to be approved, and paid the regular foster care rates (Thornton 1987; Gleeson 1996). This resulted in a huge increase in the formal use of the relative care option in the USA.

Rates of relative care

The use of relative care is referenced as an increasing practice in many Western countries: Holland (Portengen and van Neut 1995); Sweden (Bergerhed 1995); Israel (Mosek and Adler 1993); and UK (Colton and Williams 1997; Thoburn 1994). Statistics that demonstrate the increase are limited, except for the USA where the practice intensified from the late 1980s. Recent reports show that between 30 per cent and 50 per cent of foster children in different jurisdictions in the USA are now placed in relative homes (Hegar 1993). The practice is prevalent, predominantly in large urban centres (Berrick, Barth and Needell 1994). In the mid-nineties New York, approximately half of the 41,283 children in foster care were in relative care (Link 1996), while the rate of children cared for by relatives rose to 59 per cent of the total care population in Illinois at the same time (Gleeson 1996). In Ireland there is evidence that relative care is now being used increasingly for children needing care. In the agency in which the study on which this chapter is based was conducted (which deals with over one-third of children in care in the country), a quarter of all children in the foster care system are now placed with relatives, and this rate is increasing annually.

Notwithstanding these indications, it is difficult to track precisely the rate of change in the use of this care option, as data on relative care are 'not always collected as a discrete entity and is not readily available' (Link 1996, p.512). In Ireland, there is an increased recognition in administrative systems of the need to collate statistics for relative care and foster care separately (Department of Health 1995b). Good information systems are an essential prerequisite if the practice and policy issues arising from this development are to be adequately identified and addressed.

It is anticipated that the increase and use of relative care will continue. Legislative changes which facilitate relative placements are now evident in many countries – the Indian Child Welfare Act 1980 (US); Children's Act 1989 (England and Wales); Children, Young Person and Families Act 1989 (New Zealand); Child Care Act 1991 (Ireland). While this reflects an increased focus on culturally appropriate placements for children in the care system, it may be argued that the increase in relative care has not occurred as a result of a coherent policy direction. There is evidence that, despite the legislative and value-based changes in practice, the role and purpose of relative care remain unclear. This is apparent in the American context, where relative care has been formally established earlier than elsewhere. The trends emerging there (connected in part with welfare cuts) are likely therefore to be replicated at a future date in other countries. Johnson asserts that, despite the changes, there is still huge resistance to the placement of children in relative care:

...despite the documented weakness of the foster care system and the risks to children of foster care placement, the reluctance of child welfare workers to place children has endured and is echoed anew in reservations about contemporary kinship foster care. (1995, p.38).

He maintains that:

relatives ushered into the formal child welfare system face the residue of ... two historical patterns of official scepticism, in that they are families which raised a neglectful or abusive parent and the overwhelming majority are poor families. (1995, p.40).

This suggests that, despite the increased use and interest in relative care, an underlying ambivalence remains towards the practice. On the one hand, the practice is welcome as it fits with current values surrounding the importance of the family. On the other, however, there is an increasing concern with the costs associated with this practice. This is linked to the question of paying family members for what many think should be done out of a sense of familial affection and obligation. Before considering this central dilemma more fully, the differences between relative and foster care are discussed. The distinction between the two provides an important context marker for those involved in the development and practice of relative care.

Differences between relative care and traditional foster care

Differences between relative and traditional foster care are considered in relation to four headings:

- Connection to the agency
- Assessment process
- Demographic profile
- The position of the agency in the network of relationships.

Connection to the agency

Available studies show that one of the principal differences between relative carers and traditional foster parents is the way they become connected with the agency (Thornton 1987; Needell 1994). In the main, traditional foster parents approach the agency as prospective foster parents. They are provided with training aimed at inducting them into the role of foster parent, and acquainted with agency expectations. They are subsequently assessed by the agency to determine their suitability. The process culminates with the placement of a child, when the agency and the prospective foster parents enter a contractual arrangement together. On the other hand, relatives are seen to respond to a set of pressing circumstances involving a dependent child within their family network. A decision is made, usually very speedily in the midst of a crisis, for the relatives to care for the child. This may happen as a result of either an approach from the family to the agency, or through the agency contacting the family. The importance of the way in which relatives connect with the agency, and the ensuing practice implications, is further amplified when the route of children into relative care is considered. In the Irish study one-third of the children entered care directly from their birth parents' home, another third were already in the care system and moved either as part of a planned move or following disruption in a previous place-ment, and the remaining third were already in the informal care of the relatives at the time the child was received into care.

(The Irish study did not distinguish between children on statutory care orders and accommodation (voluntary care). The study population consisted of ninety-two children placed in care where the assessment was finally formalised following the placement. The distinction between court-mandated care and accommodation only provides a snapshot of a care population, and fails to take account of the movement that occurs between these two care options when children enter the system. For that reason, it was decided to include both categories in the study, first because of the exploratory nature of the study and second to examine the underlying processes surrounding the connection with the agency and the eventual formalising of the placement.)

Assessment process

The assessment process in traditional foster care normally takes a period of nine months, although there is variation within and between agencies. In tra-ditional foster care, the assessment is completed before a child is placed with the foster family. In relative care, the placement of the child usually occurs during a crisis, and before the start of the main assessment. Relative assess-ment is usually in two phases. The first phase involves a preliminary assessment of the relatives, which if satisfactory leads to the placement. This is followed by a formal assessment process, conducted when the child is already placed and is living in the relative's family. This represents a major challenge to the relationship between the agency and the relative carers. The Irish study showed that relatives did not understand the process, and found it largely threatening, intrusive, unwieldy and unnecessary. The confusion is evident in these relatives' views:

> Liz: I was saying, my God, I didn't think all this was involved, and then I'd say to myself, well they have to you know, they have to look after where they're putting these kids, because there are foster families who do abuse these kids and don't treat them the same way ... and yet I dreaded it, I really did. I suppose I did not understand what they were on about.

and

> Mark: I had no idea why they wanted that information, or what use it would be to them. I just went along with it. I could not see what it was all about.

Social workers experienced major role confusion between their assessment and support roles, and were uncomfortable with many aspects of the process that the relatives had to contend with (O'Brien 1997a). They questioned the validity of the current model of working, and yet recognised the dilemma facing the agency:

> Margaret: One of the greatest challenges is convincing the people of the validity of it [relative care] – the need for it – that certainly is a challenge. (Social Worker)

and

> Pauline: ... leaves the agency open and leaves them vulnerable in case anything went wrong in the placement. (Social Worker)

Highlighting the difference in the assessment process needed for both groups raises a question at the heart of the issue. Should relatives be viewed as a unique and special group of foster carers, with needs distinct from the general population of foster care, and if so, should assessment of them be built upon different criteria?

Demographic profile

The demographic profile of relative carers and traditional foster parents comprises a third difference between the two groups. Studies in the field from the USA and UK show that relatives are older, poorer, and comprise a higher number of families headed by single women than do traditional foster parents (Rowe et al. 1984; Dubowitz, Feigelman and Zuvarim 1993; Iglehart 1994; LeProhn 1994). Relatives also receive fewer services (Berrick et al. 1994) and are generally 'approved by the agency predominantly to care for their own family member rather than foster unrelated children' (Rowe, Hundleby and Garnett 1989, p.121). This difference is of major importance, and the issue of adequate support for relatives and other participants is discussed more fully later.

Position of the agency in the network of relationships

The fourth principal difference between relative and traditional foster care relates to the structure of relationships among the network of participants involved. In traditional foster care, the social worker is positioned centrally in all the relationships (Portengen and van Neut 1995), and is engaged in exchanging information between the participants, i.e. birth parents, foster carers, children and agency. The foster carer and birth parent are quite separate. In relative care, the carer is aligned both to the private domain of family through the relationship with the birth parents, and to the public domain through their role as foster carer for the agency. In this context, the social worker is involved in a family system that shares a mutual history, and the social worker will therefore always hold a more peripheral position to the family members. This has implications for practice, and raises a question about current practice in UK and Ireland whereby different social workers carry responsibility for the separate participants in the network. (The two-worker model, which involves one social worker having responsibility for the child and the other worker carrying principal responsibility for the foster carers, is a common feature of contemporary practice in foster care.) A skill base in systemic thinking and practice, which stresses the importance of context, language and meaning, would equip practitioners to take greater account of the different position of the agency in relative care if, as suggested, a greater emphasis is placed on the network of relationships.

The four principal differences between relative and traditional foster care outlined above represent a major challenge to existing case management and social work practice. The role of the social worker, and the service and support needs of the various participants, challenge the applicability of existing modes of working, based on and derived largely from traditional foster care. This is especially relevant when it is considered that relative care did not emerge as a coherent or planned policy direction, but could be characterised as emerging in response to a particular set of circumstances. As such, relative care developed and was grafted onto the existing system of foster care, rather than emerging from its own custom-made system.

Five central concerns in relative care

The approach to resolving the practice issues arising from the differences between relative and traditional foster carers needs to be considered against a backdrop of five principal concerns with relative care. The central concerns emerging in relative care are seen as:

- level of support services
- financial equity
- adoption and reunification rates
- protection of children
- applicability of traditional foster care structures.

These issues are discussed in the context of the advantages for children placed in relative care. The advantages, identified through research and practice, are generally considered as:

- the availability of familiar care in a time of crisis (Thornton 1987)
- placement in a familiar ethnic and racial community (Hegar and Scannapieco 1995)
- avoidance of trauma of being placed with strangers (Dubowitz 1994)
- greater facilitation of access with birth parents (Berrick *et al.* 1994)
- lower disruption rates (Iglehart 1994)
- greater opportunity for sibling unity (Johnson 1995)
- greater adjustment in alternative care (Iglehart 1994).

It is not the intention in this chapter to consider in depth the advantages for children in relative care, but it is important that the central concerns regarding this care option are considered against this backdrop. Caution is needed generally as research which examines the outcome of children placed with relatives remains at an early stage, and is fraught with methodological difficulties. The next part of this chapter will now consider the five central concerns in relative care, and suggestions are made for improved practice.

Services and support

There is evidence from USA studies that relatives receive less services from the agencies than traditional foster parents (Berrick *et al.* 1994; Dubowitz *et al.* 1993; Iglehart 1994; LeProhn 1994; Task Force 1990; Thornton 1987,

1991). The profile of relative foster carers (as older, poorer and headed predominantly by single women) providing homes for large groups of sibling children who have special health, educational and psychological needs has important implications for the types of services provided, and the spirit in which these are offered. Consideration of service needs of relatives, and the children placed in their care, and the children's birth parents is crucial to successful relative care.

To date, the research shows the differentials in the rates of support service offered, while the Irish study extends an understanding of the processes underlying service provision. Family members (relative carers) did not make a distinction between support and supervision, and tended to see the agency in a monitoring role, rather than a supporting one in its contacts. The lower levels of contact from the agency after the completion of the assessment was welcomed by the relatives, along with relief at the decision that the child was to remain with them, and the message that the agency was satisfied with their work. However the relatives who welcomed the limited contact showed a lack of understanding of the availability of services, and expressed a high level of ambivalence about asking for help, in case their motivations were misinterpreted. Interpreting lack of contact from the agency as a belief that they were expected to manage independently undoubtedly influenced the way the relatives negotiated service requirements with the agency.

The principal findings arising in the Irish study concerning support in relative care which practitioners need to take account of are as follows:

- Support in relative care is a broad concept similar to foster care, and refers to the range of services designed to meet the financial, emotional and practical needs of the different participants.

- The increased number of sibling placements, and the demographic profile of the relative networks, point to a high level of support needs in relative care.

- The participants' need for support varies over time, according to their position and relationships in the network.

- Support is of crucial importance, being the most significant issue in bringing families who are already caring informally into contact with the agency.

- Confusion exists between support and supervision/protection needs by both relatives and social workers, and was evident at multiple levels and in a range of relationships.

Financial equity

A most important issue surrounding support and relative care is the issue of financial equity, and debates arising from pressures for budgetary stability/restraint. In the USA, relative care has come under the microscope particularly due to the huge increase in the number of children placed in this care option, combined with the lower rates of reunification (Link 1996). Gleeson (1996) draws comparisons between general welfare reforms and the relative care debate. He suggests that the recipients of support in both spheres are portrayed as the cause of the problem for which the service was created, rather than the response to a problem. Concerns with the cost of relative care can be traced to the early 1990s, when questions were first raised regarding the equity of a state paying different rates of financial support to birth parents, relatives and foster parents to care for children.

In her report to US Congress, Spar said:

> Moreover, a policy that encourages compensation of kinship providers at higher levels than available to biological parents ... could be viewed as an incentive to break up parent–child families and a disincentive to reunite such families after the children are placed in kinship care. Particularly if parents continue to have uninhibited access to their children, they might be reluctant to seek resumed custody if it would result in reduced income. (Spar 1993, p.34)

The differential allowance paid to traditional foster parents compared to relatives is also addressed by Link, who asks:

> Can we in all conscience pay more to strangers to care for children than we do for relatives? At the same time can we create a system that gives more to a grandparent to support her grandchildren than we give to her daughter on welfare to support her daughter. (1996, p.520)

Relative care clearly exemplifies the link between care and poverty, by exemplifying the different range of supports offered to families to rear a child.

The development of relative care within alternative care systems through budgetary-driven measures needs to take full account of the likely impact of such interventions. Savings associated with lower recruitment costs and lower placement turnover, which probably makes relative care the 'somewhat less expensive alternative to administer', are not adequately taken into consideration in addressing the cost differential between relative and traditional foster care (Hegar and Scannapieco 1995). Efforts need to be made to support relatives who have a commitment to care for the children, but the barriers facing them cannot be overlooked (Gleeson 1996). Particular attention needs to be drawn to the assertion that 'perhaps the major role for the government in the future should be to provide minimal supports and intrusions to allow traditional family care to take place naturally' (Link 1996, p.528). Finch and Mason (1993), however, through their study of family responsibilities, have shown the error of considering care-giving in families as being part of a natural process.

The emphasis on the financial costs of relative care and the concerns about financial equity expressed in the American literature have not yet emerged in the limited literature about relative care in other countries. However, concerns about the possible cost implication of formal relative care as a placement option, and its impact on informal family care, is likely to emerge in other countries as relative care increases.

Adoption and reunification rates

Another issue in relative care, which needs to be seen in the context of the adoption concern, and in its own right, is the rate of reunification of children with their birth parents. Research has shown that the longer children spend in care, the higher is the risk that reunification will not occur. In examining the longer periods which children spend in relative care compared with traditional care, there is a need to consider the evidence that the re-entry rates to care are lower in relative care than for children returned from other placement options (Fein *et al.* 1983; Wulczyn, Poulin and Staller 1995). Further research is needed to ascertain if the dynamics and processes in relative care affect reunification rates.

While lower reunification rates and adoption in relative care are a central concern in the American studies, it is not expressed as a major issue in those few studies available elsewhere. This may reflect the policy preference in the USA for adoption, aimed at securing permanency, an approach which is not accorded such prominence in other jurisdictions. Adoption of related children is a critical issue, particularly as it has been suggested that the policy is designed to cut costs by removing them from the formal support systems. The point is also made that it fails to take account of the impact on intra-familial relationships (Link 1996; Ingram 1996). The image of 'shotgun' adoptions (Link 1996), in which relatives agree to adopt children whom they fear may otherwise be lost to them in the care system, raises profound ethical questions about power and control in the family/state relationship. Permanency is an important concept in child care, and provision needs to be made to provide security. However, other legal provisions, such as the Residence Orders and Guardianship proceedings under the UK Children's Act 1989, are examples of ways of providing a level of security for children in relative care (Department of Health 1995a). Caution is also needed in this sphere, as these provisions may work against the service needs of relatives and the children placed with them, if they are designed to minimise state involvement, even where a range of discretionary supports and services are provided. (Under the provisions of a residence order in the UK, the local authority are only required to review the financial supports provided on a yearly basis, and no provision is made to consider the child's care.)

The welfare of the child in relative care: Protection concerns

Concerns about the welfare of the child in relative care arise in a context where there is a lack of rigorous pre-placement review, combined with less monitoring of relative placements (Kusserow 1992); confusion regarding assessment frameworks to determine suitability of relative homes (Killackey 1992); and an implicit questioning among professionals of the relatives' ability to protect the child in light of the difficulties of the birth parents (Thornton 1987, 1991). Given these concerns, the evidence which shows that the relative homes receive less contact and services from child welfare agencies than traditional foster families (Berrick *et al.* 1994), and that they are older and poorer, is especially interesting. Establishing adequate levels of protection for children in relative care is part of a wider discourse, which is shaped by the uncertain relationship between the private domain of family and the public domain of child abuse. Parton draws attention to this central question when he asks:

> How can the state establish the health, development and, hence, rights of individual family members who are weak and dependent, particularly children, while promoting the family as the 'natural' sphere for caring for those individuals, and thus not intervening in all families, which would destroy the autonomy of the private sphere. (Parton 1994, pp.16–17)

In this ambivalent space, protection and supervision of the relative home remains a recurring theme at all stages of the evolution of the network. It was seen in the Irish study as a particularly acute issue at the decision-making and assessment stage. The diversity of family types and lifestyles, the continued influence/impact of the dysfunctional family theory, and the current emphasis on child abuse and protection were juxtaposed by the social workers with

the perceived benefits of relative care, such as the importance of family connections for children's identity, and relative care offering children greater
continuity of placement and sibling unity. As the placements developed, the
social workers saw the benefit of many relative home placements for the children, and even in the most distressed networks, many of the previous
concerns were dissipated. However, unease about protection, and the
agency's vulnerability in an era of inquiries, remained a particular issue, and
reflects the fact that a specific model for working with relative care has not
been developed to date. This confusion is compounded where the care plan
for the child is unclear, or where major differences in participants' views of
the plan have never been adequately articulated.

Operating in this paradoxical space, relative care is further complicated
by the social worker's fundamentally different position in the networks
compared to traditional foster care. The relative carer operates simul-
taneously in both the public domain of the state and the private domain of
the family. A reiteration of the idea that family remains the first line of
protection for children may help in resolving this dilemma (Wilcox *et al.*
1991, Ryburn 1994, 1996; Family Rights Group 1994; Hudson *et al.* 1996).
The fact that a large percentage of relatives contacted the child welfare
agencies with concerns about the children is testament to families' desire and
capacity to protect (Berrick *et al.* 1994).

Applicability of traditional foster care structures

The concerns surrounding support, financial equity, reunification and adoption rates and protection point to the fifth concern, which is the applicability
of traditional foster care practice, criteria and structure in relative care. The
'awkward fit' between relative and foster care is particularly relevant when
the different routes to care, the assessment practices required, and the service
and support needs are considered.

Takas (1992) identifies dangers in relative care if attention is not paid to
the structures required. Less carefully designed policies 'can undermine
parent–child unity, subject some children to risk of harm and subject some
families to unnecessary state intervention into family life' (Takas 1992, p.92).
It is also important if comparing an emerging system to an existing one that
the limitations of the existing system are not lost. Ample evidence is available
that the traditional foster-care system is not without difficulties in terms of
role confusion of foster parents (Kadushin 1980; LeProhn 1994); adequacy
of support services (Sellick 1992); stability of placements (Berridge and

Cleaver 1987; Fratter *et al.* 1991); and assessment practices (Rhodes 1992: Ryburn 1991, 1995).

Relative care: A different type of case management?

Countries currently developing relative care as a formal child placement option can learn much from the policy and practice issues which have already emerged from the American experience. It is to be expected that issues identified as significant in the American context, and highlighted in this chapter, may emerge for policy makers, practitioners and families in their attempts to resolve complex issues relating to decision making, assessment practices and the subsequent development of relative care placements. In addition to the five central issues identified and discussed above, which have both policy and practice implications, a number of research findings from the Irish study point to the type of case management model needed for relative care.

Changes in the current case management model

The limitations of current relative care systems, identified through this chapter, can be traced to the context in which they emerged. It was shown that the increased use of relative care placements is due to a combination of factors connected with a preference for foster care over residential care, a shortage of traditional foster parents, the emergence of partnership as a key principle in child welfare, greater emphasis on family connection as a means to enhance children's identity, and positive research outcomes. However, it was also shown that its early development in the USA arose out of legislative duties and other constraints. The existence of a value system among individual workers which reflected an ideological preference for family unity, and a placement crisis which left little choice but to use this care option, were the driving forces, rather than a coherently formulated social policy which provided specific guidance and regulation for the developing practice. It is also important to stress that, as relative care has expanded, it has been developing within the existing foster-care system, which in itself is characterised by multiple challenges, as pointed to in Berridge's review of the latest foster care literature (1997), in terms of role confusion, placement breakdown, recruitment and retention of foster carers, and meeting children's needs.

The Irish study shows that the current relative care case management system in the agency are based primarily on traditional foster care. An understanding/appreciation of the diverse range of relative networks identified in the Irish study (O'Brien 1999) is required in designing a different system. The study shows that four different types of networks can evolve over time, ranging from co-operative to conflictual categories. By examining the evolution of the various networks over time, the study shows that all placements commence in a co-operative state, but that increased marginalisation and exclusion of the birth parents leads to a distressed network. The conflicts which underlie the ongoing disputes were traced to confusion and disagreement about the care plan, and these conflicts were played out in large part through access arrangements. This led to an intensification of conflict, in which participants felt confused, misunderstood and not respected. The study emphasises the fluidity of the network of relationships, and the importance of being vigilant about the changing configuration of relationships, as participants strive to manage sometimes very difficult, turbulent situations.

Towards improved practice

Arising from the study findings, and bearing in mind the principal issues identified in this chapter, it is suggested that a case management system specifically for relative care needs to:

- Address the difference between relative and the traditional foster parent population in terms of demographic profile, the routes by which children enter the system, and the more peripheral position of the agency.

- Take more account of the contradictory and complex social discourses that surround relative care. In particular the discourses surrounding the family/state relationship, as exemplified by confusion between social control and family privacy and family and state responsibilities, can lead to confused roles and expectations for the participants. Strenuous effort is needed in examining the contradictory discourses surrounding relative care, so that the inherent difficulties of partnership in terms of power differentials are not masked.

- Utilise and build upon the level of co-operation that exists at the outset and build on the principle of inclusive decision making. The Family Group Conference would provide a valuable approach, if applied to the decision making/assessment stages. (The Family Group Conference technique is being increasingly used in a range of settings since it was developed in New Zealand. The key principles are: the professionals share their concerns with the family; the family have time to plan in private; the plan is accepted unless the child is put at risk; and the process is facilitated by an independent co-ordinator.)

- Develop an assessment system attuned to the particular circumstances of relative care. Families are generally only motivated to care for their own, and will generally make workable and safe plans. Agencies need to make explicit the criteria on which decisions are made. Social workers have a wealth of knowledge and practice experience to be tapped to benefit families and children in need of alternative care. However, they also have an ethical responsibility to examine the ways in which their knowledge is professionally enclosed, and how this influences them when presenting 'expert' opinions, particularly as it relates to assessment. A short time-frame is essential for conducting the assessment process because of the uncertainty hanging over the future of the child who is already placed, and to avoid the ambivalence arising from a dual assessment/support role. The two-worker model needs to be examined critically. A systemic framework in conjunction with the principles of the Family Group Conference is currently being developed to construct an appropriate assessment model (O'Brien 1999b). The framework, which comprises both the family group conference and systemic thinking, is currently being developed and will be piloted in two areas in Ireland in 1999. Systemic thinking with its focus on context, interaction and meaning is particularly appropriate at a theoretical and skills level.

- Considering the demographic profile of relatives as older and poorer than foster carers, there is need for a recognition of the enormous burden on some relatives in continuing to care for children in relative care. Positive, user-friendly support services directed to all participants could lead to more harmonious network of relationships. The relative care system also needs to develop appropriate training, as well as support networks among the participant groups. There is a need to distinguish adequately between *support* and *protection* requirements. A conceptual framework is needed which distinguishes between networks/cases which needed high and low support and high and low supervision. It is suggested that such a framework would provide greater clarity about support and supervision requirements, and could enhance the co-operation that exists at the initial decision-making stage of the networks, if taken in conjunction with the proposals for redeploying resources currently used in extended assessment. This framework can guide policy and practice in formulating the service requirements and protection needs of the individual participants in the relative networks as these arise over time. This could enhance case management, and help especially to diffuse many of the difficulties associated with conflictual networks.

- There is a need to examine critically if relative placements can be diverted out of the formal care system, either at the initial decision-making stage, or when placements are stabilised. It is essential in devising such a scheme that children's and families' support and protection needs are safeguarded, and that cost reduction is not the driving force.

Creating the change

In considering the changes required to improve practice, the issues about relative care raised in this chapter present many challenges for both the child welfare agencies and individual workers. Introducing changes for relative care at an organisational and practice level involves the management of change, and recognition of the tasks arising from incorporating change into a system. However, releasing the energy currently absorbed by the problems of superimposing the traditional foster-care system on relative care can provide space to learn the new skills, and bring about the attitudinal and practice changes needed. The challenge lies in the opening of possibilities in which the certainties and uncertainties can be examined, the strengths of families can be explored and practitioners equipped to work in a practice of partnership, creativity, openness and respect.

Relative care has emerged as an important and growing care option for children. It is embedded in complex relationships at a family/state, and intra-familial level. Relative care will not be a solution for all children requiring care. It may be unsuitable due to the unavailability of appropriate resources in the child's network, or excessive risks associated with the proposed placement. The diverse needs of children will continue to warrant a range of care options in residential, foster and relative care.

Relative care, if operated properly, will not be a cheap care option. If it is used primarily because of perceived budgetary savings, or as a response to the shortage of other alternative care options, and good practice does not develop, then unfortunate results can be predicted.

However by considering the benefits for the children and families and by analysing the practical, ideological, economic and social forces that both militate against and support relative care, an effective child-centred care option may be successfully developed for many children. Willingness, commitment and vision are required to embrace 'this age-old tradition and new departure' in a way that is advantageous to all.

References

Bergerhed, E. (1995) Kinship and network care in Sweden. In H. Thelen (ed) *Foster Children in a Changing World.* Documentation of The 1994 European I.F.C.O. Conference in Berlin. Berlin, Arbeitskreis Zur Forderung Von Pflegekindern E.V.

Berrick, J.D., Barth, R.P. and Needell, B. (1994) A comparison of kinship foster homes and foster family homes – implications for kinship foster-care as family. *Preservation Children And Youth Services Review 16,* 33–63.

Berridge, D. (1997) *Foster Care: A Research Review.* London: HMSO.

Berridge, D. and Cleaver, H. (1987) *Foster Home Breakdown.* Oxford: Blackwell.

Colton, M. (1989) *Dimensions of Substitute Child Care.* Aldershot: Gower.

Colton, M. and Williams, M. (1997) The nature of foster care: International trends. *Adoption and Fostering 21,* 44–49.

Department of Health (1995a) *The Children's Act 1989: Residence Order Study: A Study of the Experiences of Local Authorities of Public Law Residence Orders.* London: Social Service Inspectorate.

Department of Health (1995b) *Child Care Regulations. (Placement of Children with Relatives).* S.I. No. 130 of 1995. Dublin: Stationery Office.

Dingwall, R. (1986) The Jasmine Beckford Affair. *Modern Law Review 10,* 489–507.

Dubowitz, H. (1994) Suggestions for future research. Special Issue: A research agenda for child welfare. *Child Welfare 73,* 553–564.

Dubowitz, H., Feigelman, S. and Zuvarim, S. (1993) A profile of kinship care. *Child Welfare 72,* 153–169.

Family Rights Group (1994) Family Group Conferences: A Report Commissioned by the Department of Health. London: Family Rights Group.

Fein, E., Maluccio, A., Hamilton, J. and Ward, D. (1983) After foster care: Outcomes of permanence planning for children. *Child Welfare 6,* 485–556.

Finch, J. and Mason, J. (1993) *Negotiating Family Responsibilities.* London: Tavistock/Routledge.

Fratter, J., Rowe, J., Sapsford, D. And Thoburn, J. (1991) *Permanent Family Placement: A Decade of Experience.* London: British Agencies for Adoption and Fostering.

Gilligan, R. (1990) *Foster Care for Children in Ireland: Issues and Challenges for the 1990s.* Occasional paper No.2. University of Dublin: Trinity College.

Gleeson, J.P. (1996) Kinship care as a child welfare service: The policy debate in an era of welfare reform. *Child Welfare, 75,* 419–449.

Hegar, R.L. (1993) Assessing attachment, permanence and kinship in choosing permanent homes. *Child Welfare, 72,* 367–379.

Hegar, R. and Scannapieco, M. (1995) From family duty to family foster care: The evolution of kinship care. *Child Welfare 64,* 200–216.

Hudson, J., Morris, A., Maxwell, G. and Galaway, B. (eds) (1996) *Family Group Conferences.* Leichhardt, Australia: Federation Press.

Iglehart, A. (1994) Kinship foster care: placement, service and outcome issues. *Social Service Review 16,* 107–122.

Ingram, C. (1996) Kinship care: From last resort to first choice. *Child Welfare, 75,* 550–566.

Johnson, H.J. (1995) *Traditions in a New Time: Stories of Grandmothers.* PhD Thesis. New York: Columbia University.

Kadushin, A. (1980) *Child Welfare Services.* New York: Macmillan.

Killackey, E. (1992) Kinship foster care. *Family Law Quarterly 26,* 211–220.

Kusserow, R. (1992) *Using Relatives for Foster Care.* Washington DC: US Department of Health and Human Services, Office of the Inspector General. OEI. 16–90–2391.

LeProhn, N. (1994) The role of the kinship foster parent: A comparison of the role conceptions of relative and non relative foster parents. *Social Service Review 16,* 65–84.

Link, M.K. (1996) Permanency outcomes in kinship care: A study of children placed in kinship care in Erie County, New York. *Child Welfare 75,* 509–529.

Miller v. *Youakim* (1979) Supreme Court 440 US 125.

Mosek, A. and Adler, L. (1993) Identity Development of Adolescent Girls in Foster Care – Comparison of Adolescents Placed in Kinship vs. Unrelated Foster Families. Unpublished Paper Presented at I.F.C.O. Conference, Dublin.

Needell, B. (1994) Kinship care: rights and responsibilities, services and standard, In P.B. Barth, M. Courtney, J.D. Berrick and V. Albert (eds) (1994) *From Child Abuse To Permanency Planning.* New York: Aldine De Gruyter.

O'Brien, V. (1997a) *Fostering the Family: A New Systemic Approach to Evolving Networks of Relative Care.* PhD Thesis submitted to National University of Ireland.

O'Brien, V. (1997b) Relative foster care – a family/state discourse. *Feedback, the Magazine of the Family Therapy Association 7,* Spring, 16–23.

O'Brien, V. (1999a) Evolving networks of relative care: Some findings from an Irish study. In R. Grieff (ed) *Kinship Care* (forthcoming). Ashgate: Arena.

O'Brien, V. (1999b) Training Manual for Pilot Project in Relative Care, in Mid Western Health Board, Ireland.

Portengen, R. and Van Neut, B. (1995) Foster care in family and social networks, In D. McTeigue (ed) *A Journey Through Fostering.* Dublin: Irish Foster Care Association.

KING ALFRED'S COLLEGE
LIBRARY

Rhodes, P.J. (1992) *Racial Matching in Fostering.* Aldershot: Avebury.

Rowe, J., Cain, H., Hundleby, M. and Keane, A. (1984) *Long Term Foster Care.* London: Batsford.

Rowe, J., Hundleby, M. and Garnett, L. (1989) *Child Care Now: A Survey of Placement Patterns.* London: British Agencies For Adoption And Fostering.

Ryburn, M. (1991) The myth of assessment. *Fostering and Adoption 15,* 20–27.

Ryburn, M. (1993) *Empowering Practise in Family Placement.* Paper delivered at the Eighth International Foster Care Conference, Dublin (July).

Ryburn, M. (1994) Planning for children here and in New Zealand. A comparison of the legislation in Family Rights Group (1994) *Family Group Conferences: A Report Commissioned by the Dept. Of Health.* London: Family Rights Group.

Ryburn, M. (1995) *Partnership and Child Care.* Unpublished Paper presented to the International Foster Care Conference, July, Bergen, Norway.

Ryburn, M. (1996) Family Group Conferences: partnership in practice. *Adoption and Fostering 20,* 16–23.

Sellick, C. (1992) *Supporting Foster Parents.* Aldershot, Avebury.

Spar, K. (1993) *Kinship Foster Care: An Emerging Federal Issue.* Washington, DC: Library of Congress, Congressional Research Service.

Takas, M. (1992) Kinship care: developing a safe and effective framework for protective placements of children with relatives. *Children's Legal Rights Journal 13,* 12–19.

Task Force on Permanency Planning for Children (1990) *Kinship Care: The Double Edged Dilemma.* Rochester, New York.

Thoburn, J. (1994) *Child Placement: Principles and Practice.* (2nd edition). Aldershot: Gower.

Thornton, J. (1987) *An Investigation Into The Nature of Kinship Foster Care.* Unpublished Doctoral Dissertation, Yeshiva University, New York.

Thornton, J.L. (1991) Permanency planning for children in kinship foster homes. *Child Welfare 70,* 593–601.

Triseliotis, J. (1989) Foster care outcomes: A review of key research findings. *Adoption and Fostering, 13,* 5–17.

Wilcox, R., Smith, D., Moore, J., Hewitt, A., Allan, G., Walker, H., Ropata, M., Monu, L. and Featherstone, T. (1991) *Family Decision Making: Family Group Conferences – Practitioners Views.* Lower Hutt, New Zealand/Wellington: Practitioners Publishing.

Wulczyn, F.H., Poulin, S. and Staller, K. (1995) *Kinship Foster Care in New York City.* Pre-publication Manuscript, Grant Aided by Robert Sterling Clark Foundation, Columbia University School of Social Work, New York.

The Contributors

Robbie Gilligan is Senior Lecturer in Social Work in the Department of Social Studies and Academic Co-Director of The Children's Research Centre at Trinity College Dublin. He is also a former foster carer. He has written widely on child welfare and has recently co-authored with Brigid Daniel and Sally Wassell *Promoting Child Development: A Guide for Child Care and Protection Workers*, also published by Jessica Kingsley.

Stan Houston is a Lecturer in the Department of Social Work at Queen's University Belfast. He has lead responsibility for post qualifying courses. He was recently the Eastern Health and Social Services Board's commissioner for training for the Children (NI) Order and prior to that a senior social worker in adolescent and child care teams in Belfast.

Greg Kelly is a senior lecturer in the Department of Social Work at Queen's University Belfast. He is programme director for the Masters in Social Work / DipSW Programme. He is currently researching, writing and providing training in the area of 'permanence' for children in care and is chair of the Children's Law Centre for Northern Ireland.

Ken P. Kerr is the Director of Training for the charity Parents' Education as Autism Therapists (PEAT) in Northern Ireland. His interests include behaviour analysis in the area of autism, establishing behavioural management programmes in home, devising behavioural parent training courses, and the general application of behavioural principles to promote acceleration in learning.

Stephen Nixon is Senior Lecturer in Applied Social Studies and Deputy Head of the School of Continuing Studies at the University of Birmingham. He has been a social worker, lecturer and researcher in the field of foster care for a number of years. He is actively involved in the preparation, training and further development of both foster carers and social workers.

Dr Valerie O'Brien currently lectures at the Department of Social Policy and Social Work at University College Dublin. She worked previously as a social worker in the area of child protection and child placement. She is currently involved in developing pilot projects in the area of family group conferences, kinship care and intercountry adoption assessment practices in child welfare agencies in Ireland.

Dr Pinkerton is Senior Research Fellow at the Centre for Child Care Research, Department of Social Work, Queen's University Belfast. Having worked in statutory social services, he has been involved in professional training and research for the last twenty years. He has a specialist interest in needs and services relating to young people leaving state care. He has written extensively in these areas.

Subject Index

Author index